PREPARE!

A Weekly Worship Planbook for Pastors and Musicians 2009–2010

David L. Bone

and

Mary J. Scifres

Abingdon Press
Nashville

PREPARE! A WEEKLY WORSHIP PLANBOOK FOR PASTORS AND MUSICIANS

This book is printed on acid-free, recycled paper.

ISBN 978-0-687-64936-5

09 10 11 12 13 14 15 16 16 18—10 9 8 7 6 5 4 3 2 1

MANUFACTURED IN THE UNITED STATES OF AMERICA

CONTENTS

USING *PREPARE!*

Prepare! has been created to give you as many ideas as possible about a given worship service. It is designed to be used along with a worship plan notebook that you create, and a copy of your church's hymnal. Features of *Prepare!* include:

- Each week, **Primary Hymns and Songs for the Day** are suggested first. These suggestions include various helps for singing the hymns. These hymns and songs have the closest relationship to the scriptures and are widely known.
- **Additional Hymns Suggestions** and **Additional Contemporary Suggestions** are given to offer more options for worship planning. Some of these suggestions may bring to mind anthems that you may want to consider. Selected stanzas or refrains from these lists may provide shorter musical responses for use in a service.
- The suggestions for each week are chosen to suggest a wide variety of styles.
- Each item is referenced to Scripture or occasion.
- At least one **Communion hymn** is recommended for the first Sunday of each month and liturgical season. Where space permits, communion hymns appropriate to the lections are suggested on other Sundays as well.
- **Opening (O) and Closing (C) hymns** are suggested for each worship service.
- The copyright status of a particular item is noted in the suggestion lists. If a hymn is in the public domain, it is marked (PD). This means that you may legally copy this hymn without obtaining further permission. You may find this useful if a hymn is not in your hymnal. Please be advised: The (PD) mark only refers to the hymn that it follows, not all hymns in the listing. Often, an arrangement in one hymnal may be public domain, but an arrangement of the same hymn tune in a different hymnal may be under copyright.
- **Visual Suggestions** are offered for each service. These suggestions are discussed in the following article. They are found in each week's "Other Suggestions" list. Ashley M. Calhoun of Knoxville, Tennessee compiled these. Ashley is known for his inventive use of "found" items in creating visual worship settings. Worship committees and altar guilds can use these ideas to create unique worship centers and altar pieces.
- *Prepare!* also includes **Contemporary Suggestions** for use in contemporary or blended worship services. The resources listed there include suggestions for several nontraditional styles of worship music. Praise music, Taizé and meditative music, folk music, and ethnic music from around the globe are all included in this section. Several resources are referenced in this section. Information about these resources can be found on page 7.

Be sure to consult all the suggestions regardless of the type of service you are planning. Many items that are used in contemporary services are listed under **Hymn Suggestions,** and resources for traditional services can be found in the **Contemporary Suggestions** list. Vocal solo ideas may come from the list of **Anthems,** or a beloved song for your congregation may be found in the "Vocal Solos" list. Don't let the designation deter you from using any item that will enhance your worship service.

All the scriptures in the Revised Common Lectionary are listed for each day. From the Second Sunday after Pentecost to Christ the King Sunday, the lectionary includes two patterns of readings.

1. One pattern includes semicontinuous readings from the Hebrew Scriptures, Epistles, and Gospels. These readings are not necessarily related to one another, but allow for a sequential experience of the biblical narrative. This is the pattern used to determine which scripture texts are printed in *Prepare!* It is the pattern followed by most users of the hymnals referenced.

2. In the second pattern, the Hebrew Scripture is chosen to relate to the Gospel passage. This pattern is used primarily in traditions where Communion is celebrated at every service of worship. These lections are noted at the beginning of the **Other Suggestions.** Some items are also referenced to these lections.

Worship planners may certainly choose to follow the pattern that best serves their needs. However, the patterns should not be mixed. This only results in losing the benefits of the individual patterns.

When planning any worship service, it is always best to start with the scripture and let it guide your thoughts and plans. If your church is not using the Revised Common Lectionary, but you know what the scripture will be for a service, look up that scripture in the Scripture Index on page 130. Nonlectionary worship planners may wish to keep the three most recent volumes of *Prepare!* on hand.

As you read and study the scripture passages, read all of the suggested hymn texts. The hymns may remind you of anthems, solos, or keyboard selections. It is wise to mark your hymnal with the dates individual hymns are sung to avoid singing some too frequently. The "Hymn

Resources" (see page 7) can enhance congregational singing, but should be used sparingly.

Use a three-ring binder to organize your plans. For each service of worship, include a copy of one of the **Worship Planning Sheets** found on pages 134–36 (or design your own!) along with blank paper for listing further ideas. Do not simply fill in the blanks for each service, but use the Planning Sheet to guide your work.

If *Prepare!* is new to you, you will want to be aware of several other items. The **Vocal Solos** are taken from a group of ten collections that range from contemporary settings of hymn texts to well-known classics (see page 7). You may also find vocal solo ideas from *The Faith We Sing,* as you introduce new songs to your congregation. Where theme and space permits, songs are listed several times within a season in order for your congregation to gain familiarity with the new songs.

The **Anthems** include new works, as well as generally known works that are already in many church choral libraries. Your study of the scripture and hymn texts will lead you to anthems in your church library that are appropriate.

The **Other Suggestions** for each service are varied in their intent and function, but will often add to the non-musical aspects of planning worship. Here, you will find visual ideas, words for worship, and occasional ideas for choral introits and benedictions. Add to this list as you study the scripture and hymn texts.

Use the suggestions in *Prepare!* along with your own page of ideas to begin making decisions about worship. Will the choir sing a "Call to Worship"? Can a hymn verse serve as a prayer response? Can a particular anthem or vocal solo give direction to the sermon? What prayers will be used?

Once your decisions are made, complete the Worship Planning Sheet. Make a separate list of tasks related to that service. Planning worship is an awesome responsibility, but one that can be accomplished with an organized effort along with spiritual guidance.

VISUALS IN WORSHIP

Ashley M. Calhoun

The suggestions for visuals in *Prepare!* are meant to help worship leaders use objects and images to increase the impact of the gospel on a people who are increasingly oriented to visual forms of communication. These suggestions can be incorporated into many visual elements: hanging and processional banners, worship settings (whether on the altar, in the chancel or narthex), worship folder covers, and bulletin boards. Classical and contemporary works of art, sculpture, needlework, and photography can also be a meaningful addition to the worship service.

With more churches incorporating screens and video walls into their worship space, there is a tremendous potential for the use of still or moving imagery. Also, interpretive movement and drama can be very strong in their visual impact.

The visual suggestions in *Prepare!* have several characteristics.

- The suggestions are not meant to give detailed plans, but to spark your imagination and creativity.
- Some are drawn literally from the lessons; others are thematic.
- The suggestions are organized by reference to the lectionary passages:

O	Old Testament reading
P	Psalm reading or Canticle
E	Epistle or New Testament reading
G	Gospel reading

- Chapter and verse numbers are sometimes given to indicate actual phrases in the scripture passage that can serve as visual elements.
- Themes such as "forgiveness," "love," "rejoicing," and so on are offered to encourage creative use of video and photographic images of people engaged in demonstrating those themes.

So much about worship is visual and intended to strengthen the proclamation of the gospel. The worship space is filled with visual elements that send a message, positive or negative. The Christian Year itself is a treasure trove of color, texture, symbolism, and visual imagery. The special Sundays and special days in the cultural and denominational calendars also give the opportunity for visual expression. Evaluate the visual aspects of your worship services and find ways to enhance the worship experience with a more thoughtful use of visual elements.

PLANNING WORSHIP IN ALTERNATIVE STYLES

Mary J. Scifres

Various forms of nontraditional worship have become increasingly popular in the last thirty years, mass labeled as "contemporary." For the traditional worship planner, these alternative styles of worshiping may be foreign to your experience. Nevertheless, the popularity of modern music and public events, the increasing diversity of today's culture, the growing comfort with informal approaches to worship, and the high energy of young people may encourage you to use contemporary resources and alternative styles in one or more of your worship services.

Planning alternative worship provides an exciting opportunity for church staff members and volunteers to work together as a team. Such planning can also provide a vehicle in which worship committees find opportunity for ministry.

If alternative or contemporary worship is new to you, spend time in prayer and planning long before your first service. Know your own gifts and those of your congregation, and observe what other churches and worship leaders are doing around your community and around the country. If you're beginning an additional worship service, build the necessary groundwork to support this new mission of the church by recruiting leadership from within your congregation, advertising the event before it happens, and setting a goal for this mission. If you are integrating new elements into an existing worship service, include your current leadership alongside young adults and new leadership in planning for the changes. As you embark on this new venture, be careful not to abandon your current worshiping congregation or set up a competition between existing worship services and new ones. As you explore the possibility of new worship styles, be open not only to contemporary praise music and alternative Christian music, but also to global praise music or quieter forms of contemporary worship using folk music or Taizé music. Secular resources and music may also be of help in developing new styles of worship. With these things in mind, you are ready to begin the planning process.

As you design your alternative worship service, several decisions need to be made:

- Whom do you want to reach?
  (traditions, faith backgrounds, ages, theology?)
- What type of worship experience shall you start or improve? (You may want to consider blending styles.)
- How much are you willing to spend?

With those decisions in mind, you are ready to build your planning team. "Team?" you may ask. "Our pastor does all the worship planning!" If that is the case, this is the perfect opportunity to explore a new model of planning worship. Contemporary expressions of worship are foreign to many pastors and musicians. Increasing the number of planners will expand the diversity and creativity of ideas—important elements of alternative worship! With this resource, we hope that many pastors, musicians, and worship leaders find encouragement and assistance planning worship in advance and in cooperation with one another.

Planning team members may include musicians, artists, organizers, writers, and pastors. All members of the worship planning team meet regularly, at least bi-annually. Some worship teams find weekly, monthly, or seasonal planning meetings helpful, but even two meetings a year can improve communication and coordination efforts immensely. Planning meetings are common, necessary, and often frequent in alternative worship planning.

However often one plans, pastors need to know the time requirements for planning music and other artistic elements of worship. Each pianist or song leader can communicate to the pastor the average length of time needed to pick new songs, order the music or songbooks, obtain copyright permissions, and rehearse the songs prior to Sunday morning. Each drama coordinator can decide the length of time needed to write or find a vignette to illustrate the scripture or sermon topic. Visual coordinators can let worship planners know the time needed to locate photographs, develop altar displays, or prepare electronic slide shows for worship. Finally, the musicians and artists can communicate with the pastor their visions for music and art ministry in the context of worship.

Pastors, likewise, need to inform musicians of special needs for musical and visual support. Some pastors establish cues to alert the musician that light background music is needed during an unexpected situation in worship. A pastor can tell the artists what expectations are regarding worship leadership roles (to listen attentively to the sermon, to smile during the opening songs, to stand or kneel during the prayer). Additionally, pastors can communicate their visions for the music and worship arts ministry of the church. These initial communications are essential when the worship planners begin to work together and when there are personnel changes in the worship planning team.

Many models for the actual planning might be used, but we offer one model to help a team in starting integrated planning. In order to use this model, the team needs several copies of *Prepare!* (particularly for use of scripture readings and song lists), a Bible (if lectionary is not being used or for team members who do not have access to a copy of *Prepare!*), hymnals and/or songbooks. Musicians may find it helpful to have in hand copies of each of the music collections suggested in this guide as well as a single copy file of the song collection of your church. Copies of the planning sheet from page136 can be distributed to each team member for each Sunday being discussed.

1. Before the meeting, the pastor(s) prepare Scripture and sermon outlines; musicians prepare repertoire lists as well as repertoire wish lists.
2. Team meets for a designated time period. (A retreat setting is appropriate, especially if this is to be only a bi-annual event.)
3. Open meeting with prayer and discussion of worship.
4. Read Scriptures (perhaps in advance to meeting) and select specific Scriptures for each Sunday being planned.
5. The pastor(s) introduces and outliines sermon topics or emphases.
6. Discuss and outline seasonal needs.
7. Choose songs and/or hymns, keeping in mind; thematic and scriptural emphases, musical abilities, sermon topics, congregational music preferences, and desire for introduction of new songs in a helpful way.
8. Visual artists begin outlining plans for visual emphases or focal points.
9. Introduce and discuss special ideas or plans for specific worship services (e.g., Easter, new member celebration, children's Sunday, stewardship Sunday).
10. Write or choose spoken prayers, responses, and other worship words (full team or subgroup, depending on number of people participating).
11. Choose vocal and instrumental music (full team or subgroup, depending on number of people participating).
12. Review services for integration and unity as well as diversity.
13. Discsuss concerns regarding specific services and plans for improvement.
14. Close meeting with song and prayer.

In planning alternative worship, you want to offer a quality experience; planning with a team can help you to do so. At any step, members of the team may have valuable input. A pastor may have an idea for a dramatic sketch to enhance the sermon; a musician may have an insight into a sermon topic. All members of the team will find helpful suggestions in *Prepare!* The text of each scripture reading is provided, season and color are noted, music and visual suggestions are offered, liturgical suggestions are offered, and other ideas are mentioned that may spark interest in innovations for your worship service.

When planning alternative worship, try to:

- Offer a high-quality experience of worship.
- Employ your heritage creatively.
- Offer as many opportunities for participation as possible.
- Use language and theology that affirms.
- Use creative, diverse, understandable language and music.
- Be honest, open, and genuine in word and action.
- Offer a welcoming experience for visitors.
- Utilize a variety of media (video, drama, live music, visual arts).
- Avoid dependence on handouts (such as bulletins).
- Obtain a copyright license if you plan to duplicate for overhead projection or bulletins (Christian Copyright License 800-234-2446, ccli.com or OneLicense at onelicense.net or LicenSing 800-328-0200).
- Have fun!

Alternative worship planning need not be a point of departure for a worship staff. Rather, it can be a point of unity and team building. The team that works together models corporate worship for the congregation. If we want people to walk in the church doors on Sunday mornings from their many walks of life to have a corporate experience, we need to offer worship that incorporates many ideas from different voices to connect with our congregation's diverse journeys of faith. In so doing, we will find that the Holy Spirit has found a new freedom in which to work.

RESOURCE KEY

HYMNALS

- B Forbis, Wesley, ed. *The Baptist Hymnal.* Nashville: Convention Press, 1991.
- C Merrick, Daniel and Polk, David, ed. *Chalice Hymnal.* St. Louis: Chalice Press, 1996.
- E *The Hymnal 1982.* New York: The Church Hymnal Corporation, 1985.
- F Bock, Fred, ed. *Hymns for the Family of God.* Nashville: Paragon Associates, Inc., 1976.
- L *Lutheran Book of Worship.* Minneapolis: Augsburg Publishing House, 1978.
- N Clyde, Arthur G., ed. *The New Century Hymnal.* Cleveland, Oh.: The Pilgrim Press, 1995.
- P McKim, LindaJo, ed. *The Presbyterian Hymnal.* Louisville: Westminster/John Knox Press, 1990.
- S Hickman, Hoyt L., ed. *The Faith We Sing.* Nashville: Abingdon Press, 2000.
- SF Hickman, Hoyt L., ed. *We Sing Faith.* Nashville: Abingdon Press, 2000.
- UM Young, Carlton R., ed. *The United Methodist Hymnal.* Nashville: The United Methodist Publishing House, 1989.
- VU Ambrose, John E., ed. *Voices United.* Etobicoke, Ontario, Canada: The United Church Publishing House, 1996.
- W Batastini, Robert J., ed. *Worship.* Chicago: GIA Publications, Inc., 1986.

HYMN RESOURCES

- S-1 Smith, Gary Alan, ed. *The United Methodist Hymnal: Music Supplement.* Nashville: Abingdon Press, 1991. Cokesbury Order #431476.
- S-2 Bennett, Robert C., ed. *The United Methodist Hymnal: Music Supplement II.* Nashville: Abingdon Press, 1993. Cokesbury Order #430135.
- H-3 Hopson, Hal H. *The Creative Church Musician Series.* Carol Stream, IL: Hope Publishing Co.
  Hbl—Vol. 1. The Creative Use of Handbells in Worship, 1997. Cokesbury Order #921992.
  Chr—Vol. 2. The Creative Use of Choirs in Worship, 1999. Cokesbury Order #732807.
  Desc—The Creative Use of Descants in Worship, 1999. Cokesbury Order #732864.
  Org—The Creative Use of the Organ in Worship (1997). Cokesbury Order #323904.

VOCAL SOLOS RESOURCES

- V-1 Kimbrough, Steven, ed. *Sweet Singer,* Chapel Hill, NC: Hinshaw Music, 1987. Catalogue #CV-1. #811712
- V-2 Handel, George Frideric. *Messiah.* Various editions available.
- V-3 Inman, Bryce. *I Can Only Imagine: 25 Modern Praise Favorites.* Nashville: Word Music, 2002. Catalogue #080689-43228. Cokesbury Order #513622.
- V-4 Scott, K. Lee. *Sing a Song of Joy.* Minneapolis, MN: Augsburg Fortress, 1989. Catalogue #0800647882 (Medium High Voice) Cokesbury Catalog #9780800647889 or #0800652827 (Medium Low Voice) Cokesbury Catalog #9780800652821.
- V-5 Courtney, Craig. *Music for the Master.* Beckenhorst VC1 #508872.
- V-6 Walters, Richard, arr. *Hymn Classics: Concert Arrangements of Traditional Hymns for Voice and Piano.* Hal Leonard Publishing, 1993. Catalogue #740033 (High Voice) or #740032 (Low Voice).
- V-7 Johnson, Hall, arr. *Thirty (30) Spirituals.* G. Shirmer, Inc., 1949. Catalogue #HL50328310.
- V-8 Wilson, John F., Don Doig, Jack Schrader, ed. *Everything for the Church Soloist.* Carol Stream, IL: Hope Publishing Company, 1980. Catalogue #804. Cokesbury Order #810103.
- V-9 Scott, K. Lee. *Rejoice Now My Spirit: Vocal Solos for the Church Year.* Augsburg Fortress, 1992. Catalogue #0800651081. Cokesbury Order #9780800651084
- V-10 Hayes, Mark et al. *From the Manger to the Cross*: Seasonal Solos for Medium Voice. Dayton, OH: The Lorenz Corporation, 2006. Catalogue #30/2157L. Cokesbury Order #526369.
- V-11 Pote, Allen. *A Song of Joy.* Carol Stream, IL: Hope Publishing, 2003. Catalogue #8135. Cokesbury Order #515068.

CONTEMPORARY RESOURCES

- R Webber, Robert, et al., ed. *Renew! Songs & Hymns for Blended Worship.* Carol Stream, IL: Hope Publishing Co., 1995. Accompaniment Edition: (#1998) #735812. Singer's Edition: (#1997) #735878.
- SP Various. *Songs for Praise and Worship Singalong Edition.* Waco, TX: Word Music, 1992. Catalogue #080689-006395.
- M1-M55 Barker, Ken, ed. *More Songs for Praise and Worship. Choir/Worship Team Edition.* Catalogue #0-80689-31317-2. *Keyboard Edition.* Catalogue #0-80689-39087-6. *Piano/Guitar/Vocal Edition.* Catalogue #0-80689-31018-8) Waco, TX: Word Music, 2000.
- M56-M115 Baker, Ken, ed. *More Songs for Praise and Worship 2. Choir/Worship Team Edition.* Catalogue #0-80689-35117-4. *Keyboard Edition.* Catalogue #0-80689-41187-8. *Piano/Guitar/Vocal Edition.* Catalogue #0-80689-31418-6. Waco, TX: Word Music, 2002.
- M116-M168 Barker, Ken, ed. *More Songs for Praise and Worship 3 Choir/Worship Team Edition.* Catalogue #0-80689-36917-5. *Keyboard Edition* Catalog #0-80689-45187-4. *Piano/Guitar/Vocal Edition* #0-80689-31818-4. Waco, TX: Word Music, 2005.
- M169-M219 Barker, Ken, ed. *More Songs for Praise and Worship 4 Choir/Worship Team Edition.* Catalog #0-80689-41217-2. *Keyboard Edition.* Catalogue #0-80689-47276-9. *Piano/Guitar/Vocal Edition* #0-80689-32018-7. Cokesbury Order #529198. Waco, TX: Word Music, 2006.

Proverbs 22:1-2, 8-9, 22-23

[1]A good name is to be chosen rather than great riches, and favor is better than silver or gold. [2]The rich and the poor have this in common: the LORD is the maker of them all.

[8]Whoever sows injustice will reap calamity, and the rod of anger will fail. [9]Those who are generous are blessed, for they share their bread with the poor.

[22]Do not rob the poor because they are poor, or crush the afflicted at the gate; [23]for the LORD pleads their cause and despoils of life those who despoil them.

Psalm 125

[1]Those who trust in the LORD are like Mount Zion, which cannot be moved, but abides forever. [2]As the mountains surround Jerusalem, so the LORD surrounds his people, from this time on and forevermore. [3]For the scepter of wickedness shall not rest on the land allotted to the righteous, so that the righteous might not stretch out their hands to do wrong. [4]Do good, O LORD, to those who are good, and to those who are upright in their hearts. [5]But those who turn aside to their own crooked ways the LORD will lead away with evildoers. Peace be upon Israel!

James 2:1-10 (11-13), 14-17

[1]My brothers and sisters, do you with your acts of favoritism really believe in our glorious Lord Jesus Christ? [2]For if a person with gold rings and in fine clothes comes into your assembly, and if a poor person in dirty clothes also comes in, [3]and if you take notice of the one wearing the fine clothes and say, "Have a seat here, please," while to the one who is poor you say, "Stand there," or, "Sit at my feet," [4]have you not made distinctions among yourselves, and become judges with evil thoughts? [5]Listen, my beloved brothers and sisters. Has not God chosen the poor in the world to be rich in faith and to be heirs of the kingdom that he has promised to those who love him? [6]But you have dishonored the poor. Is it not the rich who oppress you? Is it not they who drag you into court? [7]Is it not they who blaspheme the excellent name that was invoked over you?

[8]You do well if you really fulfill the royal law according to the scripture, "You shall love your neighbor as yourself." [9]But if you show partiality, you commit sin and are convicted by the law as transgressors. [10]For whoever keeps the whole law but fails in one point has become accountable for all of it. [11]For the one who said, "You shall not commit adultery," also said, "You shall not murder." Now if you do not commit adultery but if you murder, you have become a transgressor of the law. [12]So speak and so act as those who are to be judged by the law of liberty. [13]For judgment will be without mercy to anyone who has shown no mercy; mercy triumphs over judgment.

[14]What good is it, my brothers and sisters, if you say you have faith but do not have works? Can faith save you? [15]If a brother or sister is naked and lacks daily food, [16]and one of you says to them, "Go in peace; keep warm and eat your fill," and yet you do not supply their bodily needs, what is the good of that? [17]So faith by itself, if it has no works, is dead.

Mark 7:24-37

[24]From there he set out and went away to the region of Tyre. He entered a house and did not want anyone to know he was there. Yet he could not escape notice, [25]but a woman whose little daughter had an unclean spirit immediately heard about him, and she came and bowed down at his feet. [26]Now the woman was a Gentile, of Syrophoenician origin. She begged him to cast the demon out of her daughter. [27]He said to her, "Let the children be fed first, for it is not fair to take the children's food and throw it to the dogs." [28]But she answered him, "Sir, even the dogs under the table eat the children's crumbs." [29]Then he said to her, "For saying that, you may go—the demon has left your daughter." [30]So she went home, found the child lying on the bed, and the demon gone.

[31]Then he returned from the region of Tyre, and went by way of Sidon towards the Sea of Galilee, in the region of the Decapolis. [32]They brought to him a deaf man who had an impediment in his speech; and they begged him to lay his hand on him. [33]He took him aside in private, away from the crowd, and put his fingers into his ears, and he spat and touched his tongue. [34]Then looking up to heaven, he sighed and said to him, "Ephphatha," that is, "Be opened." [35]And immediately his ears were opened, his tongue was released, and he spoke plainly. [36]Then Jesus ordered them to tell no one; but the more he ordered them, the more zealously they proclaimed it. [37]They were astounded beyond measure, saying, "He has done everything well; he even makes the deaf to hear and the mute to speak."

Notes

Primary Hymns and Songs for the Day

"When the Church of Jesus" (Prov, Jas) (O)
B396, C470, UM592
H-3 Chr-35; Org-65
S-2 #99 Descant
"Cuando El Pobre" ("When the Poor Ones") (Prov, Jas)
C662, P407, UM434, VU702
"Where Cross the Crowded Ways of Life" (Jas)
C665, E609, F665, L429, N543, P408, UM427 (PD), VU681
H-3 Chr-178, 180; Org-44
S-1 #141-3 Various treatments
"Open My Eyes, That I May See" (Jas, Mark)
B502, C586, F486, P324, UM454, VU371
H-3 Chr-157; Org-108
"The Power of Your Love" (Jas, Mark)
M26
"Heal Me, Hands of Jesus" (Mark)
C504, UM262, VU621
"Open Our Eyes, Lord" (Mark)
B499, R91, S2086, SF2086, SP199
"Sent Forth by God's Blessing" (Jas) (C)
L221, N76, R307, UM664, VU481
H-3 Chr-125; Org-9
S-1 #327. Descant

Additional Hymn Suggestions

"All Things Bright and Beautiful" (Prov)
C61, E405, N31, P267, UM147 (PD), VU291, W505
"Lord, Whose Love Through Humble Service" (Prov, Jas, Mark)
C461, L423, UM581, R286
"Forth in Thy Name, O Lord" (Jas)
L505, UM438 (PD), VU416
"Now Let Us from This Table Rise" (Jas, Communion)
R242, UM634, VU483, W625
"Sunday's Palms Are Wednesday's Ashes" (Jas)
S2138, SF2138, VU107
"Living for Jesus" (Jas)
B282, C610, F462, S2149, SF2149
"Together We Serve" (Jas, Mark)
S2175, SF2175
"Healer of Our Every Ill" (Jas)
C506, S2213, SF2213, VU619
"Within the Day-to-Day" ("A Hymn for Deacons") (Jas)
S2245, SF2245
"In Remembrance of Me" (Jas, Communion)
B365, C403, S2254
"Taste and See" (Jas, Communion)
S2267, SF2267
"When Jesus the Healer Passed Through Galilee" (Mark)
UM263, VU358
"O Christ, the Healer" (Mark)
C503, L360, N175, P380, R191, UM265, W747
"Jesus' Hands Were Kind Hands" (Mark)
B477, UM273, VU570
"He Touched Me" (Mark)
C564, F628, UM367
"Go Forth for God" (Pss) (C)
E347, R291, UM670, VU418

Additional Contemporary Suggestions

"Live in Charity" ("Ubi Caritas") (Jas)
C523, R226, S2179, SF2179, W604
"Song of Hope" (Prov, Jas, Mark)
P432, S2186, VU424
"Change My Heart, O God" (Prov, Pss, Jas)
R143, SP195, S2152, SF2152
"Jesu, Jesu" (Jas)
B501, C600, E602, N498, P367, R289, UM432, VU593, W431
"Awesome God" (Mark)
R245, S2040, SF2040, SP11
"Open the Eyes of My Heart" (Mark)
M57; V-3 p. 162 Vocal Solo
"O Lord, You're Beautiful" (Mark)
S2064, SF2064

Vocal Solos

"Lord, Take Control of Me" (Prov)
V-8 p. 320
"Jesus Revealed in Me" (Jas)
V-8 p. 347
"O For a Thousand Tongues to Sing" (Mark)
V-1 p. 32

Anthems

"Healer of Our Every Ill" (Jas, Mark)
Marty Haugen; GIA G-3478
Two-part with keyboard

"God Is Able" (Mark)
Mark A. Miller; Abingdon Press 9780687030224
SATB, solo with piano

Other Suggestions

Visuals:
O Bread, generosity, ministering hands
P Mountain(s), scepter, ministry, (river, bird, snare)
E Rich/poor, hands, ministry w/ poor, clothes, food, blanket
G Sick child/well child, healing hands, hearing impaired

This would be an appropriate day to schedule a healing service in relation to the Mark reading.
Call to Prayer: C456. Prayer from the Heart (Jas)
Prayer: C653, UM639. Bread and Justice (Prov, Jas, Communion)
Prayer: C505. Prayer for Healing
Responsive Prayer: F74. A Pledge of Trust (Pss)
Alternate Lessons: Isa 35:4-7a; Ps 146 (see Scripture Index in this, or previous, editions of *Prepare!*).

PLANNING NOTES

Also Available from Abingdon Press

A trusted planning resource for traditional and contemporary worship . . . now includes interactive CD!

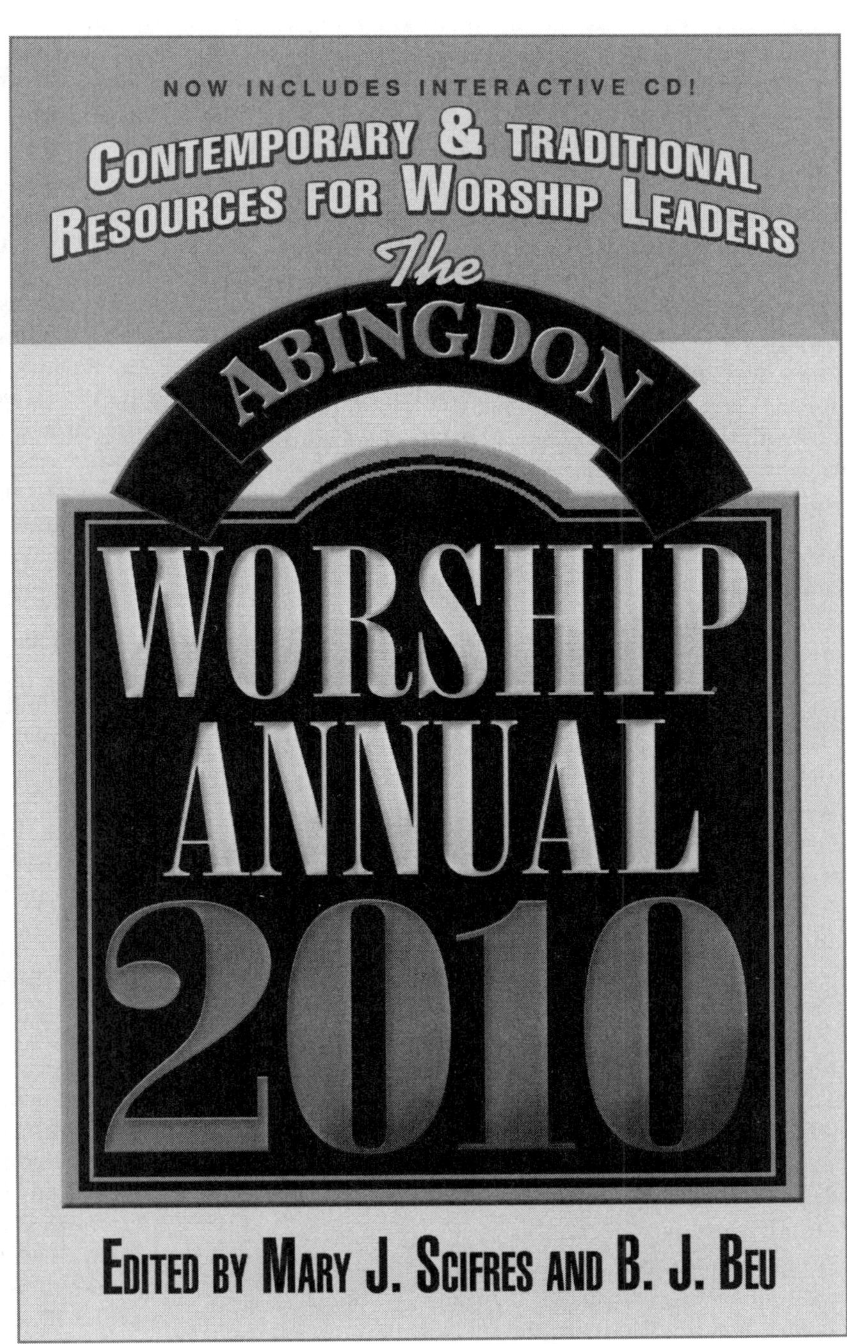

Theme Idea based on the lectionary readings, each week's offering of prayers and litanies follows a basic pattern of Christian worship:

- Gathering and Praise
- Proclamation and Response
- Thanksgiving and Communion
- Sending Forth

Plus . . .

- Praise Sentences
- Contemporary Gathering Words

Included CD-ROM in searchable PDF format:

- Full print text with hyperlinked table of contents
- Song suggestions for each week.
- Annotated resource list linked to worship planning websites
- Prayers and Liturgies for Communion

Proverbs 1:20-33

[20]Wisdom cries out in the street; in the squares she raises her voice. [21]At the busiest corner she cries out; at the entrance of the city gates she speaks: [22]"How long, O simple ones, will you love being simple? How long will scoffers delight in their scoffing and fools hate knowledge? [23]Give heed to my reproof; I will pour out my thoughts to you; I will make my words known to you. [24]Because I have called and you refused, have stretched out my hand and no one heeded, [25]and because you have ignored all my counsel and would have none of my reproof, [26]I also will laugh at your calamity; I will mock when panic strikes you, [27]when panic strikes you like a storm, and your calamity comes like a whirlwind, when distress and anguish come upon you. [28]Then they will call upon me, but I will not answer; they will seek me diligently, but will not find me. [29]Because they hated knowledge and did not choose the fear of the LORD, [30]would have none of my counsel, and despised all my reproof, [31]therefore they shall eat the fruit of their way and be sated with their own devices. [32]For waywardness kills the simple, and the complacency of fools destroys them; [33]but those who listen to me will be secure and will live at ease, without dread of disaster."

Psalm 19

[1]The heavens are telling the glory of God; and the firmament proclaims his handiwork. [2]Day to day pours forth speech, and night to night declares knowledge. [3]There is no speech, nor are there words; their voice is not heard; [4]yet their voice goes out through all the earth, and their words to the end of the world. In the heavens he has set a tent for the sun, [5]which comes out like a bridegroom from his wedding canopy, and like a strong man runs its course with joy. [6]Its rising is from the end of the heavens, and its circuit to the end of them; and nothing is hid from its heat. [7]The law of the LORD is perfect, reviving the soul; the decrees of the LORD are sure, making wise the simple; [8]the precepts of the LORD are right, rejoicing the heart; the commandment of the LORD is clear, enlightening the eyes; [9]the fear of the LORD is pure, enduring forever; the ordinances of the LORD are true and righteous altogether. [10]More to be desired are they than gold, even much fine gold; sweeter also than honey, and drippings of the honeycomb. [11]Moreover by them is your servant warned; in keeping them there is great reward. [12]But who can detect their errors? Clear me from hidden faults. [13]Keep back your servant also from the insolent; do not let them have dominion over me. Then I shall be blameless, and innocent of great transgression. [14]Let the words of my mouth and the meditation of my heart be acceptable to you, O LORD, my rock and my redeemer.

James 3:1-12

[1]Not many of you should become teachers, my brothers and sisters, for you know that we who teach will be judged with greater strictness. [2]For all of us make many mistakes. Anyone who makes no mistakes in speaking is perfect, able to keep the whole body in check with a bridle. [3]If we put bits into the mouths of horses to make them obey us, we guide their whole bodies. [4]Or look at ships: though they are so large that it takes strong winds to drive them, yet they are guided by a very small rudder wherever the will of the pilot directs. [5]So also the tongue is a small member, yet it boasts of great exploits.

How great a forest is set ablaze by a small fire! [6]And the tongue is a fire. The tongue is placed among our members as a world of iniquity; it stains the whole body, sets on fire the cycle of nature, and is itself set on fire by hell. [7]For every species of beast and bird, of reptile and sea creature, can be tamed and has been tamed by the human species, [8]but no one can tame the tongue—a restless evil, full of deadly poison. [9]With it we bless the Lord and Father, and with it we curse those who are made in the likeness of God. [10]From the same mouth come blessing and cursing. My brothers and sisters, this ought not to be so. [11]Does a spring pour forth from the same opening both fresh and brackish water? [12]Can a fig tree, my brothers and sisters, yield olives, or a grapevine figs? No more can salt water yield fresh.

Mark 8:27-38

[27]Jesus went on with his disciples to the villages of Caesarea Philippi; and on the way he asked his disciples, "Who do people say that I am?" [28]And they answered him, "John the Baptist; and others, Elijah; and still others, one of the prophets." [29]He asked them, "But who do you say that I am?" Peter answered him, "You are the Messiah." [30]And he sternly ordered them not to tell anyone about him.

[31]Then he began to teach them that the Son of Man must undergo great suffering, and be rejected by the elders, the chief priests, and the scribes, and be killed, and after three days rise again. [32]He said all this quite openly. And Peter took him aside and began to rebuke him. [33]But turning and looking at his disciples, he rebuked Peter and said, "Get behind me, Satan! For you are setting your mind not on divine things but on human things."

[34]He called the crowd with his disciples, and said to them, "If any want to become my followers, let them deny themselves and take up their cross and follow me. [35]For those who want to save their life will lose it, and those who lose their life for my sake, and for the sake of the gospel, will save it. [36]For what will it profit them to gain the whole world and forfeit their life? [37]Indeed, what can they give in return for their life? [38]Those who are ashamed of me and of my words in this adulterous and sinful generation, of them the Son of Man will also be ashamed when he comes in the glory of his Father with the holy angels."

Primary Hymns and Songs for the Day

"How Great Thou Art" (Pss) (O)
B10, C33, F2, L532, N35, P467, R250, UM77, VU238 (Fr.)
H-3 Chr-103; Org-105
S-1 #163. Harmonization

"Be Thou My Vision" (Prov, Pss)
B60, C595, E488, F468, N451, P339, R151, UM451, VU642
H-3 Hbl-15, 48; Chr-36; Org-153
S-1 #319. Arr. for organ and voices in canon

"God of Wonders" (Pss)
M80; V-3 p. 184 Vocal Solo

"Let It Be Said of Us" (Mark)
M53

"I Have Decided to Follow Jesus" (Mark)
B305, C344, S2129, SF2129

"Take Up Thy Cross" (Mark) (C)
B494, E675, L398, N204, P393, UM415 (PD), VU561, W634

Additional Hymn Suggestions

"Lift High the Cross" (Mark) (O)
B594, C108, E473, L377, N198, P371, R297, UM159, VU151, W704

"O Word of God Incarnate" (Prov)
C322, E632, L231, N315, P327, R97, UM598 (PD), VU499

"Praise the Source of Faith and Learning" (Pss)
N411, S2004, SF2004

"Cantemos al Señor" ("Let's Sing Unto the Lord") (Pss)
B38, C60, N39, R11, UM149

"God, Who Stretched the Spangled Heavens" (Pss)
B47, C651, E580, L463, N556, P268, UM150, W648

"Now, On Land and Sea Descending" (Pss)
P545, UM685 (PD), VU432

"Let Us with a Joyful Mind" (Pss)
E389, N16, P244, S2012, SF2012, VU234

"Lord, Speak to Me" (Jas)
B568, F625, L403, N531, P426, UM463 (PD), VU589

"Where Charity and Love Prevail" (Jas)
E581, L126, N396, UM549

"Woke Up This Morning" (Jas)
C623, N85, S2082, SF2082

"Where He Leads Me" (Mark)
B288, C346, F607, UM338 (PD)

"Must Jesus Bear the Cross Alone" (Mark)
B475, F504, SF2112, UM424 (PD)

"Nearer, My God, to Thee" (Mark)
B458, C577, N606, UM528 (PD), VU497 (Fr.)

"Two Fishermen" (Mark)
S2101, SF2101, W633

"Swiftly Pass the Clouds of Glory" (Mark)
P73, S2102

"Living for Jesus" (Mark)
B282, C610, F462, S2149, SF2149

"Christ for the World We Sing" (Mark) (C)
E537, F686, R299, UM568 (PD)

Additional Contemporary Suggestions

"I Will Call Upon the Lord" (Pss, Jas)
R15, S2002, SF2002, SP224

"More Precious than Silver" (Pss)
S2065, SF2065, SP99

"Praise the Name of Jesus" (Pss)
R7, S2066, SF2066, SP87

"All Heaven Declares" (Pss)
M58, R163

"The Heavens Shall Declare" (Pss)
M111

"Cry of My Heart" (Mark)
S2165, SF2165, M39

"Every Move I Make" (Mark)
M122

"Everyday" (Mark)
M150

Vocal Solos

"The Heavens Declare His Glory" (Pss)
V-8 p. 248

"Courage, My Heart" (Mark)
V-9 p. 20

Anthems

"The Heavens Are Telling" (Pss)
Richard McKinney; Concordia 98-3517
SAB with keyboard

"The Heavens Declare Thy Glory" (Pss)
arr. Barbara Owen; Choristers Guild CGA261
Unison with Organ and opt. trumpets

Other Suggestions

Visuals:
- **O** Crowded street corner, gates, storm, tornado, listening
- **P** Light/darkness, rising/setting sun, gold, honeycomb, honey
- **E** Teaching, bridle, ship rudder, fire
- **G** Christ, teaching, rugged cross, descending Christ/angels

This would be an appropriate day to dedicate new church schoolteachers and/or celebrate Christian Education Sunday in relation to the Prov and Jas readings.

Greeting: N824 (Pss)
Canticle: UM112. "Canticle of Wisdom" (Prov)
Prayer of Confession: N837 (Jas)
Words of Assurance: N840 (Pss)
Prayer: C1, C256, or N851 (Prov)
Prayer: C89. Christ Comes as One Unknown (Mark)
Reading: C57. Feast of a Hundred Hills (Pss)
Alternate Lessons: Isa 50:4-9a; Ps 116:1-9 (see Scripture Index in this, or previous, editions of *Prepare!*)..

Proverbs 31:10-31

[10]A capable wife who can find? She is far more precious
than jewels. [11]The heart of her husband trusts in her, and
he will have no lack of gain. [12]She does him good, and not
harm, all the days of her life. [13]She seeks wool and flax,
and works with willing hands. [14]She is like the ships of the
merchant, she brings her food from far away. [15]She rises
while it is still night and provides food for her household
and tasks for her servant-girls. [16]She considers a field and
buys it; with the fruit of her hands she plants a vineyard.
[17]She girds herself with strength, and makes her arms
strong. [18]She perceives that her merchandise is profitable.
Her lamp does not go out at night. [19]She puts her hands
to the distaff, and her hands hold the spindle. [20]She
opens her hand to the poor, and reaches out her hands
to the needy. [21]She is not afraid for her household when it
snows, for all her household are clothed in crimson. [22]She
makes herself coverings; her clothing is fine linen and
purple. [23]Her husband is known in the city gates, taking
his seat among the elders of the land. [24]She makes linen
garments and sells them; she supplies the merchant with
sashes. [25]Strength and dignity are her clothing, and she
laughs at the time to come. [26]She opens her mouth with
wisdom, and the teaching of kindness is on her tongue.
[27]She looks well to the ways of her household, and does
not eat the bread of idleness. [28]Her children rise up and
call her happy; her husband too, and he praises her:
[29]"Many women have done excellently, but you surpass
them all." [30]Charm is deceitful, and beauty is vain, but a
woman who fears the LORD is to be praised. [31]Give her a
share in the fruit of her hands, and let her works praise
her in the city gates.

Psalm 1

[1]Happy are those who do not follow the advice of the
wicked, or take the path that sinners tread, or sit in the
seat of scoffers; [2]but their delight is in the law of the
LORD, and on his law they meditate day and night. [3]They
are like trees planted by streams of water, which yield
their fruit in its season, and their leaves do not wither. In
all that they do, they prosper. [4]The wicked are not so, but
are like chaff that the wind drives away. [5]Therefore the
wicked will not stand in the judgment, nor sinners in the
congregation of the righteous; [6]for the LORD watches
over the way of the righteous, but the way of the wicked
will perish.

James 3:13–4:3, 7-8*a* 4:1-8

[13]Who is wise and understanding among you? Show by
your good life that your works are done with gentleness
born of wisdom. [14]But if you have bitter envy and selfish
ambition in your hearts, do not be boastful and false to
the truth. [15]Such wisdom does not come down from
above, but is earthly, unspiritual, devilish. [16]For where
there is envy and selfish ambition, there will also be
disorder and wickedness of every kind. [17]But the wisdom
from above is first pure, then peaceable, gentle, willing to
yield, full of mercy and good fruits, without a trace of partiality or hypocrisy. [18]And a harvest of righteousness is
sown in peace for those who make peace.

[1]Those conflicts and disputes among you, where do they
come from? Do they not come from your cravings that are
at war within you? [2]You want something and do not have
it; so you commit murder. And you covet something and
cannot obtain it; so you engage in disputes and conflicts.
You do not have, because you do not ask. [3]You ask and do
not receive, because you ask wrongly, in order to spend
what you get on your pleasures.

[7]Submit yourselves therefore to God. Resist the devil,
and he will flee from you. [8]Draw near to God, and he will
draw near to you.

Mark 9:30-37

[30]They went on from there and passed through Galilee.
He did not want anyone to know it; [31]for he was teaching
his disciples, saying to them, "The Son of Man is to be
betrayed into human hands, and they will kill him, and
three days after being killed, he will rise again." [32]But they
did not understand what he was saying and were afraid to
ask him.

[33]Then they came to Capernaum; and when he was in
the house he asked them, "What were you arguing about
on the way?" [34]But they were silent, for on the way they
had argued with one another who was the greatest. [35]He
sat down, called the twelve, and said to them, "Whoever
wants to be first must be last of all and servant of all."
[36]Then he took a little child and put it among them; and
taking it in his arms, he said to them, [37]"Whoever welcomes one such child in my name welcomes me, and
whoever welcomes me welcomes not me but the one
who sent me."

Notes

Primary Hymns and Songs for the Day

"Praise the Source of Faith and Learning" (Prov, Jas) (O)
N411, S2004, SF2004
H-3 Hbl-46; Chr-26, 134; Desc-53; Org-56
S-1 #168-171. Various treatments
"O Word of God Incarnate" (Prov, Pss)
C322, E632, L231, N315, P327, R97, UM598 (PD), VU499
H-3 Hbl-86; Chr-153; Org-95
S-1 #243. Harmonization
"Lord, I Want to Be a Christian" (Jas, Mark)
B489, C589, F421, N454, P372 (PD), R145, UM402
H-3 Chr-130
"Jesu, Jesu" (Mark)
B501, C600, E602, N498, P367, R289, UM432, VU593
H-3 Chr-114; Org-19
S-1 #63. Vocal part
"Make Me a Servant" (Mark)
S2176, SF2176, SP193
"Make Me a Captive, Lord" (Mark) (C)
B278, P378, UM421 (PD)

Additional Hymn Suggestions

"Morning Glory, Starlit Sky" (Prov)
E585, UM194, W587
"All Who Love and Serve Your City" (Prov, Mark)
C670, E570 and E571, L436, P413, UM433, W621
"I Sing a Song of the Saints of God" (Prov, Mark)
E293, N712, P364, UM712 (PD)
"I Surrender All" (Jas)
B275, F408, UM354
"Blessed Assurance" (Jas)
B334, C543, F67, N473, P341, UM369 (PD), VU337
"We Utter Our Cry" (Jas)
B631, UM439
"We Need a Faith" (Jas)
S2181, SF2181
"Together We Serve" (Jas, Mark)
S2175, SF2175
"O For a Heart to Praise My God" (Jas, Mark)
F357, UM417 (PD)
"Jesus, United by Thy Grace" (Jas, Mark)
UM561 (PD), VU591 (PD)
"Jesus Loves Me" (Mark)
B344 (PD), C113, F226, N327, P304, UM191, VU365
"Are Ye Able" (Mark)
C621, UM530 (PD)
"Like a Child" (Mark)
C133, S2092, SF2092, VU366
"Within the Day-to-Day" (Mark)
S2245, SF2245
"As We Gather at Your Table" (Mark, Communion)
S2268, SF2268. N332, VU457
"Lord, Whose Love Through Humble Service" (Mark) (C)
C461, L423, UM581, R286

Additional Contemporary Suggestions

"I Will Enter His Gates" (Pss)
S2270, SF2270, SP168
"Thy Word is a Lamp" (Pss)
C326, R94, SP183, UM601
"Humble Thyself in the Sight of the Lord" (Jas)
S2131, SF2131, R188, SP223
"Song of Hope" (Jas)
P432, S2186, VU424
"They'll Know We Are Christians" (Jas)
C494, S2223, SF2223
"Make Me a Channel of Your Peace" (Jas)
S2171, SF2171, VU684
"The Power of Your Love" (Jas)
M26
"The Servant Song" (Mark)
C490, N539, R148, S2222, SF2222, SP193, VU595

Vocal Solos

"A Worthy Woman" (Prov)
V-8 p. 364
"Ye Servants of God" (Mark)
V-1 p. 41

Anthems

"God Be in My Head" (Jas)
Kenneth Kosche; GIA G-3720
SATB a cappella

"Like a Child" (Mark)
arr. David Cherwien; Hope C5013
Two-part with piano and opt. flute
Other Suggestions

Visuals:

O Jewels, women at work, speaking, laughing, praise
P Open Bible, chaff/wind, scales of justice
E Gentle touch, fruit/harvest, conflict/treaty, James 3:8
G Crucifixion/resurrection, arguing, child, Mark 9:37

Introit: N332, VU457, S2268, SF2268. "As We Gather at Your Table" (Mark, Communion)
Prayer: UM401. For Holiness of Heart (Jas)
Prayer: UM570. Prayer of Ignatius of Loyola (Mark)
Greeting: N820 (Jas)
Prayer: C31. Prayer of St. Augustine (Jas)
Prayer: UM401. For Holiness of Heart (Jas)
Prayer: UM570. Prayer of Ignatius of Loyola (Mark)
Prayer: N851 (Jas)
If dedicating church schoolteachers, consider:
Song: C511. "Strong Gentle Children"
Song: F537. "The Wise May Bring Their Learning"
Blessing: F536. Children as a Trust
Alternate lessons: Wis 1:16 - 2:1, 12-22 (or Jer 11:18-20); Ps 54 (see Scripture Index in this, or previous, editions of *Prepare!*).

Esther 7:1-6, 9-10; 9:20-22

[1]So the king and Haman went in to feast with Queen Esther. [2]On the second day, as they were drinking wine, the king again said to Esther, "What is your petition, Queen Esther? It shall be granted you. And what is your request? Even to the half of my kingdom, it shall be fulfilled." [3]Then Queen Esther answered, "If I have won your favor, O king, and if it pleases the king, let my life be given me—that is my petition—and the lives of my people—that is my request. [4]For we have been sold, I and my people, to be destroyed, to be killed, and to be annihilated. If we had been sold merely as slaves, men and women, I would have held my peace; but no enemy can compensate for this damage to the king." [5]Then King Ahasuerus said to Queen Esther, "Who is he, and where is he, who has presumed to do this?" [6]Esther said, "A foe and enemy, this wicked Haman!" Then Haman was terrified before the king and the queen.

[9]Then Harbona, one of the eunuchs in attendance on the king, said, "Look, the very gallows that Haman has prepared for Mordecai, whose word saved the king, stands at Haman's house, fifty cubits high." And the king said, "Hang him on that." [10]So they hanged Haman on the gallows that he had prepared for Mordecai. Then the anger of the king abated.

[20]Mordecai recorded these things, and sent letters to all the Jews who were in all the provinces of King Ahasuerus, both near and far, [21]enjoining them that they should keep the fourteenth day of the month Adar and also the fifteenth day of the same month, year by year, [22]as the days on which the Jews gained relief from their enemies, and as the month that had been turned for them from sorrow into gladness and from mourning into a holiday; that they should make them days of feasting and gladness, days for sending gifts of food to one another and presents to the poor.

Psalm 124

[1]If it had not been the LORD who was on our side—let Israel now say— [2]if it had not been the LORD who was on our side, when our enemies attacked us, [3]then they would have swallowed us up alive, when their anger was kindled against us; [4]then the flood would have swept us away, the torrent would have gone over us; [5]then over us would have gone the raging waters. [6]Blessed be the LORD, who has not given us as prey to their teeth. [7]We have escaped like a bird from the snare of the fowlers; the snare is broken, and we have escaped. [8]Our help is in the name of the LORD, who made heaven and earth.

James 5:13-20

[13]Are any among you suffering? They should pray. Are any cheerful? They should sing songs of praise. [14]Are any among you sick? They should call for the elders of the church and have them pray over them, anointing them with oil in the name of the Lord. [15]The prayer of faith will save the sick, and the Lord will raise them up; and anyone who has committed sins will be forgiven. [16]Therefore confess your sins to one another, and pray for one another, so that you may be healed. The prayer of the righteous is powerful and effective. [17]Elijah was a human being like us, and he prayed fervently that it might not rain, and for three years and six months it did not rain on the earth. [18]Then he prayed again, and the heaven gave rain and the earth yielded its harvest.

[19]My brothers and sisters, if anyone among you wanders from the truth and is brought back by another, [20]you should know that whoever brings back a sinner from wandering will save the sinner's soul from death and will cover a multitude of sins.

Mark 9:38-50

[38]John said to him, "Teacher, we saw someone casting out demons in your name, and we tried to stop him, because he was not following us." [39]But Jesus said, "Do not stop him; for no one who does a deed of power in my name will be able soon afterward to speak evil of me. [40]Whoever is not against us is for us. [41]For truly I tell you, whoever gives you a cup of water to drink because you bear the name of Christ will by no means lose the reward.

[42]"If any of you put a stumbling block before one of these little ones who believe in me, it would be better for you if a great millstone were hung around your neck and you were thrown into the sea. [43]If your hand causes you to stumble, cut it off; it is better for you to enter life maimed than to have two hands and to go to hell, to the unquenchable fire. [45]And if your foot causes you to stumble, cut it off; it is better for you to enter life lame than to have two feet and to be thrown into hell. [47]And if your eye causes you to stumble, tear it out; it is better for you to enter the kingdom of God with one eye than to have two eyes and to be thrown into hell, [48]where their worm never dies, and the fire is never quenched.

[49]"For everyone will be salted with fire. [50]Salt is good; but if salt has lost its saltiness, how can you season it? Have salt in yourselves, and be at peace with one another."

Notes

Primary Hymns and Songs for the Day
"Sing Praise to God Who Reigns Above" (Esth, Jas) (O)
B20, C6, E408, F343, N6, P483, R52, UM126 (PD), VU216, W528
H-3 Hbl-92; Chr-173; Desc-76; Org-91
S-1 #237. Descant
"If It Had Not Been for the Lord" (Esth, Pss)
S2053, SF2053
"They'll Know We Are Christians" (Jas)
C494, S2223, SF2223
"Rescue the Perishing" (Jas, Mark)
B559, F661, UM591 (PD)
"Sois la Semilla" ("You Are the Seed") (Mark)
C478, N528, UM583
"Go Forth for God" (Pss) (C)
R291, UM670, VU418
S-1 #138-9. Harmonization with descant
#140. Harmonization
H-3 Hbl-77; Chr-63; Org-106

Additional Hymn Suggestions
"God of Many Names" (Esth)
C13, UM105
"Wellspring of Wisdom" (Esth)
C596, UM506, VU287
"Lift Every Voice and Sing" (Esth, Pss)
B627, C631, E599, L562, N593, P563, UM519, W641
"His Eye Is on the Sparrow" (Esth, Pss)
C82, N475, S2146, SF2146
"Joy Comes with the Dawn" (Esth, Pss)
S2210, SF2210, VU166
"We Sing to You, O God" (Esth, Jas)
N9, S2001, SF2001
"God, How Can We Forgive" (Esth, Jas)
S2169, SF2169
"Come Away with Me" (Jas)
S2202, SF2202
"The Fragrance of Christ" (Jas)
S2205, SF2205
"Come Back Quickly to the Lord" (Jas)
P381, UM343
"There's a Spirit in the Air" (Mark)
B393, C257, N292, P433, R282, UM192, VU582, W531
"Cuando El Pobre" ("When the Poor Ones") (Mark)
C662, P407, UM434, VU702
"God of Grace and God of Glory" (Mark)
B395, C464, E594, F528, L415, N436, P420, R301, UM577, VU686
"Blessed Jesus, at Thy Word" (Mark)
E440, N74, P454, R93, UM596 (PD), VU500
"Living for Jesus" (Mark)
B282, C610, F462, S2149, SF2149
"For One Great Peace" (Mark)
S2185, SF2185
"Deep in the Shadows of the Past" (Mark)
N320, P330, S2246

Additional Contemporary Suggestions
"Trading My Sorrows" (Esth)
M75
"Lord, Listen to Your Children Praying" (Jas)
C305, S2193, SF2193, VU400
"Lord, Listen to Your Children" (Jas)
S2207, SF2207
"Someone Asked the Question" (Jas)
N523, S2144
"Make Me a Servant" (Jas, Mark)
S2176, SF2176, SP193
"The Lord's Prayer" (Jas, Mark)
S2278, SF2278
C308, P589, R180, UM271
"Make Me a Channel of Your Peace" (Mark)
S2171, SF2171, VU684
"Song of Hope" (Mark)
P432, S2186, VU424

Vocal Solos
"Jesus, Thou Art Watching Ever" (Pss)
V-4 p. 6
"This Is My Commandment" (Jas)
V-8 p. 284
"In Jesus' Name" (Mark)
V-8 p. 188

Anthems
"Born from the Gospel" (Mark)
Rob Glover; GIA G-4587
SATB with organ and C instrument

"Let Us Talents and Tongues Employ" (Mark)
arr. Austin Lovelace; Choristers Guild CGA 619
Two-part with piano and opt. guitar, bongo drums

Other Suggestions
Visuals:
O Hand, crown, festival, joy, food, gifts
P Flood, bird, snare
E Praying hands, oil, James 5:15a, parched earth/rain/harvest, return
G Cup of water, stumbling block, millstone/sea, hand/foot, eye, fire salt
Greeting: N819 (Pss)
Prayer: C394. That the Church May Be One (World Communion)
Response: S2200, SF2200. "O Lord, Hear My Prayer" (Jas)
Response: C663, E648, N572, P334, UM448, W508, stanza 11, without refrain. "Go Down, Moses" (Esth)
Alternate Lessons: Num 11:4-6, 10-16, 24-29; Ps 19 (see Scripture Index in this, or previous, editions of *Prepare!*).

Job 1:1; 2:1-10

1There was once a man in the land of Uz whose name was Job. That man was blameless and upright, one who feared God, and turned away from evil.

1One day the heavenly beings came to present themselves before the LORD, and Satan also came among them to present himself before the LORD. 2The LORD said to Satan, "Where have you come from?" Satan answered the LORD, "From going to and fro on the earth, and from walking up and down on it." 3The LORD said to Satan, "Have you considered my servant Job? There is no one like him on the earth, a blameless and upright man who fears God and turns away from evil. He still persists in his integrity, although you incited me against him, to destroy him for no reason." 4Then Satan answered the LORD, "Skin for skin! All that people have they will give to save their lives. 5But stretch out your hand now and touch his bone and his flesh, and he will curse you to your face." 6The LORD said to Satan, "Very well, he is in your power; only spare his life."

7So Satan went out from the presence of the LORD, and inflicted loathsome sores on Job from the sole of his foot to the crown of his head. 8Job took a potsherd with which to scrape himself, and sat among the ashes.

9Then his wife said to him, "Do you still persist in your integrity? Curse God, and die." 10But he said to her, "You speak as any foolish woman would speak. Shall we receive the good at the hand of God, and not receive the bad?" In all this Job did not sin with his lips.

Psalm 26

1Vindicate me, O LORD, for I have walked in my integrity, and I have trusted in the LORD without wavering. 2Prove me, O LORD, and try me; test my heart and mind. 3For your steadfast love is before my eyes, and I walk in faithfulness to you. 4I do not sit with the worthless, nor do I consort with hypocrites; 5I hate the company of evildoers, and will not sit with the wicked. 6I wash my hands in innocence, and go around your altar, O LORD, 7singing aloud a song of thanksgiving, and telling all your wondrous deeds. 8O LORD, I love the house in which you dwell, and the place where your glory abides. 9Do not sweep me away with sinners, nor my life with the bloodthirsty, 10those in whose hands are evil devices, and whose right hands are full of bribes. 11But as for me, I walk in my integrity; redeem me, and be gracious to me. 12My foot stands on level ground; in the great congregation I will bless the LORD.

Hebrews 1:1-4; 2:5-12

1Long ago God spoke to our ancestors in many and various ways by the prophets, 2but in these last days he has spoken to us by a Son, whom he appointed heir of all things, through whom he also created the worlds. 3He is the reflection of God's glory and the exact imprint of God's very being, and he sustains all things by his powerful word. When he had made purification for sins, he sat down at the right hand of the Majesty on high, 4having become as much superior to angels as the name he has inherited is more excellent than theirs.

5Now God did not subject the coming world, about which we are speaking, to angels. 6But someone has testified somewhere, "What are human beings that you are mindful of them, or mortals, that you care for them? 7You have made them for a little while lower than the angels; you have crowned them with glory and honor, 8subjecting all things under their feet." Now in subjecting all things to them, God left nothing outside their control. As it is, we do not yet see everything in subjection to them, 9but we do see Jesus, who for a little while was made lower than the angels, now crowned with glory and honor because of the suffering of death, so that by the grace of God he might taste death for everyone.

10It was fitting that God, for whom and through whom all things exist, in bringing many children to glory, should make the pioneer of their salvation perfect through sufferings. 11For the one who sanctifies and those who are sanctified all have one Father. For this reason Jesus is not ashamed to call them brothers and sisters, 12saying, "I will proclaim your name to my brothers and sisters, in the midst of the congregation I will praise you."

Mark 10:2-16

2Some Pharisees came, and to test him they asked, "Is it lawful for a man to divorce his wife?" 3He answered them, "What did Moses command you?" 4They said, "Moses allowed a man to write a certificate of dismissal and to divorce her." 5But Jesus said to them, "Because of your hardness of heart he wrote this commandment for you. 6But from the beginning of creation, 'God made them male and female.' 7'For this reason a man shall leave his father and mother and be joined to his wife, 8and the two shall become one flesh.' So they are no longer two, but one flesh. 9Therefore what God has joined together, let no one separate."

10Then in the house the disciples asked him again about this matter. 11He said to them, "Whoever divorces his wife and marries another commits adultery against her; 12and if she divorces her husband and marries another, she commits adultery."

13People were bringing little children to him in order that he might touch them; and the disciples spoke sternly to them. 14But when Jesus saw this, he was indignant and said to them, "Let the little children come to me; do not stop them; for it is to such as these that the kingdom of God belongs. 15Truly I tell you, whoever does not receive the kingdom of God as a little child will never enter it." 16And he took them up in his arms, laid his hands on them, and blessed them.

Primary Hymns and Songs for the Day
"Tell Me the Stories of Jesus" (Mark) (O)
B129, C190, F212, UM277 (PD), VU357
"Through It All" (Job)
C555, F43, UM507
"Rejoice in God's Saints" (Job)
C476, UM708
H-3 Hbl-90, 105; Chr-221; Desc-49; Org-51
S-2 #71-74. Introduction and harmonizations
"The Family Prayer Song" (Pss, Mark)
M54, S2188, SF2188
"One Bread, One Body" (World Communion)
C393, UM620, VU467
H-3 Chr-156
"How Firm a Foundation" (Job, Pss) (C)
B338, C618, E636, F32, L507, N407, P361, UM529 (PD), VU660, W585
H-3 Hbl-27, 69; Chr-102; Desc-41; Org-41
S-1 #133. Harmonization
#134. Performance note

Additional Hymn Suggestions
"When Our Confidence is Shaken" (Job)
C534, UM505
"Wellspring of Wisdom" (Job)
C596, UM506, VU287
"By Gracious Powers" (Job)
E695 and E696, N413, P342, UM517, W577
"Lift Every Voice and Sing" (Job)
B627, C631, E599, L562, N593, P563, UM519, W641
"Jesus, Tempted in the Desert" (Job)
S2105, SF2105, VU115
"When We Are Called to Sing Your Praise" (Job)
S2216, SF2216
"My Hope is Built" (Job, Pss)
B406, C537, F92, L293, L294 (PD), N368, P379, UM368 (PD)
"I Will Trust in the Lord" (Job, Pss)
B420, N416, UM464
"I Want Jesus to Walk with Me" (Job, Pss)
B465, C627, N490, P363, UM521
"Children of the Heavenly Father" (Pss, Heb, Mark)
B55, F89, L474, N487, UM141
"All Praise to Thee, for Thou, O King Divine" (Heb)
B229, UM166, VU327
"And Can It Be that I Should Gain" (Heb)
B147, F260, R193, UM363 (PD)
"Jesus Loves Me" (Mark)
B344 (PD), C113, F226, N327, P304, UM191, VU365
"Jesus' Hands Were Kind Hands" (Mark)
B477, UM273, VU570
"Our Parent, by Whose Name" (Mark)
E587, L357, UM447, VU555, W570
"Jesus, Lover of My Soul (Mark)
B180, C542, E699, F222, N546, P303, UM479 (PD), VU669
"Like a Child" (Mark)
C133, S2092, SF2092, VU366
"Lord of All Hopefulness" (Mark)
E482, L469, R174, S2197, SF2197, W568

"The Head That Once Was Crowned" (Heb) (C)
E483, L173, P149, UM326 (PD), VU190, W464

Additional Contemporary Suggestions
"Blessed Be the Name" (Job)
B206, UM63
"Blessed Be Your Name" (Job)
M163
"My Tribute" ("To God Be the Glory") (Job, Heb)
B153, C39, F365, N14, R68, UM99; V-8 p. 5 Vocal Solo
"How Majestic Is Your Name" (Heb)
C63, R98, S2023, SF2023, SP14
"Blessing, Honour, and Glory" (Heb)
M21, R81
"That's Why We Praise Him" (Heb)
M94
"The Power of Your Love" (Pss, Mark)
M26
"Where Children Belong" (Mark)
S2233, SF2233
"Bind Us Together" (World Communion)
R292, S2226, SF2226, SP140

Vocal Solos
"A Contrite Heart" (Pss)
V-4 p. 10
"Agnus Dei" (Heb)
V-3 p. 156

Anthems
"Blessed Be the Name of the Lord" (Job, Heb)
David Brazzeal; Choristers Guild CGA810
Unison or 2-part with piano

"One Bread, One Body" (World Communion)
arr. Douglas E. Wagner; Hope Publishing Co. C-5354
SATB with keyboard or 3-5 octave handbells

Other Suggestions
Visuals:
O Hand, sores, suffering, potsherd, ashes, man/woman
P Walking, heart, washing hands, singing, foot, broom
E Jesus, angels, crown, cross, pioneer
G Divorce decree, marriage (wedding rings, certificate), children, Mark 10:14, blessing
Greeting: N824 (Heb)
Reading: N887. A New Creed (World Communion)
Response: "He's Got the Whole World In His Hands" (Job, Mark)
Alternate Lessons: Gen 2:18-24; Ps 8 (see Scripture Index in this, or previous, editions of *Prepare!*).

Job 23:1-9, 16-17

[1]Then Job answered: [2]"Today also my complaint is bitter; his hand is heavy despite my groaning. [3]Oh, that I knew where I might find him, that I might come even to his dwelling! [4]I would lay my case before him, and fill my mouth with arguments. [5]I would learn what he would answer me, and understand what he would say to me. [6]Would he contend with me in the greatness of his power? No; but he would give heed to me. [7]There an upright person could reason with him, and I should be acquitted forever by my judge. [8]"If I go forward, he is not there; or backward, I cannot perceive him; [9] on the left he hides, and I cannot behold him; I turn to the right, but I cannot see him.

[16]"God has made my heart faint; the Almighty has terrified me; [17]If only I could vanish in darkness, and thick darkness would cover my face!"

Psalm 22:1-15

[1]My God, my God, why have you forsaken me? Why are you so far from helping me, from the words of my groaning? [2]O my God, I cry by day, but you do not answer; and by night, but find no rest. [3]Yet you are holy, enthroned on the praises of Israel. [4]In you our ancestors trusted; they trusted, and you delivered them. [5]To you they cried, and were saved; in you they trusted, and were not put to shame. [6]But I am a worm, and not human; scorned by others, and despised by the people. [7]All who see me mock at me; they make mouths at me, they shake their heads; [8]"Commit your cause to the LORD; let him deliver—let him rescue the one in whom he delights!" [9]Yet it was you who took me from the womb; you kept me safe on my mother's breast. [10]On you I was cast from my birth, and since my mother bore me you have been my God. [11]Do not be far from me, for trouble is near and there is no one to help. [12]Many bulls encircle me, strong bulls of Bashan surround me; [13]they open wide their mouths at me, like a ravening and roaring lion. [14]I am poured out like water, and all my bones are out of joint; my heart is like wax; it is melted within my breast; [15]my mouth is dried up like a potsherd, and my tongue sticks to my jaws; you lay me in the dust of death.

Hebrews 4:12-16

[12]Indeed, the word of God is living and active, sharper than any two-edged sword, piercing until it divides soul from spirit, joints from marrow; it is able to judge the thoughts and intentions of the heart. [13]And before him no creature is hidden, but all are naked and laid bare to the eyes of the one to whom we must render an account.

[14]Since, then, we have a great high priest who has passed through the heavens, Jesus, the Son of God, let us hold fast to our confession. [15]For we do not have a high priest who is unable to sympathize with our weaknesses, but we have one who in every respect has been tested as we are, yet without sin. [16]Let us therefore approach the throne of grace with boldness, so that we may receive mercy and find grace to help in time of need.

Mark 10:17-31

[17]As he was setting out on a journey, a man ran up and knelt before him, and asked him, "Good Teacher, what must I do to inherit eternal life?" [18]Jesus said to him, "Why do you call me good? No one is good but God alone. [19]You know the commandments: 'You shall not murder; You shall not commit adultery; You shall not steal; You shall not bear false witness; You shall not defraud; Honor your father and mother.' " [20]He said to him, "Teacher, I have kept all these since my youth." [21]Jesus, looking at him, loved him and said, "You lack one thing; go, sell what you own, and give the money to the poor, and you will have treasure in heaven; then come, follow me." [22]When he heard this, he was shocked and went away grieving, for he had many possessions.

[23]Then Jesus looked around and said to his disciples, "How hard it will be for those who have wealth to enter the kingdom of God!" [24]And the disciples were perplexed at these words. But Jesus said to them again, "Children, how hard it is to enter the kingdom of God! [25]It is easier for a camel to go through the eye of a needle than for someone who is rich to enter the kingdom of God." [26]They were greatly astounded and said to one another, "Then who can be saved?" [27]Jesus looked at them and said, "For mortals it is impossible, but not for God; for God all things are possible."

[28]Peter began to say to him, "Look, we have left everything and followed you." [29]Jesus said, "Truly I tell you, there is no one who has left house or brothers or sisters or mother or father or children or fields, for my sake and for the sake of the good news, [30]who will not receive a hundredfold now in this age—houses, brothers and sisters, mothers and children, and fields, with persecutions—and in the age to come eternal life. [31]But many who are first will be last, and the last will be first."

Notes

Primary Hymns and Songs for the Day

"Lord, Speak to Me" (Job, Mark) (O)
B568, F625, L403, N531, P426, UM463 (PD), VU589
H-3 Hbl-75; Chr-131; Desc-22; Org-18
S-1 #52. Descant
"Precious Lord, Take My Hand" (Job, Pss)
B456, C628, F611, N472, P404, UM474, VU670
H-3 Chr-164; Org-116
"Out of the Depths I Cry to You" (Job, Pss)
L295, P240, UM515
"O Jesus, I Have Promised" (Mark)
B276, C612, F402, N493, P388, UM396 (PD)
S-2 #9. Descant
E655, L503 (PD), P389, VU120
"Lord, I Want to Be a Christian" (Mark)
B489, C589, F421, N454, P372 (PD), R145, UM402
"Take My Life, and Let It Be" (Mark) (C)
B277, C609, P391
H-3 Chr-34, 177; Desc-51; Org-53
S-2 #78-80. Various treatments
B283, E707, L406, N448, R133, UM399 (PD), VU506

Additional Hymn Suggestions

"My Faith Looks Up to Thee" (Job, Pss)
B416, C576, E691, F84, L479, P383, UM452 (PD), VU663
"Why Stand So Far Away, My God?" (Job, Pss)
C671, S2180, SF2180
"By the Babylonian Rivers" (Job)
P246, S2217, VU859, W426
"I Want Jesus to Walk With Me" (Pss)
B465, C627, N490, P363, UM521
"Lead Me, Lord" (Pss, Heb)
C593, N774, R175, UM473 (PD), VU662
"Hope of the World" (Heb)
C538, E472, L493, N46, P360, UM178, VU215, W565
"Come, Thou Fount of Every Blessing" (Heb)
B15, C16, E686, F318, L499, N459, P356, UM400 (PD), VU559
"By Gracious Powers" (Heb)
E695 and E696, N413, P342, UM517, W577
"O Word of God Incarnate" (Heb)
C322, E632, L231, N315, P327, R97, UM598 (PD), VU499
"Womb of Life" (Heb)
C14, N274, S2046, SF2046
"Mothering God, You Gave Me Birth" (Heb)
C83, N467, S2050, SF2050, VU320
"Come, Let Us with Our Lord Arise" (Heb)
E49, R18, S2084, SF2084
"Take Up Thy Cross" (Mark)
B494, E675, L398, N204, P393, UM415 (PD), VU561, W634
"The Summons" (Mark)
S2130, SF2130, VU567
"As We Gather at Your Table" (Mark, Communion)
S2268, SF2268. N332, VU457

Additional Contemporary Suggestions

"Word of God, Speak" (Job, Pss, Heb)
M148
"When It's All Been Said and Done" (Job, Pss, Mark)
M115
"Thy Word is a Lamp" (Heb)
C326, R94, SP183, UM601
"People Need the Lord" (Heb, Mark)
B557, S2244, SF2244
"Give Thanks" (Mark)
C528, R266, S2036, SF2036, SP170
"Cry of My Heart" (Mark)
S2165, SF2165, M39
"I Will Never Be" (the Same Again) (Mark)
M34
"All Things are Possible" (Mark)
M92
"Take This Life" (Mark)
M98
"Every Move I Make" (Mark)
M122
"Be the Centre" (Mark)
M156

Vocal Solos

"He Trusted in God" (Job, Pss)
V-2
"Oh, Graveyard" (Job, Pss)
V-7 p. 64

Anthems

"Come, Thou Fount of Every Blessing" (Heb)
John Helgen; Kjos 9071
SATB with keyboard

"Take My Life, and Let It Be" (Mark)
Arr. Margaret R. Tucker; Choristers Guild CGA1111
Unison/Two-Part with organ and opt. handbells

Other Suggestions

Visuals:
O Briefcase, Job 23:3, courtroom, judge, scales, darkness
P Crying, worm, birth, nursing, bulls, lion, water, melted wax, dust
E Heb 4:12, open Bible, sword, scales, heart, Christ
G Kneeling, Jesus, 10 commandments, rich/poor, camel/needle
Call to Confession: N833 (Heb)
Response: C299, S2277, SF2277. "Lord, Have Mercy" (Heb)
Words of Assurance: N840 (Heb)
Reading: C325 or UM595 (Job, Heb)
Prayer: N859. Thankfulness and Hope (Job, Pss)
Prayer: C89. Christ Comes as One Unknown (Mark)
Alternate Lessons: Amos 5:6-7, 10-15; Ps 90:12-17 (see Scripture Index in this, or previous, editions of *Prepare!*).

Job 38:1-7 (34-41)

[1]Then the LORD answered Job out of the whirlwind: [2]"Who is this that darkens counsel by words without knowledge? [3]Gird up your loins like a man, I will question you, and you shall declare to me. [4]Where were you when I laid the foundation of the earth? Tell me, if you have understanding. [5]Who determined its measurements—surely you know! Or who stretched the line upon it? [6]On what were its bases sunk, or who laid its cornerstone [7]when the morning stars sang together and all the heavenly beings shouted for joy?

[34]"Can you lift up your voice to the clouds, so that a flood of waters may cover you? [35]Can you send forth lightnings, so that they may go and say to you, 'Here we are'? [36]Who has put wisdom in the inward parts, or given understanding to the mind? [37]Who has the wisdom to number the clouds? Or who can tilt the waterskins of the heavens, [38]when the dust runs into a mass and the clods cling together? [39]Can you hunt the prey for the lion, or satisfy the appetite of the young lions, [40]when they crouch in their dens, or lie in wait in their covert? [41]Who provides for the raven its prey, when its young ones cry to God, and wander about for lack of food?"

Psalm 104:1-9, 24, 35*c*

[1]Bless the LORD, O my soul. O LORD my God, you are very great. You are clothed with honor and majesty, [2]wrapped in light as with a garment. You stretch out the heavens like a tent, [3]you set the beams of your chambers on the waters, you make the clouds your chariot, you ride on the wings of the wind, [4]you make the winds your messengers, fire and flame your ministers. [5]You set the earth on its foundations, so that it shall never be shaken. [6]You cover it with the deep as with a garment; the waters stood above the mountains. [7]At your rebuke they flee; at the sound of your thunder they take to flight. [8]They rose up to the mountains, ran down to the valleys to the place that you appointed for them. [9]You set a boundary that they may not pass, so that they might not again cover the earth.

[24]O LORD, how manifold are your works! In wisdom you have made them all; the earth is full of your creatures.

[35c]Praise the LORD!

Hebrews 5:1-10

[1]Every high priest chosen from among mortals is put in charge of things pertaining to God on their behalf, to offer gifts and sacrifices for sins. [2]He is able to deal gently with the ignorant and wayward, since he himself is subject to weakness; [3] and because of this he must offer sacrifice for his own sins as well as for those of the people. [4]And one does not presume to take this honor, but takes it only when called by God, just as Aaron was.

[5]So also Christ did not glorify himself in becoming a high priest, but was appointed by the one who said to him, "You are my Son, today I have begotten you"; [6]as he says also in another place, "You are a priest forever, according to the order of Melchizedek."

[7]In the days of his flesh, Jesus offered up prayers and supplications, with loud cries and tears, to the one who was able to save him from death, and he was heard because of his reverent submission. [8]Although he was a Son, he learned obedience through what he suffered; [9]and having been made perfect, he became the source of eternal salvation for all who obey him, [10]having been designated by God a high priest according to the order of Melchizedek.

Mark 10:35-45

[35]James and John, the sons of Zebedee, came forward to him and said to him, "Teacher, we want you to do for us whatever we ask of you." [36]And he said to them, "What is it you want me to do for you?" [37]And they said to him, "Grant us to sit, one at your right hand and one at your left, in your glory." [38]But Jesus said to them, "You do not know what you are asking. Are you able to drink the cup that I drink, or be baptized with the baptism that I am baptized with?" [39]They replied, "We are able." Then Jesus said to them, "The cup that I drink you will drink; and with the baptism with which I am baptized, you will be baptized; [40]but to sit at my right hand or at my left is not mine to grant, but it is for those for whom it has been prepared."

[41]When the ten heard this, they began to be angry with James and John. [42]So Jesus called them and said to them, "You know that among the Gentiles those whom they recognize as their rulers lord it over them, and their great ones are tyrants over them. [43]But it is not so among you; but whoever wishes to become great among you must be your servant, [44]and whoever wishes to be first among you must be slave of all. [45]For the Son of Man came not to be served but to serve, and to give his life a ransom for many."

Notes

Primary Hymns and Songs for the Day

"I Sing the Almighty Power of God" (Job) (O)
B42, E398, UM152 (PD)
H-3 Hbl-44; Chr-21; Desc-40; Org-40
S-1 #131-132. Introduction and descant
C64, N12, P288 (PD), R54
H-3 Hbl-16, 22, 68; Chr-101; Desc-37
S-1 #115. Harmonization
VU231 (PD), W502 (PD)
"Hallelujah! What a Savior" (Heb)
B175, F246, UM165 (PD)
H-3 Chr-134
"Jesu, Jesu" (Mark)
B501, C600, E602, N498, P367, R289, UM432, VU593, W431
H-3 Chr-114; Org-19
S-1 #63. Vocal part
"The Servant Song" (Mark)
C490, N539, R148, S2222, SF2222, SP193, VU595
"Are Ye Able" (Mark, Laity Sunday) (C)
C621, UM530 (PD)
S-2 #23. Introduction

Additional Hymn Suggestions

"How Great Thou Art" (Job)
B10, C33, F2, L532, N35, P467, R250, UM77, VU238 (Fr.)
"This is My Father's World" (Job)
B43, C59, E651, F6, L554, P293, UM144, VU296
"God, Who Stretched the Spangled Heavens" (Job)
B47, C651, E580, L463, N556, P268, UM150, W648
"Praise the Source of Faith and Learning" (Job)
N411, S2004, SF2004
"O Worship the King" (Pss)
B16, C17, E388, F336, L548 (PD), N26, P476, UM73, VU235
"Joyful, Joyful, We Adore Thee" (Job, Pss)
B7, C2, E376, F377, L551, N4, P464, UM89 (PD), VU232, W525
"Many and Great, O God" (Job, Pss)
B49, C58, E385, N3, N341, P271 (PD), UM148, VU308, W503
"All Hail the Power of Jesus' Name" (Heb)
B202, C91, E450, F325, L328, N304, P142, R45, UM154 (PD), W494
B200, C92, F326, P143, UM155 (PD)
B201, E451, F327, L329 (PD), VU334
"Glorious Things of Thee are Spoken" (Heb)
B398, C709, E522 (or 523), F376, L358, N307, P446, UM731 (PD)
"My Song Is Love Unknown" (Heb)
E458, L94, N222, P76, S2083, SF2083, VU143, W439
"Living for Jesus" (Heb)
B282, C610, F462, S2149, SF2149
"Now Praise the Hidden God of Love" (Heb, Mark)
P402, S2027, SF2027
"Thou Didst Leave Thy Throne" (Heb, Mark)
B121, F170, S2100, SF2100
"All Praise to Thee, for Thou, O King Divine" (Heb, Mark)
B229, UM166, VU327
"Ye Servants of God" (Mark)
B589, C110, E535, F360, N305, P477, UM181 (PD), VU342
"Make Me a Captive, Lord" (Mark)
B278, P378, UM421 (PD)
"Lord, Whose Love Through Humble Service" (Mark)
C461, L423, UM581, R286

Additional Contemporary Suggestions

"My Redeemer Lives" (Job, Heb)
M73
"Once Again" (Heb)
M78
"You Are My King" ("Amazing Love") (Heb)
M82
"That's Why We Praise Him" (Heb)
M94
"I Come to the Cross" (Heb)
M106
"We Bring the Sacrifice of Praise" (Heb)
R3, S2031, SF2031, SP1
"Humble Thyself in the Sight of the Lord" (Mark)
S2131, SF2131, R188, SP223
"Make Me a Servant" (Mark)
S2176, SF2176, SP193
"Let It Be Said of Us" (Mark)
M53

Vocal Solos

"Ah, Holy Jesus" (Heb)
V-6 p. 24
"He Breaks the Bread, He Pours the Wine" (Mark, Communion)
V-10 p. 43

Anthems

"Many and Great, O God" (Job, Pss)
arr. Mitzi Scott; Choristers Guild CGA1122
Unison/Two- or Three-part with piano

"Bless the Lord, My Soul!" (Pss)
Dan R. Edwards; Choristers Guild CGA1118
SATB with piano and opt. percussion

Other Suggestions

Visuals:
O Whirlwind, creation, cornerstone, stars, storm
P Light, tent, clouds, wind, fire, sea, mountains
E Priest/sacrifice, Christ, Heb 5:5a, Jesus praying, cross
G Hands, chalice, baptism, cross, servant
Greeting: N824 (Pss)
Prayer: N851 or C68 (Job)
Alternate Lessons: Isa 53:4-12; Ps 91:9-16 (see Scripture Index in this, or previous, editions of *Prepare!*).

Job 42:1-6, 10-17

[1]Then Job answered the LORD: [2]"I know that you can do all things, and that no purpose of yours can be thwarted. [3]'Who is this that hides counsel without knowledge?' Therefore I have uttered what I did not understand, things too wonderful for me, which I did not know. [4]'Hear, and I will speak; I will question you, and you declare to me.' [5]I had heard of you by the hearing of the ear, but now my eye sees you; [6]therefore I despise myself, and repent in dust and ashes."

[10]And the LORD restored the fortunes of Job when he had prayed for his friends; and the LORD gave Job twice as much as he had before. [11]Then there came to him all his brothers and sisters and all who had known him before, and they ate bread with him in his house; they showed him sympathy and comforted him for all the evil that the LORD had brought upon him; and each of them gave him a piece of money and a gold ring. [12]The LORD blessed the latter days of Job more than his beginning; and he had fourteen thousand sheep, six thousand camels, a thousand yoke of oxen, and a thousand donkeys. [13]He also had seven sons and three daughters. [14]He named the first Jemimah, the second Keziah, and the third Keren-happuch. [15]In all the land there were no women so beautiful as Job's daughters; and their father gave them an inheritance along with their brothers. [16]After this Job lived one hundred and forty years, and saw his children, and his children's children, four generations. [17]And Job died, old and full of days.

Psalm 34:1-8 (19-22)

[1]I will bless the LORD at all times; his praise shall continually be in my mouth. [2]My soul makes its boast in the LORD; let the humble hear and be glad. [3]O magnify the LORD with me, and let us exalt his name together. [4]I sought the LORD, and he answered me, and delivered me from all my fears. [5]Look to him, and be radiant; so your faces shall never be ashamed. [6]This poor soul cried, and was heard by the LORD, and was saved from every trouble. [7]The angel of the LORD encamps around those who fear him, and delivers them. [8]O taste and see that the LORD is good; happy are those who take refuge in him.

[19]Many are the afflictions of the righteous, but the LORD rescues them from them all. [20]He keeps all their bones; not one of them will be broken. [21]Evil brings death to the wicked, and those who hate the righteous will be condemned. [22] The LORD redeems the life of his servants; none of those who take refuge in him will be condemned.

Hebrews 7:23-28

[23]Furthermore, the former priests were many in number, because they were prevented by death from continuing in office; [24]but he holds his priesthood permanently, because he continues forever. [25]Consequently he is able for all time to save those who approach God through him, since he always lives to make intercession for them.

[26]For it was fitting that we should have such a high priest, holy, blameless, undefiled, separated from sinners, and exalted above the heavens. [27]Unlike the other high priests, he has no need to offer sacrifices day after day, first for his own sins, and then for those of the people; this he did once for all when he offered himself. [28]For the law appoints as high priests those who are subject to weakness, but the word of the oath, which came later than the law, appoints a Son who has been made perfect forever.

Mark 10:46-52

[46]They came to Jericho. As he and his disciples and a large crowd were leaving Jericho, Bartimaeus son of Timaeus, a blind beggar, was sitting by the roadside. [47]When he heard that it was Jesus of Nazareth, he began to shout out and say, "Jesus, Son of David, have mercy on me!" [48]Many sternly ordered him to be quiet, but he cried out even more loudly, "Son of David, have mercy on me!" [49]Jesus stood still and said, "Call him here." And they called the blind man, saying to him, "Take heart; get up, he is calling you." [50]So throwing off his cloak, he sprang up and came to Jesus. [51]Then Jesus said to him, "What do you want me to do for you?" The blind man said to him, "My teacher, let me see again." [52]Jesus said to him, "Go; your faith has made you well." Immediately he regained his sight and followed him on the way.

Notes

Primary Hymns and Songs for the Day

"Wonderful Words of Life" (Job, Heb) (O)
B261, C323, F29, N319, UM600 (PD)
H-3 Chr-221; Org-186
"Pass Me Not, O Gentle Savior" (Mark)
B308, F416, N551, UM351 (PD), VU665
H-3 Chr-159
"My Faith Looks Up to Thee" (Mark)
B416, C576, E691, F84, L479, P383, UM452 (PD), VU663
H-3 Hbl-77; Chr-138; Org-108
S-2 #142. Flute/violin descant
"Open My Eyes, That I May See" (Mark)
B502, C586, F486, P324, UM454, VU371
H-3 Chr-157; Org-108
"Open Our Eyes, Lord" (Mark)
B499, R91, S2086, SF2086, SP199
"A Mighty Fortress Is Our God" (Job, Reformation) (C)
B8, C65, E687 or E688, F118, L228 or L229, N439 or N440, P259 or P260, UM110 (PD), VU261 (Fr.) or VU262 or VU263, W575 or W576
H-3 Chr-19; Desc-35; Org-34
S-1 #111-113. Various treatments

Additional Hymn Suggestions

"From All That Dwell Below the Skies" (Job)
B13, C49, E380, L550, N27, P229, UM101 (PD), W521
"When Our Confidence Is Shaken" (Job)
C534, UM505
"Praise the Source of Faith and Learning" (Job)
N411, S2004, SF2004
"Joy Comes with the Dawn" (Job)
S2210, SF2210, VU166
"My Life Flows On" (Job)
C619, N476, S2212, SF2212, VU716
"Joyful, Joyful, We Adore Thee" (Job, Pss) (O)
B7, C2, E376, F377, L551, N4, P464, UM89 (PD), VU232, W525
"If Thou But Suffer God to Guide Thee" (Job, Mark)
B57, C565, E635, L453, N410, P282, UM142 (PD), VU285 (Fr.) and VU286
All Who Hunger" (Pss, Communion)
C419, S2126, SF2126, VU460
"Christ, Whose Glory Fills the Skies" (Heb)
E7, L265, P462, UM173 (PD), VU336
"My Hope Is Built" (Heb)
B406, C537, F92, L293 and L294 (PD), N368, P379, UM368 (PD)
"O How I Love Jesus" (Heb, Mark)
B217, C99, F634, N52, UM170 (PD)
"O For a Thousand Tongues to Sing" (Mark)
B216, C5, E493, F349, L559, N42, P466, R32, UM57 (PD), VU326
"O Christ, the Healer" (Mark)
C503, L360, N175, P380, R191, UM265, W747
"Be Thou My Vision" (Mark)
B60, C595, E488, F468, N451, P339, R151, UM451, VU642

Additional Contemporary Suggestions

"Through It All" (Job)
C555, F43, UM507
"In His Time" (Job)
B53, S2203, SF2203
"People Need the Lord" (Job, Mark)
B557, S2244, SF2244
"My Redeemer Lives" (Job)
M73
"How Majestic Is Your Name" (Pss)
C63, R98, S2023, SF2023, SP14
"Jesus, Name Above All Names" (Heb)
R26, SP76, S2071, SF2071
"Before the Throne of God Above" (Heb)
M65
"That's Why We Praise Him" (Heb)
M94
"Turn Your Eyes upon Jesus (Mark)
B320, F621, SP218, UM349
"Something Beautiful" (Mark)
F656, UM394
"The Power of Your Love" (Mark)
M26
"Open the Eyes of My Heart" (Mark)
M57; V-3 p. 162 Vocal Solo

Vocal Solos

"This Is My Father's World" (Job, Pss)
V-6 p. 42
"Redeeming Grace" (Mark)
V-4 p. 47

Anthems

"I Will at All Times Praise the Lord" (Pss)
Handel, arr. Hopson; Choristers Guild CGA 243
Unison with keyboard

"Thou Shalt Know Him" (Mark)
Mark Sirett; Augsburg 11-10645
SATB a cappella

Other Suggestions

Visuals:
O Dust/ashes, gold coins, rings, boys/girls
P Praise, Ps 34:8, taste: fruits, vegetables, sweets
E Christ, vestments on the altar
G Tattered cloak, blind man: dramatize, dance, mime
Opening Prayer: N831 (Job, Pss)
Litany: C488. A Litany of the Saints (Reformation)
Blessing: C268. A Sarum Blessing (Mark)
Alternate Lessons: Jer 31:7-9; Ps 126 (see Scripture Index in this, or previous, editions of *Prepare!*).

Isaiah 25:6-9

[6]On this mountain the LORD of hosts will make for all
peoples a feast of rich food, a feast of well-aged wines, of
rich food filled with marrow, of well-aged wines strained
clear. [7]And he will destroy on this mountain the shroud
that is cast over all peoples, the sheet that is spread over
all nations; [8]he will swallow up death forever. Then the
Lord GOD will wipe away the tears from all faces, and the
disgrace of his people he will take away from all the earth,
for the LORD has spoken. [9]It will be said on that day, Lo,
this is our God; we have waited for him, so that he might
save us. This is the LORD for whom we have waited; let us
be glad and rejoice in his salvation.

Psalm 24

[1]The earth is the LORD's and all that is in it, the world,
and those who live in it; [2]for he has founded it on the
seas, and established it on the rivers. [3]Who shall ascend
the hill of the LORD? And who shall stand in his holy
place? [4]Those who have clean hands and pure hearts, who
do not lift up their souls to what is false, and do not swear
deceitfully. [5]They will receive blessing from the LORD, and
vindication from the God of their salvation. [6]Such is the
company of those who seek him, who seek the face of the
God of Jacob. [7]Lift up your heads, O gates! and be lifted
up, O ancient doors! that the King of glory may come in.
[8]Who is the King of glory? The LORD, strong and mighty,
the LORD, mighty in battle. [9]Lift up your heads, O gates!
and be lifted up, O ancient doors! that the King of glory
may come in. [10]Who is this King of glory? The LORD of
hosts, he is the King of glory.

Revelation 21:1-6*a*

[1]Then I saw a new heaven and a new earth; for the first
heaven and the first earth had passed away, and the sea
was no more. [2]And I saw the holy city, the new Jerusalem,
coming down out of heaven from God, prepared as a
bride adorned for her husband. [3]And I heard a loud voice
from the throne saying, "See, the home of God is among
mortals. He will dwell with them; they will be his peoples,
and God himself will be with them; [4]he will wipe every
tear from their eyes. Death will be no more; mourning
and crying and pain will be no more, for the first things
have passed away."

[5]And the one who was seated on the throne said, "See,
I am making all things new." Also he said, "Write this, for
these words are trustworthy and true." [6a]Then he said to
me, "It is done! I am the Alpha and the Omega, the
beginning and the end."

John 11:32-44

[32]When Mary came where Jesus was and saw him, she
knelt at his feet and said to him, "Lord, if you had been
here, my brother would not have died." [33]When Jesus saw
her weeping, and the Jews who came with her also weeping, he was greatly disturbed in spirit and deeply moved.
[34]He said, "Where have you laid him?" They said to him,
"Lord, come and see." [35]Jesus began to weep. [36]So the Jews
said, "See how he loved him!" [37]But some of them said,
"Could not he who opened the eyes of the blind man
have kept this man from dying?"

[38]Then Jesus, again greatly disturbed, came to the tomb.
It was a cave, and a stone was lying against it. [39]Jesus said,
"Take away the stone." Martha, the sister of the dead
man, said to him, "Lord, already there is a stench because
he has been dead four days." [40]Jesus said to her, "Did I not
tell you that if you believed, you would see the glory of
God?" [41]So they took away the stone. And Jesus looked
upward and said, "Father, I thank you for having heard
me. [42]I knew that you always hear me, but I have said this
for the sake of the crowd standing here, so that they may
believe that you sent me." [43]When he had said this, he
cried with a loud voice, "Lazarus, come out!" [44]The dead
man came out, his hands and feet bound with strips of
cloth, and his face wrapped in a cloth. Jesus said to them,
"Unbind him, and let him go."

Notes

Primary Hymns and Songs for the Day
"For All the Saints" (Pss, All Saints) (C)
B355, C637, E287, F614, L174, N299, P526, UM711 (PD), VU705, W705
H-3 Hbl-58; Chr-65; Org-152
S-1 #314-318. Various treatments
"This is a Day of New Beginnings" (Isa, Rev, John, Communion)
B370, C518, N417, UM383
H-3 Chr-196
"Joy Comes with the Dawn" (Isa, Rev, John)
S2210, SF2210, VU166
"Holy Ground" (Pss, All Saints)
B224, C112, S2272, SF2272, SP86
"Marching to Zion" (Isa, Rev) (O)
B524, C707, F550, N382, UM733 (PD), VU714
H-3 Chr-298

Additional Hymn Suggestions
"Lift Up Your Heads, Ye Mighty Gates" (Pss) (O)
B128, C129, E436, F239, N117, P8, R59, UM213 (PD), W363
"O What Their Joy and Their Glory Must Be" (Isa, Rev)
E623, L337, N385, UM727 (PD)
"O Day of Peace That Dimly Shines" (Isa, Rev)
C711, E597, P450, UM729, VU682, W654
"All Who Hunger" (Isa, Communion)
C419, S2126, SF2126, VU460
"Love Divine, All Loves Excelling (Rev)
B208, C517, F21, N43, UM384 (PD)
E657, L315, P376, R196, VU333, W588 (PD)
"For the Healing of the Nations" (Rev)
C668, N576, UM428, VU678
"Come, Ye Disconsolate" (Rev)
B67, C502, SF2132, UM510 (PD)
"Here, O My Lord, I See Thee" (Rev Communion)
C416, E318, F567, L211, P520, UM623 (PD), VU459
"Christ the Victorious" (Rev)
E358, N653, SF2208, UM653
"O Holy City, Seen of John" (Rev)
E583, N613, P453, UM726, VU709
"Blessed Quietness" (Rev)
F145, C267, N284, S2142, SF2142
"Awake, O Sleeper" (John, All Saints)
E547, UM551, VU566, W586
"How Blest Are They Who Trust in Christ" (John, All Saints)
C646, N365, UM654
"Father, We Praise Thee" (All Saints)
E1, L267, N90, P459, UM680
"I Sing a Song of the Saints of God" (John, All Saints)
E293, N712, P364, UM712 (PD)
"When Jesus Wept" (John)
C199, E715, P312, S2106, SF2106, VU146
"Blest Are They" (All Saints)
R127, S2155, SF2155, VU896
"Deep in the Shadows of the Past" (All Saints)
N320, P330, S2246
"Rejoice in God's Saints" (All Saints) (C)
C476, UM708

Additional Contemporary Suggestions
"You Who Are Thirsty" (Isa, Rev)
S2132
"The King of Glory Comes" (Pss)
B127, R267, S2091, SF2091, W501
"We Will Glorify" (Rev)
B213, S2087, SF2087, SP68
"There's Something About That Name" (Rev)
B177, C115, F227, R26, SP89, UM171
"Spirit Song" (Rev)
C352, R248, SP134, UM347
"Soon and Very Soon" (Rev)
B192, R276, UM706; S-2 #187
"Blessing, Honor and Glory" (Rev)
M21, R81
"How Great Is Our God" (Rev)
M117
"All Who Are Thirsty" (Rev)
M159
"Jesus Is Alive" (Rev, John)
M20

Vocal Solos
"Lift Up Your Heads" (Pss)
V-10 p. 38
"Then Shall the Righteous Shine Forth" (Rev, All Saints)
V-8 p. 274
"In Bright Mansions Above" (All Saints)
V-4 p. 39

Anthems
"We Fall Down" (Isa, Rev, Contemporary)
Tomlin, arr. Schrader; Hope Publishing Co. C-5355
SATB with piano and opt. rhythm

"Psalm 24" (Pss)
Tom Mitchell; Choristers Guild CGA591
SATB with keyboard and opt. percussion

Other Suggestions
These scriptures and suggestions may also be used on Nov. 5.
Visuals:
O Banquet, sheet, handkerchief, rejoicing
P Sea, river, hill, washing hands, heart, gates/doors
E Wedding, alpha/omega, joy, tears/handkerchief
G Woman weeping, open tomb, white linen, strips of cloth
Litany: C488. A Litany of the Saints (All Saints)
Prayer: N856. Eternal Life (All Saints)
Alternate Lessons for Nov. 1 if not celebrated as All Saint's Day:
Ruth 1:1-18; Ps 146:1-10; Heb 9:11-14; Mark 12:28-34 (see Scripture Index in this, or previous, editions of *Prepare!*).

Ruth 3:1-5; 4:13-17

[1]Naomi her mother-in-law said to her, "My daughter, I
need to seek some security for you, so that it may be well
with you. [2]Now here is our kinsman Boaz, with whose
young women you have been working. See, he is winnowing barley tonight at the threshing floor. [3]Now wash and
anoint yourself, and put on your best clothes and go
down to the threshing floor; but do not make yourself
known to the man until he has finished eating and drinking. [4]When he lies down, observe the place where he lies;
then, go and uncover his feet and lie down; and he will
tell you what to do." [5]She said to her, "All that you tell me
I will do."

[13]So Boaz took Ruth and she became his wife. When
they came together, the LORD made her conceive, and she
bore a son. [14]Then the women said to Naomi, "Blessed be
the LORD, who has not left you this day without next-of-
kin; and may his name be renowned in Israel! [15]He shall
be to you a restorer of life and a nourisher of your old
age; for your daughter-in-law who loves you, who is more
to you than seven sons, has borne him." [16]Then Naomi
took the child and laid him in her bosom, and became his
nurse. [17]The women of the neighborhood gave him a
name, saying, "A son has been born to Naomi." They
named him Obed; he became the father of Jesse, the
father of David.

Psalm 127

[1]Unless the LORD builds the house, those who build it
labor in vain. Unless the LORD guards the city, the guard
keeps watch in vain. [2]It is in vain that you rise up early and
go late to rest, eating the bread of anxious toil; for he
gives sleep to his beloved. [3]Sons are indeed a heritage
from the LORD, the fruit of the womb a reward. [4]Like
arrows in the hand of a warrior are the sons of one's
youth. [5]Happy is the man who has his quiver full of them.
He shall not be put to shame when he speaks with his
enemies in the gate.

Hebrews 9:24-28

[24]For Christ did not enter a sanctuary made by human
hands, a mere copy of the true one, but he entered into
heaven itself, now to appear in the presence of God on
our behalf. [25]Nor was it to offer himself again and again,
as the high priest enters the Holy Place year after year
with blood that is not his own; [26]for then he would have
had to suffer again and again since the foundation of the
world. But as it is, he has appeared once for all at the end
of the age to remove sin by the sacrifice of himself. [27]And
just as it is appointed for mortals to die once, and after
that the judgment, [28]so Christ, having been offered once
to bear the sins of many, will appear a second time, not to
deal with sin, but to save those who are eagerly waiting
for him.

Mark 12:38-44

[38]As he taught, he said, "Beware of the scribes, who like
to walk around in long robes, and to be greeted with
respect in the marketplaces, [39]and to have the best seats
in the synagogues and places of honor at banquets!
[40]They devour widows' houses and for the sake of
appearance say long prayers. They will receive the
greater condemnation."

[41]He sat down opposite the treasury, and watched the
crowd putting money into the treasury. Many rich people
put in large sums. [42]A poor widow came and put in two
small copper coins, which are worth a penny. [43]Then he
called his disciples and said to them, "Truly I tell you, this
poor widow has put in more than all those who are con-
tributing to the treasury. [44] For all of them have con-
tributed out of their abundance; but she out of her pover-
ty has put in everything she had, all she had to live on."

Notes

Primary Hymns and Songs for the Day

"Love Divine, All Loves Excelling" (Ruth, Heb) (O)
B208, C517, F21, N43, UM384 (PD)
H-3 Chr-134; Desc-18; Org-13
S-1 #41-42. Descant and harmonization
E657, L315, P376, R196, VU333, W588 (PD)
H-3 Hbl-46; Chr-26, 134; Desc-53; Org-56
S-1 #168-171. Various treatments
"What Gift Can We Bring" (Mark)
N370, UM87
H-3 Chr-211
S-2 #10-11. Descants
"Take My Life, and Let It Be" (Mark, Stewardship)
B277, C609, P391
H-3 Chr-34, 177; Desc-51; Org-53
S-2 #78-80. Various treatments
B283, E707, L406, N448, R133, UM399 (PD), VU506
"O Master, Let Me Walk With Thee" (Mark) (C)
B279, C602, E660, F442, L492, N503, P357, UM430 (PD), VU560
H-3 Hbl-81; Chr-147; Desc-74; Org-87
S-2 #118. Descant
E659

Additional Hymn Suggestions

"By Gracious Powers" (Ruth)
E695 and E696, N413, P342, UM517, W577
"When Love Is Found" (Ruth)
C499, N362, UM643, VU489, W745
"The Care the Eagle Gives Her Young" (Ruth, Pss)
C76, N468, UM118, VU269
"Blest Be the Tie That Binds" (Ruth, Mark)
B387, C433, F560, L370, N393, P438, UM557 (PD), VU602
"Your Love, O God, Has Called Us Here" (Ruth, Mark)
B509, E353, N361, UM647
"Forth in Thy Name, O Lord" (Pss)
L505, UM438 (PD), VU416
"Happy the Home When God Is There" (Pss)
B505, F540, UM445
"Out of the Depths I Cry to You" (Pss) (See esp. stanza 2)
L295, P240, UM515
"Hallelujah! What a Savior" (Heb)
B175, F246, UM165 (PD)
"Rejoice the Lord Is King" (Heb)
E481, L171 (PD), UM716
B197, C699, F374, N303, P155, UM715 (PD), VU213, W493 (alternate tune)
"Living for Jesus" (Heb)
B282, C610, F462, S2149, SF2149
"I'm So Glad Jesus Lifted Me" (Heb)
C529, N474, S2151, SF2151
"Victim Divine" (Heb, Communion)
L202, S2259, SF2259
"All My Hope Is Firmly Grounded" (Mark)
E665, N408, UM132, VU654 and VU655
"The Gift of Love" (Mark)
B423, C526, P335, R155, UM408, VU372
"Where Cross the Crowded Ways of Life" (Mark)
C665, E609, F665, L429, N543, P408, UM427 (PD), VU681
"What Does the Lord Require" (Mark)
C659, E605, P405, UM441, W624
"O Young and Fearless Prophet" (Mark)
C669, UM444 (PD)

Additional Contemporary Suggestions

"The Family Prayer Song" (Ruth, Pss)
M54, S2188, SF2188
"Before the Throne of God Above" (Heb)
M65
"You Are My King" ("Amazing Love") (Heb)
M82
"Holy Ground" (Heb)
B224, C112, S2272, SF2272, SP86
"Give Thanks" (Mark, Stewardship)
C528, R266, S2036, SF2036, SP170
"More Precious than Silver" (Mark, Stewardship)
S2065, SF2065, SP99
"Lord, Be Glorified" (Mark, Stewardship)
B457, S2150, SF2150, R172, SP196
"Praise You" (Mark, Stewardship)
M84, S2003, SF2003

Vocal Solos

"Rejoice, The Lord is King" (Heb)
V-1 p. 66
"Take My Life" (Mark, Stewardship)
V-5 p. 28
V-8 p. 262

Anthems

"O Master, Let Me Walk with Thee" (Mark)
Gregory Hamilton; MorningStar MSM-50-6042
SATB with keyboard and opt. violin or flute

"God's Loving Call" (Mark)
Wayne Wold; Choristers Guild CGA 649
Unison with keyboard

Other Suggestions

Visuals:
O Threshing, marriage, nursing woman, Jesse tree
P Building church, rising/sleeping, newborns, arrow/quiver
E Ascension, crucifixion, 2nd coming
G Long robe, greeting, banquet, widow, 2 coins
Greeting: N822 (Ruth)
Prayer: N842 or N845 (Mark, Stewardship)
Alternate Lessons: 1 Kgs 17:8-16; Ps 146 (see Scripture Index in this, or previous, editions of *Prepare!*).

1 Samuel 1:4-20

4On the day when Elkanah sacrificed, he would give portions to his wife Peninnah and to all her sons and daughters; 5but to Hannah he gave a double portion, because he loved her, though the LORD had closed her womb. 6Her rival used to provoke her severely, to irritate her, because the LORD had closed her womb. 7So it went on year by year; as often as she went up to the house of the LORD, she used to provoke her. Therefore Hannah wept and would not eat. 8Her husband Elkanah said to her, "Hannah, why do you weep? Why do you not eat? Why is your heart sad? Am I not more to you than ten sons?"

9After they had eaten and drunk at Shiloh, Hannah rose and presented herself before the LORD. Now Eli the priest was sitting on the seat beside the doorpost of the temple of the LORD. 10She was deeply distressed and prayed to the LORD, and wept bitterly. 11She made this vow: "O LORD of hosts, if only you will look on the misery of your servant, and remember me, and not forget your servant, but will give to your servant a male child, then I will set him before you as a nazirite until the day of his death. He shall drink neither wine nor intoxicants, and no razor shall touch his head."

12As she continued praying before the LORD, Eli observed her mouth. 13Hannah was praying silently; only her lips moved, but her voice was not heard; therefore Eli thought she was drunk. 14So Eli said to her, "How long will you make a drunken spectacle of yourself? Put away your wine." 15But Hannah answered, "No, my lord, I am a woman deeply troubled; I have drunk neither wine nor strong drink, but I have been pouring out my soul before the LORD. 16Do not regard your servant as a worthless woman, for I have been speaking out of my great anxiety and vexation all this time." 17Then Eli answered, "Go in peace; the God of Israel grant the petition you have made to him." 18And she said, "Let your servant find favor in your sight." Then the woman went to her quarters, ate and drank with her husband, and her countenance was sad no longer.

19They rose early in the morning and worshiped before the LORD; then they went back to their house at Ramah. Elkanah knew his wife Hannah, and the LORD remembered her. 20In due time Hannah conceived and bore a son. She named him Samuel, for she said, "I have asked him of the LORD."

---

1 Samuel 2:1-10

1Hannah prayed and said, "My heart exults in the LORD; my strength is exalted in my God. My mouth derides my enemies, because I rejoice in my victory. 2There is no Holy One like the LORD, no one besides you; there is no Rock like our God. 3Talk no more so very proudly, let not arrogance come from your mouth; for the LORD is a God of knowledge, and by him actions are weighed. 4The bows of the mighty are broken, but the feeble gird on strength. 5Those who were full have hired themselves out for bread, but those who were hungry are fat with spoil. The barren has borne seven, but she who has many children is forlorn. 6The LORD kills and brings to life; he brings down to Sheol and raises up. 7The LORD makes poor and makes rich; he brings low, he also exalts. 8He raises up the poor from the dust; he lifts the needy from the ash heap, to make them sit with princes and inherit a seat of honor. For the pillars of the earth are the LORD's, and on them he has set the world. 9He will guard the feet of his faithful ones, but the wicked shall be cut off in darkness; for not by might does one prevail. 10The LORD! His adversaries shall be shattered; the Most High will thunder in heaven. The LORD will judge the ends of the earth; he will give strength to his king, and exalt the power of his anointed."

Hebrews 10:11-14 (15-18), 19-25

11And every priest stands day after day at his service, offering again and again the same sacrifices that can never take away sins. 12But when Christ had offered for all time a single sacrifice for sins, "he sat down at the right hand of God," 13and since then has been waiting "until his enemies would be made a footstool for his feet." 14For by a single offering he has perfected for all time those who are sanctified. 15And the Holy Spirit also testifies to us, for after saying, 16"This is the covenant that I will make with them after those days, says the Lord: I will put my laws in their hearts, and I will write them on their minds," 17he also adds, "I will remember their sins and their lawless deeds no more." 18Where there is forgiveness of these, there is no longer any offering for sin.

19Therefore, my friends, since we have confidence to enter the sanctuary by the blood of Jesus, 20by the new and living way that he opened for us through the curtain (that is, through his flesh), 21and since we have a great priest over the house of God, 22let us approach with a true heart in full assurance of faith, with our hearts sprinkled clean from an evil conscience and our bodies washed with pure water. 23Let us hold fast to the confession of our hope without wavering, for he who has promised is faithful. 24And let us consider how to provoke one another to love and good deeds, 25not neglecting to meet together, as is the habit of some, but encouraging one another, and all the more as you see the Day approaching.

Mark 13:1-8

1As he came out of the temple, one of his disciples said to him, "Look, Teacher, what large stones and what large buildings!" 2Then Jesus asked him, "Do you see these great buildings? Not one stone will be left here upon another; all will be thrown down."

3When he was sitting on the Mount of Olives opposite the temple, Peter, James, John, and Andrew asked him privately, 4"Tell us, when will this be, and what will be the sign that all these things are about to be accomplished?" 5Then Jesus began to say to them, "Beware that no one leads you astray. 6Many will come in my name and say, 'I am he!' and they will lead many astray. 7When you hear of wars and rumors of wars, do not be alarmed; this must take place, but the end is still to come. 8For nation will rise against nation, and kingdom against kingdom; there will be earthquakes in various places; there will be famines. This is but the beginning of the birth pangs."

Primary Hymns and Songs for the Day
"O God, Our Help in Ages Past" (1 Sam) (O)
B74, C67, E680, F370, L320, N25, P210, UM117 (PD), VU806, W579
H-3 Hbl-33, 80; Chr-143; Desc-93; Org-132
S-1 #293-296. Various treatments
"My Soul Gives Glory to My God" (1 Sam)
C130, N119, P600, UM198, VU899
H-3 Chr-139, 145; Desc-77
S-1 #241-242. Orff arr. and descant
"My Lord, What a Morning" (Heb, Mark)
C708, P449, UM719, VU708
H-3 Chr-139
"How Firm a Foundation" (Mark)
B338, C618, E636, F32, L507, N407, P361, UM529 (PD), VU660, W585
H-3 Hbl-27, 69; Chr-102; Desc-41; Org-41
S-1 #133. Harmonization
#134. Performance note
"O Day of God, Draw Nigh" (Mark) (C)
B623, C700, E601, N611, P452, UM730 (PD), VU688 and VU689 (Fr.)
H-3 Hbl-79; Chr-141; Desc-95; Org-143
S-1 #306-308. Various treatments

Additional Hymn Suggestions
"I'll Praise My Maker While I've Breath" (1 Sam) (O)
B35, C20, E429 (PD), P253, UM60, VU867
"O Worship the King" (1 Sam)
B16, C17, E388, F336, L548 (PD), N26, P476, UM73, VU235
"Praise to the Lord, the Almighty" (1 Sam)
B14 (PD), C25, E390, F337, L543, N22, P482, R57, UM139, VU220 (Fr.) and VU221, W547
"The Care the Eagle Gives Her Young" (1 Sam)
C76, N468, UM118, VU269
"Give to the Winds Thy Fears" (1 Sam)
N404, P286 (PD), UM129 (PD), VU636 (PD)
"Tell Out, My Soul" (1 Sam)
B81, E437 and E438, R130, UM200, W534
"Rock of Ages, Cleft for Me" (1 Sam)
B342, C214, E685, F108, L327, N596, UM361 (PD)
"Sweet Hour of Prayer" (1 Sam)
B445, C570, F439, N505, UM496 (PD)
"Blest Are They" (1 Sam)
R127, S2155, SF2155, VU896
"I Am Thine, O Lord" (Heb)
B290, C601, F455, N455, UM419 (PD)
"Near to the Heart of God" (Heb)
B295, C581, F35, P527, UM472 (PD)
"There Are Some Things I May Not Know" (Heb)
N405, S2147, SF2147
"Living for Jesus" (Heb)
B282, C610, F462, S2149, SF2149
"Steal Away to Jesus" (Heb, Mark)
C644, N599, UM704
"Wake, Awake, for Night is Flying" (Heb, Mark)
E61, L31, P17, UM720 (PD), VU711, W371
"I Want to Be Ready" (Heb, Mark)
N616, UM722

"Stand By Me" (Mark)
C629, UM512

Additional Contemporary Suggestions
"Let the River Flow" (1 Sam 2)
M142
"Give Thanks" (1 Sam 2)
C528, R266, S2036, SF2036, SP170
"Praise to the Lord" (1 Sam 2)
S2029, SF2029, VU835
"The Family Prayer Song" (1 Sam)
M54, S2188, SF2188
"White as Snow" (Heb)
M35
"Before the Throne of God Above" (Heb)
M65
"You Are My King" ("Amazing Love") (Heb)
M82
"Did You Feel the Mountains Tremble?" (Mark)
M69; V-3 p. 140 Vocal Solo
"Days of Elijah" (Mark)
M139

Vocal Solos
"Come, Thou Fount of Every Blessing" (1 Sam)
V-6 p. 4
"My Lord, What a Mornin'" (Mark)
V-7 p. 68

Anthems
"Lord, You Have Been Our Refuge" (1 Sam)
Daniel Nelson; Kjos 9066
SATB with keyboard

"Great Day" (Heb, Mark)
Arr. Doug Denisen; Kjos 6332
Two-part with piano

Other Suggestions
Visuals:
O Woman weeping/praying, old man, couple worshiping, newborn
P Praying, rock, broken bow, 4 pillars, scales
E Cross, footstool, curtain, water, baptism, worship
G Scattered stones, war, earthquake, famine, dawn
Canticle: C131, UM199. "Magnificat" (1 Sam)
Response: C327. "Write These Words in Our Hearts (Heb)
Sung Benediction: B660, C437, R293, UM665, VU964. "Go Now in Peace" (1 Sam 1)
Alternate Lessons: Dan 12:1-3; Ps 16 (see Scripture Index in this, or previous, editions of *Prepare!*).

2 Samuel 23:1-7

[1]Now these are the last words of David: The oracle of David, son of Jesse, the oracle of the man whom God exalted, the anointed of the God of Jacob, the favorite of the Strong One of Israel: [2]The spirit of the LORD speaks through me, his word is upon my tongue. [3]The God of Israel has spoken, the Rock of Israel has said to me: One who rules over people justly, ruling in the fear of God, [4]is like the light of morning, like the sun rising on a cloudless morning, gleaming from the rain on the grassy land. [5]Is not my house like this with God? For he has made with me an everlasting covenant, ordered in all things and secure. Will he not cause to prosper all my help and my desire? [6]But the godless are all like thorns that are thrown away; for they cannot be picked up with the hand; [7]to touch them one uses an iron bar or the shaft of a spear. And they are entirely consumed in fire on the spot.

Psalm 132:1-12

[1]O LORD, remember in David's favor all the hardships he endured; [2]how he swore to the LORD and vowed to the Mighty One of Jacob, [3]"I will not enter my house or get into my bed; [4]I will not give sleep to my eyes or slumber to my eyelids, [5]until I find a place for the LORD, a dwelling place for the Mighty One of Jacob." [6]We heard of it in Ephrathah; we found it in the fields of Jaar. [7]"Let us go to his dwelling place; let us worship at his footstool." [8]Rise up, O LORD, and go to your resting place, you and the ark of your might. [9]Let your priests be clothed with righteousness, and let your faithful shout for joy. [10]For your servant David's sake do not turn away the face of your anointed one. [11]The LORD swore to David a sure oath from which he will not turn back: "One of the sons of your body I will set on your throne. [12]If your sons keep my covenant and my decrees that I shall teach them, their sons also, forevermore, shall sit on your throne."

Revelation 1:4*b*-8

[4b]Grace to you and peace from him who is and who was and who is to come, and from the seven spirits who are before his throne, [5]and from Jesus Christ, the faithful witness, the firstborn of the dead, and the ruler of the kings of the earth.

To him who loves us and freed us from our sins by his blood, [6]and made us to be a kingdom, priests serving his God and Father, to him be glory and dominion forever and ever. Amen. [7]Look! He is coming with the clouds; every eye will see him, even those who pierced him; and on his account all the tribes of the earth will wail. So it is to be. Amen.

[8]"I am the Alpha and the Omega," says the Lord God, who is and who was and who is to come, the Almighty.

John 18:33-37

[33]Then Pilate entered the headquarters again, summoned Jesus, and asked him, "Are you the King of the Jews?" [34]Jesus answered, "Do you ask this on your own, or did others tell you about me?" [35]Pilate replied, "I am not a Jew, am I? Your own nation and the chief priests have handed you over to me. What have you done?" [36]Jesus answered, "My kingdom is not from this world. If my kingdom were from this world, my followers would be fighting to keep me from being handed over to the Jews. But as it is, my kingdom is not from here." [37]Pilate asked him, "So you are a king?" Jesus answered, "You say that I am a king. For this I was born, and for this I came into the world, to testify to the truth. Everyone who belongs to the truth listens to my voice."

Notes

Primary Hymns and Songs for the Day

"Rejoice the Lord is King" (Rev, Christ the King) (O)
B197, C699, F374, N303, P155, UM715 (PD), VU213, W493
C699 Descant
H-3 Hbl-8, 53, 90; Chr-37; Desc-27; Org-24
S-1 #78-80. Various treatments
"Lo, He Comes with Clouds Descending" (2 Sam, Rev)
B199, F306
H-3 Chr-30, 48, 62; Desc-89; Org-121
S-1 #280. Descant and harmonization
E57, L27, P6, UM718 (PD), VU25
H-3 Hbl-93; Chr-129; Desc-50; Org-53
S-1 #157. Descant
"He Is Exalted" (Rev, Christ the King)
R238, S2070, SF2070, SP66
"Jesus Shall Reign" (Rev) (C)
B587, C95, E544, F238, L530, N157, P423, R296, UM157 (PD), VU330, W492
C95 Descant
H-3 Hbl-29, 58; Chr-117; Desc-31; Org-31
S-1 #100-103. Various treatments.

Additional Hymn Suggestions

"Hail to the Lord's Anointed" (2 Sam, Rev) (O)
C140, E616 (PD), L87, N104, P205, UM203 (PD), VU30
"O Morning Star, How Fair and Bright" (2 Sam)
C105, E497, L76, N158, P69, UM247, VU98, W390
"Rock of Ages, Cleft for Me" (2 Sam)
B342, C214, E685, F108, L327, N596, UM361 (PD)
"The Trees of the Field" (Pss)
R302, S2279, SF2279, SP128, VU884
"Ye Watchers and Ye Holy Ones" (Rev)
E618, L175, P451, UM90, W707
"All Hail the Power of Jesus' Name" (Rev)
B200, C92, F326, P143, UM155 (PD)
B201, E451, F327, L329 (PD), VU334 (alternate tune)
B202, C91, E450, F325, L328, N304, P142, R45, UM154 (PD), W494 (alternate tune)
"When Morning Gilds the Skies" (Rev)
B221, C100, E427, F322, L546, N86, P487, UM185, VU339 (Fr.), W675
"Of the Father's Love Begotten" (Rev, Communion)
B251, C104, E82, F172 (PD), L42, N118, P309, R252, UM184, VU61, W398
"Love Divine, All Loves Excelling" (Rev)
B208, C517, F21, N43, UM384 (PD)
E657, L315, P376, R196, VU333, W588 (PD)
"Let All Mortal Flesh Keep Silence" (John, Communion)
B80, C124, E324, F166, L198, N345, P5, R229, UM626 (PD), VU473 (Fr.), W523
"This Is the Feast of Victory" (Rev, Communion)
E417, P594, R199, UM638, VU904, W458

Additional Contemporary Suggestions

"Rock of Ages" (2 Sam)
M93
"I Will Call Upon the Lord" (2 Sam)
R15, S2002, SF2002, SP224
"Praise the Name of Jesus" (2 Sam, Christ the King)
R7, S2066, SF2066, SP87
"Awesome God" (Rev, John, Christ the King)
R245, S2040, SF2040, SP11
"Soon and Very Soon" (Rev, Christ the King)
B192, R276, UM706; S-2 #187
"We Will Glorify the King of Kings" (Rev, Christ the King)
B213, S2087, SF2087, SP68
"King of Kings" (Rev, Christ the King)
B234, R268, S2075, SF2075, VU167, SP94
"Jesus, We Crown You with Praise" (Rev, Christ the King)
M24
"Jehovah Reigns" (Rev, Christ the King)
M55
"How Great Is Our God" (Rev, Christ the King)
M117
"All Hail King Jesus" (John, Christ the King)
S2069, SF2069, SP63
"Crown Him King of Kings" (Christ the King)
M22
"We Want to See Jesus Lifted High" (Christ the King)
M67
"He Reigns" (Christ the King)
M168

Vocal Solos

"Great Day!" (Rev)
V-7 p. 14
"King of Glory, King of Peace" (Christ the King)
V-9 p. 24
"Crown Him, the Risen King" (Christ the King)
V-10 p. 55

Anthems

"Rejoice the Lord is King" (Rev, Christ the King)
arr. Joel Ramey; Hope C5483
SATB with piano and opt. organ and handbells

"Jesus Shall Reign Where'er the Sun" (Christ the King)
John Hatton; GIA G-2135
SATB with keyboard

Other Suggestions

Visuals: Cross/crown, lamb/cross
O Speaking, rock, sunrise, rain/grass, thorns, spear, fire
P Empty bed, ark, crown, throne, scepter
E Crown, scepter, cross, royal robe, fabric (gold/purple)
G Jesus/Pilate, shackles, John 18:36a, crown, listening
Greeting: N820 (John)
Opening Prayer: N827 (John)
For Thanksgiving Sunday, see Thanksgiving Day Suggestions.

Joel 2:21-27

[21]Do not fear, O soil; be glad and rejoice, for the LORD has done great things! [22]Do not fear, you animals of the field, for the pastures of the wilderness are green; the tree bears its fruit, the fig tree and vine give their full yield. [23]O children of Zion, be glad and rejoice in the LORD your God; for he has given the early rain for your vindication, he has poured down for you abundant rain, the early and the later rain, as before. [24]The threshing floors shall be full of grain, the vats shall overflow with wine and oil. [25]I will repay you for the years that the swarming locust has eaten, the hopper, the destroyer, and the cutter, my great army, which I sent against you. [26]You shall eat in plenty and be satisfied, and praise the name of the LORD your God, who has dealt wondrously with you. And my people shall never again be put to shame. [27]You shall know that I am in the midst of Israel, and that I, the LORD, am your God and there is no other. And my people shall never again be put to shame.

Psalm 126

[1]When the LORD restored the fortunes of Zion, we were like those who dream. [2]Then our mouth was filled with laughter, and our tongue with shouts of joy; then it was said among the nations, "The LORD has done great things for them." [3]The LORD has done great things for us, and we rejoiced. [4]Restore our fortunes, O LORD, like the watercourses in the Negeb. [5]May those who sow in tears reap with shouts of joy. [6]Those who go out weeping, bearing the seed for sowing, shall come home with shouts of joy, carrying their sheaves.

---

1 Timothy 2:1-7

[1]First of all, then, I urge that supplications, prayers, intercessions, and thanksgivings be made for everyone, [2]for kings and all who are in high positions, so that we may lead a quiet and peaceable life in all godliness and dignity. [3]This is right and is acceptable in the sight of God our Savior, [4]who desires everyone to be saved and to come to the knowledge of the truth. [5]For there is one God; there is also one mediator between God and humankind, Christ Jesus, himself human, [6]who gave himself a ransom for all—this was attested at the right time. [7]For this I was appointed a herald and an apostle (I am telling the truth, I am not lying), a teacher of the Gentiles in faith and truth.

Matthew 6:25-33

[25]"Therefore I tell you, do not worry about your life, what you will eat or what you will drink, or about your body, what you will wear. Is not life more than food, and the body more than clothing? [26]Look at the birds of the air; they neither sow nor reap nor gather into barns, and yet your heavenly Father feeds them. Are you not of more value than they? [27]And can any of you by worrying add a single hour to your span of life? [28]And why do you worry about clothing? Consider the lilies of the field, how they grow; they neither toil nor spin, [29]yet I tell you, even Solomon in all his glory was not clothed like one of these. [30]But if God so clothes the grass of the field, which is alive today and tomorrow is thrown into the oven, will he not much more clothe you—you of little faith? [31]Therefore do not worry, saying, 'What will we eat?' or 'What will we drink?' or 'What will we wear?' [32]For it is the Gentiles who strive for all these things; and indeed your heavenly Father knows that you need all these things. [33]But strive first for the kingdom of God and his righteousness, and all these things will be given to you as well."

Notes

Primary Hymns and Songs for the Day

"Come, Ye Thankful People, Come" (Joel, Thanksgiving) (O)
B637, C718, E290, F392, L407, N422, P551, UM694 (PD), VU516, W759
H-3 Hbl-54; Chr-58; Desc-94; Org-137
S-1 #302-303. Harmonizations with descant
"We Gather Together" (Joel, Matt, Thanksgiving)
B636, C276, E433, F387, N421, P559, UM131 (PD), W760
H-3 Chr-206; Desc-61; Org-68
S-1 #192-#194. Various treatments
"God Will Take Care of You" (Matt)
B64, F56, N460, UM130 (PD)
"His Eye Is on the Sparrow" (Matt)
C82, N475, S2146, SF2146
"Great Is Thy Faithfulness" (Pss, Matt) (C)
B54, C86, F98, N423, P276, R249, UM140, VU288
H-3 Chr-87; Desc-39; Org-39
S-2 #59. Piano arrangement

Additional Hymn Suggestions

"All Creatures of Our God and King" (Joel, Thanksgiving)
B27, C22, E400, F347, L527, N17, P455, R47, UM62, VU217 (Fr.), W520
"Now Thank We All Our God" (Joel, Thanksgiving)
B638, C715, E396 or E397, F525, L533 or L534, N419, P555, UM102 (PD), VU236 (Fr.), W560
"Una Espiga" ("Sheaves of Summer") (Joel, Communion)
C396, N338, UM637
"We Believe in One True God" (1 Tim.)
L374, P137 (PD), UM85 (PD)
"For the Fruits of This Creation" (Matt)
B643, C714, E424, L563, N425, P553, UM97, VU227, W562
"Give to the Winds Thy Fears" (Matt)
N404, P286 (PD), UM129 (PD), VU636 (PD)
"Children of the Heavenly Father" (Matt)
B55, F89, L474, N487, UM141
"You Satisfy the Hungry Heart" (Matt, Communion)
C429, P521, UM629, R217, VU478, W736
"God Be with You till We Meet Again" (Matt)
C434, F523, N81, UM672 (PD), VU422
"God Be with You till We Meet Again" (Matt)
P540, UM673 (PD), VU423
"How Lovely, Lord, How Lovely" (Matt)
C285, P207, S2042, VU801
"Praise Our God Above" (Matt, Thanksgiving)
N424, P480, S2061
"Bring Forth the Kingdom" (Matt)
R153, S2190, SF2190
"Let Us Offer to the Father" (Matt, Thanksgiving)
S2262, SF2262
"Time Now to Gather" (Thanksgiving, Communion)
S2265, SF2265
"Joyful, Joyful, We Adore Thee" (Thanksgiving)
B7, C2, E376, F377, L551, N4, P464, UM89 (PD), VU232, W525

Additional Contemporary Suggestions

"Open Our Eyes, Lord" (Joel)
B499, R91, S2086, SF2086, SP199
"Open the Eyes of My Heart" (Joel)
M57; V-3 p. 162 Vocal Solo
"Trading My Sorrows" (Pss)
M75
"God Is Good All the Time" (Matt)
M45
"God Is So Good" (Matt)
B23, S2056, SF2056
"Someone Asked the Question" (Matt)
N523, S2144
"Seek Ye First" (Matt)
B478, C354, E711, P333, UM405, SP182, VU356, W580
"Thank You, Lord" (Thanksgiving)
C531, UM84
"Give Thanks" (Thanksgiving)
C528, R266, S2036, SF2036, SP170
"Thank You, Jesus" ("Tino tenda, Jesu") (Thanksgiving)
S2081, SF2081
"Thank You Lord" (Thanksgiving)
M166

Vocal Solos

"Now Thank We All Our God" (Joel, Thanksgiving)
V-6 p. 8
"His Eye Is on the Sparrow" (Matt)
V-8 p. 166

Anthems

"Now Thank We All Our God" (Joel, Thanksgiving)
arr. Randall Thompson; E.C. Schirmer 4008
SATB and keyboard

"Consider the Lilies" (Matt)
Sleeth; arr. Marshall; CGA738
Two-part mixed with keyboard

Other Suggestions

Visuals: Cornucopia, fruit, vegetables, etc.
O Farm animals, green pastures, fruit trees, grapes
P Laughter, bounty, river, weeping/joy, sheaves
E Praying hands, one, Christ, cross, ransom note
G Food, clothing, birds, lilies, grass, water
Prayer: N858. Providence of God (Matt, Thanksgiving)
Litany: C716. A Thanksgiving (Matt, Thanksgiving)
Response: S2195, SF2195 or S2081, SF2081 (Thanksgiving)
Sung Benediction: R302, S2279, SF2279, SP128, VU884. "The Trees of the Field" (Pss)

Jeremiah 33:14-16

14The days are surely coming, says the LORD, when I will
fulfill the promise I made to the house of Israel and the
house of Judah. 15In those days and at that time I will
cause a righteous Branch to spring up for David; and he
shall execute justice and righteousness in the land. 16In
those days Judah will be saved and Jerusalem will live in
safety. And this is the name by which it will be called:
"The LORD is our righteousness."

Psalm 25:1-10

1To you, O LORD, I lift up my soul. 2O my God, in you
I trust; do not let me be put to shame; do not let my enemies exult over me. 3Do not let those who wait for you be
put to shame; let them be ashamed who are wantonly
treacherous. 4Make me to know your ways, O LORD; teach
me your paths. 5Lead me in your truth, and teach me, for
you are the God of my salvation; for you I wait all day
long. 6Be mindful of your mercy, O LORD, and of your
steadfast love, for they have been from of old. 7Do not
remember the sins of my youth or my transgressions;
according to your steadfast love remember me, for your
goodness' sake, O LORD! 8Good and upright is the LORD;
therefore he instructs sinners in the way. 9He leads the
humble in what is right, and teaches the humble his way.
10All the paths of the LORD are steadfast love and faithfulness, for those who keep his covenant and his decrees.

1 Thessalonians 3:9-13

9How can we thank God enough for you in return for
all the joy that we feel before our God because of you?
10Night and day we pray most earnestly that we may see
you face to face and restore whatever is lacking in your
faith.

11Now may our God and Father himself and our Lord
Jesus direct our way to you. 12And may the Lord make
you increase and abound in love for one another and for
all, just as we abound in love for you. 13And may he so
strengthen your hearts in holiness that you may be blameless before our God and Father at the coming of our Lord
Jesus with all his saints.

Luke 21:25-36

25"There will be signs in the sun, the moon, and the
stars, and on the earth distress among nations confused
by the roaring of the sea and the waves. 26People will faint
from fear and foreboding of what is coming upon the
world, for the powers of the heavens will be shaken.
27Then they will see 'the Son of Man coming in a cloud'
with power and great glory. 28Now when these things
begin to take place, stand up and raise your heads,
because your redemption is drawing near."

29Then he told them a parable: "Look at the fig tree and
all the trees; 30as soon as they sprout leaves you can see for
yourselves and know that summer is already near. 31So
also, when you see these things taking place, you know
that the kingdom of God is near. 32Truly I tell you, this
generation will not pass away until all things have taken
place. 33Heaven and earth will pass away, but my words
will not pass away.

34"Be on guard so that your hearts are not weighed
down with dissipation and drunkenness and the worries
of this life, and that day does not catch you unexpectedly,
35like a trap. For it will come upon all who live on the face
of the whole earth. 36Be alert at all times, praying that you
may have the strength to escape all these things that will
take place, and to stand before the Son of Man."

Notes

Primary Hymns and Songs for the Day

"O Come, O Come, Emmanuel" (Jer) (O)
B76, C119, E56, F169, L34 (PD), N116, P9, UM211, VU1 (Fr.), W357
H-3 Hbl-14, 79; Chr-141; Org-168
S-1 #342. Handbell accompaniment

"There's Something About That Name" (Luke)
B177, C115, F227, R26, SP89, UM171

"My Lord, What a Morning" (Luke)
C708, P449, UM719, VU708
H-3 Chr-139

"O Day of God, Draw Nigh" (Luke)
B623, C700, E601, N611, P452, UM730 (PD), VU688 and VU689 (Fr.)
H-3 Hbl-79; Chr-141; Desc-95; Org-143
S-1 #306-308. Various treatments

"Lift Up Your Heads, Ye Mighty Gates" (Jer) (C)
B128, C129, E436, F239, N117, P8, R59, UM213 (PD), W363
H-3 Hbl-50; Chr-47; Desc-101; Org-167
S-1 #334-5. Descant and harmonization

Additional Hymn Suggestions

"Come, Thou Long-Expected Jesus" (Jer, Luke)
B77, C125, F168, P2, UM196 (PD)
E66, L30, N122, P1 (PD), VU2, W364

"Hail to the Lord's Anointed" (Jer)
C140, E616 (PD), L87, N104, P205, UM203 (PD), VU30

"Blessed Be the God of Israel" (Jer)
C135, P602, UM209, VU901

"Lo, How a Rose E'er Blooming" (Jer)
B78, C160, E81, F174, L58, N127, P48 (PD), UM216, VU8, W374

"Lead Me, Lord" (Jer, Pss)
C593, N774, R175, UM473 (PD), VU662

"Thou Didst Leave Thy Throne" (Jer, Advent)
B121, F170, S2100, SF2100

"Lift Every Voice and Sing" (Pss, Luke)
B627, C631, E599, L562, N593, P563, UM519, W641

"Lead Me, Guide Me" (Pss)
C583, R176, S2214, SF2214

"Lord, I Want to Be a Christian" (1 Thess)
B489, C589, F421, N454, P372 (PD), R145, UM402

"I Want to Walk as a Child of the Light" (1 Thess, Luke)
E490, R152, UM206, W510

"People, Look East" (Luke)
C142, P12, UM202, VU9, W359

"In the Bleak Midwinter" (Luke)
E112, N128, P36, UM221 (PD), VU55

"I Know Whom I Have Believed" (Luke)
B337, F631, UM714 (PD)

"Rejoice the Lord is King" (Luke)
E481, L171 (PD), UM716
B197, C699, F374, N303, P155, UM715 (PD), VU213, W493

"Lo, He Comes With Clouds Descending" (Luke)
B199, F306, E57, L27, P6, UM718 (PD), VU25

"Wake, Awake, for Night Is Flying" (Luke)
E61, L31, P17, UM720 (PD), VU711, W371

"Here, O My Lord, I See Thee" (Luke, Communion)
C416, E318, F567, L211, P520, UM623 (PD), VU459

Additional Contemporary Suggestions

"You Are Holy" ("Prince of Peace") (Jer, Advent)
M129

"Sing to the King" (Jer)
M141

"The King of Glory Comes" (Jer)
B127, R267, S2091, SF2091, W501

"Cry of My Heart" (Pss)
S2165, SF2165, M39

"In the Secret" ("I Want to Know You") (Pss)
M38; V-3 p. 36 Vocal Solo

"Show Me Your Ways" (Pss)
M107

"Lead Me, Lord" (Pss)
M108

"In the Presence of Jehovah" (Pss, Advent)
M113

"Ancient of Days" (Luke)
M1

"No Greater Love" (Luke)
M25

Vocal Solos

"Lo, He Comes with Clouds Descending" (Luke)
V-1 p. 54

"My Lord, What a Mornin'" (Luke, Advent)
V-7 p. 68

Anthems

"O Come, O Come, Emmanuel" (Jer)
arr. Evelyn R. Larter; Abingdon Press 9780687650767
SATB with piano and opt. flute

"Of The Father's Love Begotten" (Advent, Communion)
Arr. James E. Clemens; Curtis Music Press C9303
SATB a cappella

Other Suggestions

Visuals:
O Branch, Jesse tree
P Teaching, leading, path, open Bible
E Joy, praying hands, Jesus, 2nd coming
G Sun, moon, earth, clouds, Christ descending, fig tree, guard, praying, Luke 21:36a

Greeting: N819 (Pss)
Prayer: C19. Prayer of an African Girl (Advent)
Prayer: N816 (1 Thess, Luke, Advent)
Advent Wreath Response: C128 "One Candle Is Lit"
Advent Antiphons: C120, UM211 (Advent)

DECEMBER 6, 2009

Malachi 3:1-4

1See, I am sending my messenger to prepare the way before me, and the Lord whom you seek will suddenly come to his temple. The messenger of the covenant in whom you delight—indeed, he is coming, says the LORD of hosts. 2But who can endure the day of his coming, and who can stand when he appears?

For he is like a refiner's fire and like fullers' soap; 3he will sit as a refiner and purifier of silver, and he will purify the descendants of Levi and refine them like gold and silver, until they present offerings to the LORD in righteousness. 4Then the offering of Judah and Jerusalem will be pleasing to the LORD as in the days of old and as in former years.

Luke 1:68-79

68"Blessed be the Lord God of Israel, for he has looked favorably on his people and redeemed them. 69He has raised up a mighty savior for us in the house of his servant David, 70as he spoke through the mouth of his holy prophets from of old, 71that we would be saved from our enemies and from the hand of all who hate us. 72Thus he has shown the mercy promised to our ancestors, and has remembered his holy covenant, 73the oath that he swore to our ancestor Abraham, to grant us 74that we, being rescued from the hands of our enemies, might serve him without fear, 75in holiness and righteousness before him all our days. 76And you, child, will be called the prophet of the Most High; for you will go before the Lord to prepare his ways, 77to give knowledge of salvation to his people by the forgiveness of their sins. 78By the tender mercy of our God, the dawn from on high will break upon us, 79to give light to those who sit in darkness and in the shadow of death, to guide our feet into the way of peace."

Philippians 1:3-11

3I thank my God every time I remember you, 4constantly praying with joy in every one of my prayers for all of you, 5because of your sharing in the gospel from the first day until now. 6I am confident of this, that the one who began a good work among you will bring it to completion by the day of Jesus Christ. 7It is right for me to think this way about all of you, because you hold me in your heart, for all of you share in God's grace with me, both in my imprisonment and in the defense and confirmation of the gospel. 8For God is my witness, how I long for all of you with the compassion of Christ Jesus. 9And this is my prayer, that your love may overflow more and more with knowledge and full insight 10to help you to determine what is best, so that in the day of Christ you may be pure and blameless, 11having produced the harvest of righteousness that comes through Jesus Christ for the glory and praise of God.

Luke 3:1-6

1In the fifteenth year of the reign of Emperor Tiberius, when Pontius Pilate was governor of Judea, and Herod was ruler of Galilee, and his brother Philip ruler of the region of Ituraea and Trachonitis, and Lysanias ruler of Abilene, 2during the high priesthood of Annas and Caiaphas, the word of God came to John son of Zechariah in the wilderness. 3He went into all the region around the Jordan, proclaiming a baptism of repentance for the forgiveness of sins, 4as it is written in the book of the words of the prophet Isaiah, "The voice of one crying out in the wilderness: 'Prepare the way of the Lord, make his paths straight. 5Every valley shall be filled, and every mountain and hill shall be made low, and the crooked shall be made straight, and the rough ways made smooth; 6and all flesh shall see the salvation of God.' "

Notes

Primary Hymns and Songs for the Day

"Blessed Be the God of Israel" (Mal, Luke 1) (O)
C135, P602, UM209, VU901
"Prepare the Way of the Lord" (Luke 3, Advent)
C121, R92, UM207, VU10, W369
"Refiner's Fire" (Mal)
M50
"He Who Began a Good Work in You" (Phil)
S2163, SF2163, SP180, R134
"Angels from the Realms of Glory" (Mal) (C)
B94, C149, E93, F190, L50, P22, UM220 (PD), VU36, W377
H-3 Chr-30, 48, 62; Desc-89; Org-121
S-1 #280. Descant and harmonization

Additional Hymn Suggestions

"Have Thine Own Way, Lord" (Mal)
B294, C588, F400, UM382 (PD)
"Love Divine, All Loves Excelling" (Mal)
B208, C517, F21, N43, UM384 (PD)
E657, L315, P376, R196, VU333, W588 (PD)
"Guide My Feet" (Luke 1)
N497, P354, S2208
"Lead Me, Guide Me" (Luke 1)
C583, R176, S2214, SF2214
"Gather Us In" (Luke 1)
C284, S2236, SF2236, W665
"Toda la Tierra" ("All Earth is Waiting") (Mal, Luke 3)
C139, N121, UM210, VU5
"Send Your Word" (Luke 1)
N317, UM195
"I Want to Walk as a Child of the Light" (Luke 1)
E490, R152, UM206, W510
"Blessed Be the God of Israel" (Luke 1)
C135, P602, UM209, VU901
"Lo, How a Rose E'er Blooming" (Luke 1)
B78, C160, E81, F174, L58, N127, P48 (PD), UM216, VU8, W374
"Lift Up Your Heads, Ye Mighty Gates" (Phil, Advent)
B128, C129, E436, F239, N117, P8, R59, UM213 (PD), W363
"More Love to Thee, O Christ" (Phil)
B473, C527, F476, N456, P359, UM453 (PD)
"Come Down, O Love Divine" (Phil)
C582, E516, L508, N289, P313, UM475 (PD), VU367, W472
"Deck Thyself, My Soul, with Gladness" (Phil, Communion)
E339, L224, P506, UM612 (PD), VU463
"People, Look East" (Luke)
C142, P12, UM202, VU9, W359
"O Come, O Come, Emmanuel" (Luke)
B76, C119, E56, F169, L34 (PD), N116, P9, UM211, VU1 (Fr.), W357
"Wild and Lone the Prophet's Voice" (Luke 3)
P409, S2089, SF2089

Additional Contemporary Suggestions

"Purify My Heart" (Mal)
M90, R187
"Purified" (Mal)
M89
"Light the Fire Again" (Mal)
M144
"Shine on Us" (Luke 1, Advent)
M19
"Hear our Praises" (Luke 1, Advent)
M64
"Here I Am to Worship" (Luke 1, Advent)
M116
"Everyday" (Luke 1, Advent)
M150
"Light of the World" (Luke 1)
S2204
"We Are Marching" ("Siyahamba") (Luke 1)
C442, N526, R306, S2235-b, SF2235-b, VU646
"Praise Adonai" (Luke 3)
M125

Vocal Solos

"And He Shall Purify" (Mal)
V-2
"Consume Me" (Mal)
V-3 p. 148
"Come, Thou Long-Expected Jesus" (Luke, Advent)
V-10 p. 11

Anthems

"Antiphonal Hosanna" (Mal, Luke3)
Smith, arr. Schrader; Hope Publishing Co. C-5262
SATB and unison choir with piano

"God of the Plains" (Advent)
Dadee Reilly; Abingdon Press 9780687648603
SABE with keyboard and opt. flute and percussion

Other Suggestions

Visuals:
O Fire, soap, silver, gold, refining
P Christ, child, dawn breaking, light/darkness
E Prayer, open Bible, heart, shackles, letter, robe
G John, baptism, Luke 3:4b, straight path, level ground, all nations
Greeting: N822 (Luke 1)
Opening Prayer: N826 (Luke 1, Advent)
Call to Confession: N832 (Advent)
Canticle: C137, F191, N733, UM208, VU900 (Luke 1)
Litany: N880. A Litany of Darkness and Light (Luke 1)
Prayer: N853 or C31 (Luke 1)

Zephaniah 3:14-20
14Sing aloud, O daughter Zion; shout, O Israel! Rejoice
and exult with all your heart, O daughter Jerusalem!
15The LORD has taken away the judgments against you, he
has turned away your enemies. The king of Israel, the
LORD, is in your midst; you shall fear disaster no more.
16On that day it shall be said to Jerusalem: Do not fear,
O Zion; do not let your hands grow weak. 17The LORD,
your God, is in your midst, a warrior who gives victory; he
will rejoice over you with gladness, he will renew you in
his love; he will exult over you with loud singing 18as on a
day of festival. I will remove disaster from you, so that you
will not bear reproach for it. 19I will deal with all your
oppressors at that time. And I will save the lame and gather the outcast, and I will change their shame into praise
and renown in all the earth. 20At that time I will bring you
home, at the time when I gather you; for I will make you
renowned and praised among all the peoples of the
earth, when I restore your fortunes before your eyes, says
the LORD.

Isaiah 12:2-6
2Surely God is my salvation; I will trust, and will not be
afraid, for the LORD GOD is my strength and my might; he
has become my salvation.
3With joy you will draw water from the wells of salvation.
4And you will say in that day: Give thanks to the LORD, call
on his name; make known his deeds among the nations;
proclaim that his name is exalted. 5Sing praises to the
LORD, for he has done gloriously; let this be known in all
the earth. 6Shout aloud and sing for joy, O royal Zion, for
great in your midst is the Holy One of Israel.

Philippians 4:4-7
4Rejoice in the Lord always; again I will say, Rejoice.
5Let your gentleness be known to everyone. The Lord is
near. 6Do not worry about anything, but in everything
by prayer and supplication with thanksgiving let your
requests be made known to God. 7And the peace of God,
which surpasses all understanding, will guard your hearts
and your minds in Christ Jesus.

Luke 3:7-18
7John said to the crowds that came out to be baptized
by him, "You brood of vipers! Who warned you to flee
from the wrath to come? 8Bear fruits worthy of repentance. Do not begin to say to yourselves, 'We have
Abraham as our ancestor'; for I tell you, God is able from
these stones to raise up children to Abraham. 9Even now
the ax is lying at the root of the trees; every tree therefore
that does not bear good fruit is cut down and thrown into
the fire."
10And the crowds asked him, "What then should we
do?" 11In reply he said to them, "Whoever has two coats
must share with anyone who has none; and whoever has
food must do likewise." 12Even tax collectors came to be
baptized, and they asked him, "Teacher, what should we
do?" 13He said to them, "Collect no more than the
amount prescribed for you." 14Soldiers also asked him,
"And we, what should we do?" He said to them, "Do not
extort money from anyone by threats or false accusation,
and be satisfied with your wages."
15As the people were filled with expectation, and all
were questioning in their hearts concerning John,
whether he might be the Messiah, 16John answered all of
them by saying, "I baptize you with water; but one who
is more powerful than I is coming; I am not worthy to
untie the thong of his sandals. He will baptize you with
the Holy Spirit and fire. 17His winnowing fork is in his
hand, to clear his threshing floor and to gather the wheat
into his granary; but the chaff he will burn with
unquenchable fire."
18So, with many other exhortations, he proclaimed the
good news to the people.

Notes

Lessons + Carols

Primary Hymns and Songs for the Day

"Hail to the Lord's Anointed" (Zeph) (O)
C140, E616 (PD), L87, N104, P205, UM203 (PD), VU30

"The First Song of Isaiah" (Isa)
R122, S2030, SF2030

"Good Christian Friends, Rejoice" (Phil, Luke)
B96, C164, E107 (PD), F177, L55, N129, P28, UM224, VU35, W391
H-3 Hbl-19, 30, 65; Chr-83; Desc-55; Org-62
S-1 #180. Rhythm instrument accompaniment

"Wild and Lone the Prophet's Voice" (Luke)
P409, S2089, SF2089

"Come, Thou Long-Expected Jesus" (Zeph) (C)
B77, C125, F168, P2, UM196 (PD)
H-3 Hbl-46; Chr-26, 134; Desc-53; Org-56
S-1 #168-171. Various treatments
E66, N122, P1 (PD), VU2, W364
H-3 Hbl-53; Chr-32; Desc-99; Org-158
S-1 #324. Descant

Additional Hymn Suggestions

"Send Your Word" (Zeph, Luke)
N317, UM195

"Tell Out, My Soul" (Zeph, Isa, Phil, Luke)
B81, E437 and E438, R130, UM200, W534

"Blessed Be the God of Israel" (Zeph, Luke)
C135, P602, UM209, VU901

"Toda la Tierra" ("All Earth is Waiting") (Zeph, Luke 3)
C139, N121, UM210, VU5

"Cantemos al Señor" ("Let's Sing Unto the Lord") (Isa)
B38, C60, N39, R11, UM149

"Rejoice, Ye Pure in Heart" (Phil)
B39, C15, E556, F394, N55, P145, UM160 (PD)
E557, N71, P146, UM161

"Rejoice, the Lord Is King" (Phil)
B197, C699, F374, N303, P155, UM715 (PD), VU213
E481, L171 (PD), UM716

"O Day of Peace That Dimly Shines" (Phil, Luke)
C711, E597, P450, UM729, VU682, W654

"Lord of All Hopefulness" (Phil, Advent)
E482, L469, R174, S2197, SF2197, W568

"In the Bleak Midwinter" (Luke)
E112, N128, P36, UM221 (PD), VU55

"Take My Life, and Let It Be" (Luke)
B277 and B283, C609, E707, L406, N448, P391, R133, UM399 (PD), VU506

"Make Me a Captive, Lord" (Luke)
B278, P378, UM421 (PD)

"Cuando El Pobre" ("When the Poor Ones") (Luke)
C662, P407, UM434, VU702

"The Voice of God Is Calling" (Luke)
C666, UM436 (PD)

"What Does the Lord Require" (Luke)
C659, E605, P405, UM441, W624

"God the Sculptor of the Mountains" (Luke)
S2060, SF2060

Additional Contemporary Suggestions

"Shout to the Lord" (Zeph, Isa)
S2074, SF2074, M16; V-3 p. 56 Vocal Solo

"Forever" (Isa)
M68

"He Is Exalted" (Isa)
R238, S2070, SF2070, SP66

"Someone Asked the Question" (Isa, Phil)
N523, S2144, SF2144

"I Will Enter His Gates" (Isa, Phil)
S2270, SF2270, SP168

"I've Got Peace Like a River" (Phil)
B418, C530, N478, P368, S2145, VU577

"Come and Fill Our Hearts" ("Confitemini Domino") (Phil)
S2157, SF2157, W561

"Let the Peace of God Reign" (Phil)
M87

"Jesus, Name Above All Names" (Luke)
R26, SP76, S2071, SF2071

"I Will Never Be" (the Same Again) (Luke)
M34

"Refiner's Fire" (Luke, Advent)
M50

Vocal Solos

"Rejoice Greatly, O Daughter of Zion" (Zeph)
V-2

"Prepare Thyself, Zion" (Zeph)
V-9 p. 2

"A Song of Joy" (Zeph, Phil)
V-11 p. 2

Anthems

"An Advent Alleluia" (Zeph)
Douglas E. Wagner; Hope Publishing Co. A680
SATB with keyboard

"Rejoice, Ye Pure in Heart" (Phil)
Mark Kellner; Hope C5461
SATB with piano

Other Suggestions

Visuals:
O Rejoicing, singing, festival, clock, saving
P Races/nations, singing, shouting, water/well
E Rejoicing, praying hands, Phil 4:4, 5b, 6a, b, peace
G Snakes, axe/root, Holy Spirit, fir, water, 2 coats, tax form, fruit, winnowing fork, wheat, service

Greeting: N823 (Advent)
Prayers: UM201 (Advent, Luke) and N854 (Phil)
Reading: VU880. Give Thanks to God (Isa)
Blessing: N872 (Zeph, Luke)
Sung Benediction: R302, S2279, SF2279, SP128, VU884. "The Trees of the Field" (Isa)

Micah 5:2-5*a*

[2]But you, O Bethlehem of Ephrathah, who are one of the little clans of Judah, from you shall come forth for me one who is to rule in Israel, whose origin is from of old, from ancient days. [3]Therefore he shall give them up until the time when she who is in labor has brought forth; then the rest of his kindred shall return to the people of Israel. [4]And he shall stand and feed his flock in the strength of the LORD, in the majesty of the name of the LORD his God. And they shall live secure, for now he shall be great to the ends of the earth; [5a] and he shall be the one of peace.

Luke 1:46*b*-55

[46b]"My soul magnifies the Lord, [47]and my spirit rejoices in God my Savior, [48]for he has looked with favor on the lowliness of his servant. Surely, from now on all generations will call me blessed; [49]for the Mighty One has done great things for me, and holy is his name. [50]His mercy is for those who fear him from generation to generation. [51]He has shown strength with his arm; he has scattered the proud in the thoughts of their hearts. [52]He has brought down the powerful from their thrones, and lifted up the lowly; [53]he has filled the hungry with good things, and sent the rich away empty. [54]He has helped his servant Israel, in remembrance of his mercy, [55]according to the promise he made to our ancestors, to Abraham and to his descendants forever."

Hebrews 10:5-10

[5]Consequently, when Christ came into the world, he said, "Sacrifices and offerings you have not desired, but a body you have prepared for me; [6]in burnt offerings and sin offerings you have taken no pleasure. [7]Then I said, 'See, God, I have come to do your will, O God' (in the scroll of the book it is written of me)." [8]When he said above, "You have neither desired nor taken pleasure in sacrifices and offerings and burnt offerings and sin offerings" (these are offered according to the law), [9]then he added, "See, I have come to do your will." He abolishes the first in order to establish the second. [10]And it is by God's will that we have been sanctified through the offering of the body of Jesus Christ once for all.

Luke 1:39-45 46-55

[39]In those days Mary set out and went with haste to a Judean town in the hill country, [40]where she entered the house of Zechariah and greeted Elizabeth. [41]When Elizabeth heard Mary's greeting, the child leaped in her womb. And Elizabeth was filled with the Holy Spirit [42]and exclaimed with a loud cry, "Blessed are you among women, and blessed is the fruit of your womb. [43]And why has this happened to me, that the mother of my Lord comes to me? [44]For as soon as I heard the sound of your greeting, the child in my womb leaped for joy. [45]And blessed is she who believed that there would be a fulfillment of what was spoken to her by the Lord."

Notes

Primary Hymns and Songs for the Day

"O Come, All Ye Faithful" (Luke) (O)
B89, C148, E83, F193, L45, N135, P41, UM234 (PD), VU60 (Fr.), W392
H-3 Hbl-78; Desc-12; Org-2
S-1 #7-13. Various treatments

"O Little Town of Bethlehem" (Mic)
B86, C144, E79, F178, L41, N133, P44, UM230, VU64, W386
H-3 Hbl-81; Chr-145; Desc-95; Org-141
S-1 #304. Harmonization
E78, P43
H-3 Hbl-44; Chr-21; Desc-40; Org-40
S-1 #131-132. Introduction and descant

"My Soul Gives Glory to My God" (Luke)
C130, N119, P600, UM198, VU899
H-3 Chr-139, 145; Desc-77
S-1 #241-242. Orff arr. and descant

"Give Thanks" (Luke)
C528, R266, S2036, SF2036, SP170

"Joy to the World" (Mic, Luke) (C)
B87, C143, E100, F171, L39, N132, P40, UM246 (PD), VU59, W399
H-3 Hbl-8, 29, 73; Chr-119; Desc-15; Org-6
S-1 #19-20. Trumpet descants

Additional Hymn Suggestions

"O Sing a Song of Bethlehem" (Mic)
B120, F208, N51, P308, UM179 (PD)

"Come, Thou Long-Expected Jesus" (Mic)
B77, C125, F168, P2, UM196 (PD)
E66, L30, N122, P1 (PD), VU2, W364

"Once In Royal David's City" (Mic)
C165, E102, N45, P49, UM250 (PD), VU62, W402

"Savior of the Nations, Come" (Mic, Luke)
E54, P14 (PD), UM214, W372

"That Boy-Child of Mary" (Mic, Luke)
B110, P55, UM241

"What Does the Lord Require" (Heb, Luke)
C659, E605, P405, UM441, W624

"Ye Who Claim the Faith of Jesus" (Luke)
E268 and E269, UM197

"Tell Out, My Soul" (Luke)
B81, E437 and E438, R130, UM200, W534

"To a Maid Engaged to Joseph" (Luke)
P19, UM215, VU14

"Lo, How a Rose E'er Blooming" (Luke)
B78, C160, E81, F174, L58, N127, P48 (PD), UM216, VU8, W374

"Sing of Mary, Pure and Lowly" (Luke)
C184, E277, UM272, W404

"The First One Ever" (Luke)
E673, UM276

"Cuando el Pobre" ("When the Poor Ones") (Luke)
C662, P407, UM434, VU702

"The Snow Lay on the Ground" (Luke)
E110, S2093, P57

"Joseph Dearest, Joseph Mine" (Luke)
N105, S2099, SF2099

"She Comes Sailing on the Wind" (Luke)
S2122, SF2122, VU380

"I'm So Glad Jesus Lifted Me" (Luke)
C529, N474, S2151, SF2151

"Blest Are They" (Luke)
R127, S2155, SF2155, VU896

Additional Contemporary Suggestions

"Ancient of Days" (Mic)
M1

"Shout to the North" (Mic, Luke)
M99

"You Are My All in All" (Mic, Heb, Luke)
SP220

"Praise to the Lord" (Luke)
S2029, SF2029, VU835

"The Virgin Mary Had a Baby Boy" (Luke)
S2098, VU73

"Holy Ground" (Luke)
B224, C112, S2272, SF2272, SP86

"Let the River Flow" (Luke)
M142

"O Magnify the Lord" (Luke)
R131, SP77

Vocal Solos

"He Shall Feed His Flock" (Mic)
V-8 p. 334

"To Touch His Tiny Hand" (Luke)
V-10 p. 22

Anthems

"Hope Came Down from Heaven" (Luke)
Ken Dosso; Abingdon Press 978068790288
SATB with piano

"Christmas is Coming" (Advent, Christmas)
Joel Raney; Hope C5471
SAB with piano and opt. handbells

Other Suggestions

Visuals:
O Bethlehem, Christ feeding sheep, globe
P Mary, arm, toppled throne, feed, full/empty bowls
E Scroll, open Bible, cross/manger
G Pregnant women, greeting, Luke 1:42b

Greeting: N825 (Luke)
Canticle: C131, N732, UM199. ("Magnificat") (Luke)
Reading: F176, N page 59. The Song of Mary (Luke)
Litany: C157. For All Who Give You a Face (Luke)
Words of Assurance: N840 (Luke)
Blessing: N873 (Luke)

DECEMBER 24/25, 2009

Isaiah 9:2-7

[2]The people who walked in darkness have seen a great light; those who lived in a land of deep darkness—on them light has shined. [3]You have multiplied the nation, you have increased its joy; they rejoice before you as with joy at the harvest, as people exult when dividing plunder. [4]For the yoke of their burden, and the bar across their shoulders, the rod of their oppressor, you have broken as on the day of Midian. [5]For all the boots of the tramping warriors and all the garments rolled in blood shall be burned as fuel for the fire. [6]For a child has been born for us, a son given to us; authority rests upon his shoulders; and he is named Wonderful Counselor, Mighty God, Everlasting Father, Prince of Peace. [7]His authority shall grow continually, and there shall be endless peace for the throne of David and his kingdom. He will establish and uphold it with justice and with righteousness from this time onward and forevermore. The zeal of the LORD of hosts will do this.

Psalm 96

[1]O sing to the LORD a new song; sing to the LORD, all the earth. [2]Sing to the LORD, bless his name; tell of his salvation from day to day. [3]Declare his glory among the nations, his marvelous works among all the peoples. [4]For great is the LORD, and greatly to be praised; he is to be revered above all gods. [5]For all the gods of the peoples are idols, but the LORD made the heavens. [6]Honor and majesty are before him; strength and beauty are in his sanctuary. [7]Ascribe to the LORD, O families of the peoples, ascribe to the LORD glory and strength. [8]Ascribe to the LORD the glory due his name; bring an offering, and come into his courts. [9]Worship the LORD in holy splendor; tremble before him, all the earth. [10]Say among the nations, "The LORD is king! The world is firmly established; it shall never be moved. He will judge the peoples with equity." [11]Let the heavens be glad, and let the earth rejoice; let the sea roar, and all that fills it; [12]let the field exult, and everything in it. Then shall all the trees of the forest sing for joy [13]before the LORD; for he is coming, for he is coming to judge the earth. He will judge the world with righteousness, and the peoples with his truth.

Titus 2:11-14

[11]For the grace of God has appeared, bringing salvation to all, [12]training us to renounce impiety and worldly passions, and in the present age to live lives that are self-controlled, upright, and godly, [13]while we wait for the blessed hope and the manifestation of the glory of our great God and Savior, Jesus Christ. [14]He it is who gave himself for us that he might redeem us from all iniquity and purify for himself a people of his own who are zealous for good deeds.

Luke 2:1-20

[1]In those days a decree went out from Emperor Augustus that all the world should be registered. [2]This was the first registration and was taken while Quirinius was governor of Syria. [3]All went to their own towns to be registered. [4]Joseph also went from the town of Nazareth in Galilee to Judea, to the city of David called Bethlehem, because he was descended from the house and family of David. [5]He went to be registered with Mary, to whom he was engaged and who was expecting a child. [6]While they were there, the time came for her to deliver her child. [7]And she gave birth to her firstborn son and wrapped him in bands of cloth, and laid him in a manger, because there was no place for them in the inn.

[8]In that region there were shepherds living in the fields, keeping watch over their flock by night. [9]Then an angel of the Lord stood before them, and the glory of the Lord shone around them, and they were terrified. [10]But the angel said to them, "Do not be afraid; for see—I am bringing you good news of great joy for all the people: [11]to you is born this day in the city of David a Savior, who is the Messiah, the Lord. [12]This will be a sign for you: you will find a child wrapped in bands of cloth and lying in a manger." [13]And suddenly there was with the angel a multitude of the heavenly host, praising God and saying, [14]"Glory to God in the highest heaven, and on earth peace among those whom he favors!"

[15]When the angels had left them and gone into heaven, the shepherds said to one another, "Let us go now to Bethlehem and see this thing that has taken place, which the Lord has made known to us." [16]So they went with haste and found Mary and Joseph, and the child lying in the manger. [17]When they saw this, they made known what had been told them about this child; [18] and all who heard it were amazed at what the shepherds told them. [19]But Mary treasured all these words and pondered them in her heart. [20]The shepherds returned, glorifying and praising God for all they had heard and seen, as it had been told them.

Notes

Primary Hymns and Songs for the Day

"Angels We Have Heard on High" (Luke) (O)
B100, C155, E96, F192, L71, P23, N125, UM238, VU38 (Fr.), W376
C155 Descant
H-3 Hbl-47; Chr-31; Desc-43; Org-45

"Away in a Manger" (Luke)
B103, C147, F185, L67, N124, P25, UM217 (PD)
H-3 Org-12
S-1 #30-32. Various treatments
S-2 #20. Descant
E101, F187, P24, VU69, W378
H-3 Org-21

"It Came Upon the Midnight Clear" (Luke)
B93, C153, E89, F197, L54, N131, P38, UM218 (PD), VU44, W400
H-3 Hbl-72; Chr-113; Desc-22; Org-19
S-2 #39. Descant

"Sing We Now of Christmas" (Luke) (C)
B111, UM237
H-3 Chr-140
S-1 #136. Orff instrument arrangement

"Silent Night" (Luke) (C)
B91, C145, E111, F195, L65, N134, P60, UM239 (PD), VU67 (Fr.), W379
H-3 Hbl-92; Chr-171; Desc-99; Org-159
S-1 #322. Descant
#323. Guitar/Autoharp chords
S-2 #167. Handbell arrangement

Additional Hymn Suggestions

"Good Christian Friends, Rejoice" (Luke)
B96, C164, E107 (PD), F177, L55, N129, P28, UM224, VU35, W391

"Infant Holy, Infant Lowly" (Luke)
B106, C163, F194, L44, P37, UM229, VU58, W393

"O Little Town of Bethlehem" (Luke)
B86, C144, E78 and E79, F178, L41, N133, P43 and P44, UM230, VU64, W386

"O Come, All Ye Faithful" (Luke)
B89, C148, E83, F193, L45, N135, P41, UM234 (PD), VU60 (Fr.), W392

"While Shepherds Watched Their Flocks" (Luke)
C154, F175, P59, UM236 (PD)
E94 and E95, P58, VU75, W382

"The First Noel" (Luke)
B85, C151, E109, F179, L56, N139, P56, UM245 (PD), VU90 (Fr.) and VU91, W408

"Like a Child" (Luke)
C133, S2092, SF2092, VU366

"The Snow Lay on the Ground" (Luke)
E110, S2093, P57

"Joseph Dearest, Joseph Mine" (Luke)
N105, S2099, SF2099

"Glory to God in the Highest" (Luke)
S2276, SF2276

Additional Contemporary Suggestions

"King of Kings" (Isa)
B234, R268, S2075, SF2075, VU167, SP94

"How Majestic Is Your Name" (Isa)
C63, R98, S2023, SF2023, SP14

"Jesus, Name Above All Names" (Isa)
R26, SP76, S2071, SF2071

"His Name Is Wonderful" (Isa)
B203, F230, R30, SP90, UM174

"Shine on Us" (Isa)
M19

"You Are Holy" ("Prince of Peace") (Isa)
M129

"Blessed Be the Name of the Lord" (Pss)
M12, S2034, SF2034

"I Sing Praises to Your Name" (Pss)
R79, S2037, SF2037, SP27

"Shout to the Lord" (Pss)
S2074, SF2074, M16; V-3 p. 56 Vocal Solo

"Majesty" (Pss)
B215, R63, SP73, UM176

"Lord, I Lift Your Name on High" (Luke)
M2, R4, S2088, SF2088

"O Praise Him" ("All This for a King") (Luke)
M133

"Offering" (Christmas)
M130

Vocal Solos

"A Scottish Christmas Song" (Luke)
V-4 p. 4

"Sing Noel!" (Luke)
V-11 p. 13

"Sleep, Little Baby" (Luke)
V-10 p. 27

Anthems

"While Shepherds Watched Their Flocks" (Luke)
Franklin D. Ashdown; Kjos 9074
SATB with keyboard and opt. cello

"One Small Child" (Luke)
Meece; arr. Larson; Hope C5467
SAB with piano and opt. handbells

Other Suggestions

Visuals:
O Light, yoke, rod, infant Jesus, Isa 9:6b, crown
P All nature, gifts and offerings, gold
E Gold cross, glory, sacrifice
G Infant Jesus, manger, nativity scene, shepherds, angels

Prayer: UM231 or F188. Christmas (Titus)
Reading: F196. For Unto Us (Isa)
Readings: C152, F186, F204 (Luke)

1 Samuel 2:18-20, 26

18 Samuel was ministering before the LORD, a boy wearing a linen ephod. 19 His mother used to make for him a little robe and take it to him each year, when she went up with her husband to offer the yearly sacrifice. 20 Then Eli would bless Elkanah and his wife, and say, "May the LORD repay you with children by this woman for the gift that she made to the LORD"; and then they would return to their home.

26 Now the boy Samuel continued to grow both in stature and in favor with the LORD and with the people.

Psalm 148

1 Praise the LORD! Praise the LORD from the heavens; praise him in the heights! 2 Praise him, all his angels; praise him, all his host! 3 Praise him, sun and moon; praise him, all you shining stars! 4 Praise him, you highest heavens, and you waters above the heavens! 5 Let them praise the name of the LORD, for he commanded and they were created. 6 He established them forever and ever; he fixed their bounds, which cannot be passed. 7 Praise the LORD from the earth, you sea monsters and all deeps, 8 fire and hail, snow and frost, stormy wind fulfilling his command! 9 Mountains and all hills, fruit trees and all cedars! 10 Wild animals and all cattle, creeping things and flying birds! 11 Kings of the earth and all peoples, princes and all rulers of the earth! 12 Young men and women alike, old and young together! 13 Let them praise the name of the LORD, for his name alone is exalted; his glory is above earth and heaven. 14 He has raised up a horn for his people, praise for all his faithful, for the people of Israel who are close to him. Praise the LORD!

Colossians 3:12-17

12 As God's chosen ones, holy and beloved, clothe yourselves with compassion, kindness, humility, meekness, and patience. 13 Bear with one another and, if anyone has a complaint against another, forgive each other; just as the Lord has forgiven you, so you also must forgive. 14 Above all, clothe yourselves with love, which binds everything together in perfect harmony. 15 And let the peace of Christ rule in your hearts, to which indeed you were called in the one body. And be thankful. 16 Let the word of Christ dwell in you richly; teach and admonish one another in all wisdom; and with gratitude in your hearts sing psalms, hymns, and spiritual songs to God. 17 And whatever you do, in word or deed, do everything in the name of the Lord Jesus, giving thanks to God the Father through him.

Luke 2:41-52

41 Now every year his parents went to Jerusalem for the festival of the Passover. 42 And when he was twelve years old, they went up as usual for the festival. 43 When the festival was ended and they started to return, the boy Jesus stayed behind in Jerusalem, but his parents did not know it. 44 Assuming that he was in the group of travelers, they went a day's journey. Then they started to look for him among their relatives and friends. 45 When they did not find him, they returned to Jerusalem to search for him. 46 After three days they found him in the temple, sitting among the teachers, listening to them and asking them questions. 47 And all who heard him were amazed at his understanding and his answers. 48 When his parents saw him they were astonished; and his mother said to him, "Child, why have you treated us like this? Look, your father and I have been searching for you in great anxiety." 49 He said to them, "Why were you searching for me? Did you not know that I must be in my Father's house?" 50 But they did not understand what he said to them. 51 Then he went down with them and came to Nazareth, and was obedient to them. His mother treasured all these things in her heart.

52 And Jesus increased in wisdom and in years, and in divine and human favor.

Notes

Primary Hymns and Songs for the Day

"Once in Royal David's City" (Luke, Christmas) (O)
C165, E102, N45, P49, UM250 (PD), VU62, W402
H-3 Hbl-83; Chr-68, 156; Desc-57; Org-63
S-1 #182-184. Various treatments
"O Sing a Song of Bethlehem" (Luke)
B120, F208, N51, P308, UM179 (PD)
H-3 Hbl-15, 20, 34, 84; Chr-150; Org-67
S-2 #100-103. Various treatments
"Infant Holy, Infant Lowly" (Luke, Christmas)
B106, C163, F194, L44, P37, UM229, VU58, W393
H-3 Chr-113; Desc-102; Org-171
S-1 #345. Handbell/keyboard arrangement
"That Boy-Child of Mary" (Luke, Christmas)
B110, P55, UM241
H-3 Chr-179
S-1 #45. Guitar/autoharp chords
S-2 #28. Flute descant
"Go, Tell It on the Mountain" (Christmas) (C)
B95, C167, E99, F205, L70, N154, P29, UM251, VU43, W397
H-3 Hbl-17, 28, 61; Chr-73; Desc-45; Org-46

Additional Hymn Suggestions

"Blest Are They" (1 Sam)
R127, S2155, SF2155, VU896
"Let All Things Now Living" (Pss)
B640, C717, F389, L557, P554, R48, S2008, VU242, W559
"How Great Thou Art" (Pss)
B10, C33, F2, L532, N35, P467, R250, UM77, VU238 (Fr.)
"At the Font We Start Our Journey" (Col, New Year)
N308, S2114, SF2114
"Together We Serve" (Col)
S2175, SF2175
"For One Great Peace" (Col)
S2185, SF2185
"Healer of Our Every Ill" (Col)
C506, S2213, SF2213, VU619
"We Are God's People" (Col)
B383, F546, S2220, SF2220
"Love Came Down at Christmas" (Luke, Christmas)
B109, E84, N165, UM242
"We Meet You, O Christ" (Luke)
C183, P311, UM257, VU183
"Our Parent, by Whose Name" (Luke)
E587, L357, UM447, VU555, W570
"Like a Child" (Luke)
C133, S2092, SF2092, VU366
"Lord of All Hopefulness" (Luke)
E482, L469, R174, S2197, SF2197, W568

Additional Contemporary Suggestions

"Praise to the Lord" (1 Sam)
S2029, SF2029, VU835
"Let Everything That Has Breath" (Pss)
M59
"God of Wonders" (Pss)
M80; V-3 p. 184 Vocal Solo
"Praise Adonai" (Pss)
M125
"Indescribable" (Pss)
M127
"Dwell" (Col)
M154
"Give Thanks" (Col)
C528, R266, S2036, SF2036, SP170
"There's a Song" (Col)
S2141, SF2141
"Make Me a Channel of Your Peace" (Col)
S2171, SF2171, VU684
"Song of Hope" (Col)
P432, S2186, VU424
"Make Us One" (Col)
S2224, SF2224, SP137
"Bind Us Together" (Col)
R292, S2226, SF2226, SP140

Vocal Solos

"All Creatures of Our God and King" (Pss)
V-6 p. 55
"Because You Are God's Chosen Ones" (Col)
V-8 p. 286
"Gentle Jesus, Meek and Mild" (Luke, Christmas)
V-1 p. 11
"Sing for Christ Is Born" (Luke, Christmas)
V-10 p. 16

Anthems

"It Came Upon the Midnight Clear" (Christmas)
Mark Patterson; Kjos 9070
SATB divisi with piano

"Come and Sing the Christmas Story" (Christmas)
arr. Allen Pote; Hope C5469
SATB with keyboard

Other Suggestions

Visuals:
O Twelve-year-old boy, growing children, graduated sizes (clothes)
P Stars, planets, moon; nature imagery, single horn
E Clothes, compassion, forgiveness, singing, Col 3:16, 17b
G Growing boy, parents, child with teachers, glue or cord
Introit: C575, S2128, SF2128, VU374. "Come and Find the Quiet Center" (Col)
Canticle: UM646. "Canticle of Love" (Col)
Reading: F3. Praise Hymn (Pss)
Call to Confession: N832 (Christmas)
Prayer of Confession: N837 (Col)
Words of Assurance: N839 (Christmas)
For New Year's suggestions, see page 47.

Ecclesiastes 3:1-13

1For everything there is a season, and a time for every matter under heaven: 2a time to be born, and a time to die; a time to plant, and a time to pluck up what is planted; 3a time to kill, and a time to heal; a time to break down, and a time to build up; 4a time to weep, and a time to laugh; a time to mourn, and a time to dance; 5a time to throw away stones, and a time to gather stones together; a time to embrace, and a time to refrain from embracing; 6a time to seek, and a time to lose; a time to keep, and a time to throw away; 7a time to tear, and a time to sew; a time to keep silence, and a time to speak; 8a time to love, and a time to hate; a time for war, and a time for peace.

9What gain have the workers from their toil? 10I have seen the business that God has given to everyone to be busy with. 11He has made everything suitable for its time; moreover he has put a sense of past and future into their minds, yet they cannot find out what God has done from the beginning to the end. 12I know that there is nothing better for them than to be happy and enjoy themselves as long as they live; 13moreover, it is God's gift that all should eat and drink and take pleasure in all their toil.

Psalm 8

1O LORD, our Sovereign, how majestic is your name in all the earth! You have set your glory above the heavens. 2Out of the mouths of babes and infants you have founded a bulwark because of your foes, to silence the enemy and the avenger. 3When I look at your heavens, the work of your fingers, the moon and the stars that you have established; 4what are human beings that you are mindful of them, mortals that you care for them? 5Yet you have made them a little lower than God, and crowned them with glory and honor. 6You have given them dominion over the works of your hands; you have put all things under their feet, 7all sheep and oxen, and also the beasts of the field, 8the birds of the air, and the fish of the sea, whatever passes along the paths of the seas. 9O LORD, our Sovereign, how majestic is your name in all the earth!

Revelation 21:1-6*a*

1Then I saw a new heaven and a new earth; for the first heaven and the first earth had passed away, and the sea was no more. 2And I saw the holy city, the new Jerusalem, coming down out of heaven from God, prepared as a bride adorned for her husband. 3And I heard a loud voice from the throne saying, "See, the home of God is among mortals. He will dwell with them; they will be his peoples, and God himself will be with them; 4he will wipe every tear from their eyes. Death will be no more; mourning and crying and pain will be no more, for the first things have passed away."

5And the one who was seated on the throne said, "See, I am making all things new." Also he said, "Write this, for these words are trustworthy and true." 6aThen he said to me, "It is done! I am the Alpha and the Omega, the beginning and the end."

Matthew 25:31-46

31"When the Son of Man comes in his glory, and all the angels with him, then he will sit on the throne of his glory. 32All the nations will be gathered before him, and he will separate people one from another as a shepherd separates the sheep from the goats, 33and he will put the sheep at his right hand and the goats at the left. 34Then the king will say to those at his right hand, 'Come, you that are blessed by my Father, inherit the kingdom prepared for you from the foundation of the world; 35for I was hungry and you gave me food, I was thirsty and you gave me something to drink, I was a stranger and you welcomed me, 36I was naked and you gave me clothing, I was sick and you took care of me, I was in prison and you visited me.' 37Then the righteous will answer him, 'Lord, when was it that we saw you hungry and gave you food, or thirsty and gave you something to drink? 38And when was it that we saw you a stranger and welcomed you, or naked and gave you clothing? 39And when was it that we saw you sick or in prison and visited you?' 40And the king will answer them, 'Truly I tell you, just as you did it to one of the least of these who are members of my family, you did it to me.' 41Then he will say to those at his left hand, 'You that are accursed, depart from me into the eternal fire prepared for the devil and his angels; 42for I was hungry and you gave me no food, I was thirsty and you gave me nothing to drink, 43I was a stranger and you did not welcome me, naked and you did not give me clothing, sick and in prison and you did not visit me.' 44Then they also will answer, 'Lord, when was it that we saw you hungry or thirsty or a stranger or naked or sick or in prison, and did not take care of you?' 45Then he will answer them, 'Truly I tell you, just as you did not do it to one of the least of these, you did not do it to me.' 46And these will go away into eternal punishment, but the righteous into eternal life."

Notes

Primary Hymns and Songs for the Day
"O God, Our Help in Ages Past" (Pss, Rev) (O)
B74, C67, E680, F370, L320, N25, P210, UM117 (PD), VU806, W579
H-3 Hbl-33, 80; Chr-143; Desc-93; Org-132
S-1 #293-296. Various treatments
"Hymn of Promise" (Eccl)
C638, N433, UM707, VU703
H-3 Chr-112; Org-117
S-1 #270. Descant
"How Great Thou Art" (Pss)
B10, C33, F2, L532, N35, P467, R250, UM77, VU238 (Fr.)
H-3 Chr-103; Org-105
S-1 #163. Harmonization
"This is a Day of New Beginnings" (Rev)
B370, C518, N417, UM383
H-3 Chr-196
"In Remembrance of Me" (Matt, Communion)
B365, C403, S2254
"Joy in the Morning" (Rev) (C)
S2284, SF2284

Additional Hymn Suggestions
"Love Divine, All Loves Excelling" (Rev)
B208, C517, F21, N43, UM384 (PD)
E657, L315, P376, R196, VU333, W588 (PD)
"Come, Ye Disconsolate" (Rev)
B67, C502, SF2132, UM510 (PD)
"We've a Story to Tell to the Nations" (Rev)
B586, C484, F659, UM569 (PD)
"O What Their Joy and Their Glory Must Be" (Rev)
E623, L337, N385, UM727 (PD)
"There's a Spirit in the Air" (Rev, Matt)
B393, C257, N292, P433, R282, UM192, VU582, W531
"For the Healing of the Nations" (Rev, Matt)
C668, N576, UM428, VU678
"Cuando El Pobre" ("When the Poor Ones") (Matt)
C662, P407, UM434, VU702
"Rescue the Perishing" (Matt)
B559, F661, UM591 (PD)
"God Weeps" (Matt)
S2048, SF2048
"Carol of the Epiphany" (Matt)
S2094, SF2094
"Star-Child" (Matt)
S2095, SF2095
All Who Hunger" (Matt)
C419, S2126, SF2126, VU460
"Together We Serve" (Matt)
S2175, SF2175
"Here Am I" (Matt)
C654, S2178, SF2178
"As We Gather at Your Table" (Matt, Communion)
S2268, SF2268. N332, VU457
"We Shall Overcome" (Rev) (C)
C630, N570, UM533

Additional Contemporary Suggestions
"In His Time" (Eccl)
B53, S2203, SF2203
"I Could Sing of Your Love Forever" (Eccl)
M63; V-3 p. 22 Vocal Solo
"We Will Dance" (Eccl)
M140
"Be Glorified" (Eccl)
M152
"God of Wonders" (Pss)
M80; V-3 p. 184 Vocal Solo
"How Majestic Is Your Name" (Pss)
C63, R98, S2023, SF2023, SP14
"There's Something about That Name" (Rev)
B177, C115, F227, R26, SP89, UM171
"Spirit Song" (Rev)
C352, R248, SP134, UM347
"Soon and Very Soon" (Rev)
B192, R276, UM706; S-2 #187
"You Are Holy" ("Prince of Peace") (Rev)
M129
"All Who Are Thirsty" (Rev)
M159
"People Need the Lord" (Matt)
B557, S2244, SF2244

Vocal Solos
"I Will Sing of Thy Great Mercies" (Eccl)
V-4 p. 43
"Reach Out to Your Neighbor" (Matt)
V-8 p. 372

Anthems
"A Time and a Purpose" (Eccl)
Charles W. Ore: MorningStar 80-845
SATB with keyboard

"Whoever Welcomes You, Welcomes Me" (Matt)
Larry E. Schultz; Choristers Guild CGA1067
Unison/Two-part with piano

Other Suggestions
Visuals:
O Seasons, birth/death, workers, time piece, joy, gift
P Ps 8:1, infants, moon, stars, people, crown, sheep, birds, sea
E Heaven/earth, bride, handkerchief, newness, Alpha/Omega
G Christ, angels, nations, sheep/goats, ministry, fire,
Greeting: N824 (Pss)
Prayer of Confession: N836 (Matt, New Year)
Litany: C157. For All Who Give You a Face (Matt)
Reading: B617, C473, or F308 (Matt)
Blessing: C401. Communion Affirmation (Matt, New Year)

Isaiah 60:1-6

1Arise, shine; for your light has come, and the glory of the LORD has risen upon you. 2For darkness shall cover the earth, and thick darkness the peoples; but the LORD will arise upon you, and his glory will appear over you. 3Nations shall come to your light, and kings to the brightness of your dawn. 4Lift up your eyes and look around; they all gather together, they come to you; your sons shall come from far away, and your daughters shall be carried on their nurses' arms. 5Then you shall see and be radiant; your heart shall thrill and rejoice, because the abundance of the sea shall be brought to you, the wealth of the nations shall come to you. 6A multitude of camels shall cover you, the young camels of Midian and Ephah; all those from Sheba shall come. They shall bring gold and frankincense, and shall proclaim the praise of the LORD.

Psalm 72:1-7, 10-14

1Give the king your justice, O God, and your righteousness to a king's son. 2May he judge your people with righteousness, and your poor with justice. 3May the mountains yield prosperity for the people, and the hills, in righteousness. 4May he defend the cause of the poor of the people, give deliverance to the needy, and crush the oppressor. 5May he live while the sun endures, and as long as the moon, throughout all generations. 6May he be like rain that falls on the mown grass, like showers that water the earth. 7In his days may righteousness flourish and peace abound, until the moon is no more.

10May the kings of Tarshish and of the isles render him tribute, may the kings of Sheba and Seba bring gifts. 11May all kings fall down before him, all nations give him service. 12For he delivers the needy when they call, the poor and those who have no helper. 13He has pity on the weak and the needy, and saves the lives of the needy. 14From oppression and violence he redeems their life; and precious is their blood in his sight.

Ephesians 3:1-12

1This is the reason that I Paul am a prisoner for Christ Jesus for the sake of you Gentiles— 2for surely you have already heard of the commission of God's grace that was given me for you, 3and how the mystery was made known to me by revelation, as I wrote above in a few words, 4a reading of which will enable you to perceive my understanding of the mystery of Christ. 5In former generations this mystery was not made known to humankind, as it has now been revealed to his holy apostles and prophets by the Spirit: 6that is, the Gentiles have become fellow heirs, members of the same body, and sharers in the promise in Christ Jesus through the gospel.

7Of this gospel I have become a servant according to the gift of God's grace that was given me by the working of his power. 8Although I am the very least of all the saints, this grace was given to me to bring to the Gentiles the news of the boundless riches of Christ, 9and to make everyone see what is the plan of the mystery hidden for ages in God who created all things; 10so that through the church the wisdom of God in its rich variety might now be made known to the rulers and authorities in the heavenly places. 11This was in accordance with the eternal purpose that he has carried out in Christ Jesus our Lord, 12in whom we have access to God in boldness and confidence through faith in him.

Matthew 2:1-12

1In the time of King Herod, after Jesus was born in Bethlehem of Judea, wise men from the East came to Jerusalem, 2asking, "Where is the child who has been born king of the Jews? For we observed his star at its rising, and have come to pay him homage." 3When King Herod heard this, he was frightened, and all Jerusalem with him; 4and calling together all the chief priests and scribes of the people, he inquired of them where the Messiah was to be born. 5They told him, "In Bethlehem of Judea; for so it has been written by the prophet: 6'And you, Bethlehem, in the land of Judah, are by no means least among the rulers of Judah; for from you shall come a ruler who is to shepherd my people Israel.' "

7Then Herod secretly called for the wise men and learned from them the exact time when the star had appeared. 8Then he sent them to Bethlehem, saying, "Go and search diligently for the child; and when you have found him, bring me word so that I may also go and pay him homage." 9When they had heard the king, they set out; and there, ahead of them, went the star that they had seen at its rising, until it stopped over the place where the child was. 10When they saw that the star had stopped, they were overwhelmed with joy. 11On entering the house, they saw the child with Mary his mother; and they knelt down and paid him homage. Then, opening their treasure chests, they offered him gifts of gold, frankincense, and myrrh. 12And having been warned in a dream not to return to Herod, they left for their own country by another road.

Notes

Primary Hymns and Songs for the Day

"Angels from the Realms of Glory" (Matt) (O)
B94, C149, E93, F190, L50, P22, UM220 (PD), VU36, W377
H-3 Chr-30, 48, 62; Desc-89; Org-121
S-1 #280. Descant and harmonization

"What Child Is This" (Matt)
B118, C162, E115, F180, L40, N148, P53, UM219 (PD), VU74, W411
H-3 Hbl-102; Chr-210; Desc-46; Org-47
S-1 #150. Guitar chords

"We Three Kings" (Matt)
B113, C172, E128, F206, P66, UM254 (PD), W406
H-3 Chr-208; Org-65
S-2 #97-98. Various treatments

"The First Noel" (Matt) (C)
B85, C151, E109, F179, L56, N139, P56, UM245 (PD), VU90 (Fr.) and VU91, W408
H-3 Hbl-95; Chr-182; Desc-100; Org-161
S-1 #328-330. Various treatments

Additional Hymn Suggestions

"Gather Us In" (Isa, Epiphany)
C284, S2236, SF2236, W665

"O Splendor of God's Glory Bright" (Isa)
E5, N87, P474, UM679, VU413

"Jesus Shall Reign" (Pss)
B587, C95, E544, F238, L530, N157, P423, R296, UM157 (PD), VU330, W492 Ps 72

"Hail to the Lord's Anointed" (Pss)
C140, E616 (PD), L87, N104, P205, UM203 (PD), VU30

"Here Am I" (Pss)
C654, S2178, SF2178

"Make Me a Captive Lord" (Eph)
B278, P378, UM421 (PD)

"Christ for the World We Sing" (Eph)
E537, F686, R299, UM568 (PD)

"O Zion, Haste" (Eph)
B583, C482, E539, F658, L397, UM573 (PD)

"Lo, How a Rose E'er Blooming" (Matt)
B78, C160, E81, F174, L58, N127, P48 (PD), UM216, VU8, W374

"De Tierra Lejana Venimos" ("From a Distant Home") (Matt)
P64, UM243, VU89

"O Morning Star, How Fair and Bright" (Matt)
C105, E497, L76, N158, P69, UM247, VU98, W390

"On This Day Earth Shall Ring" (Matt)
E92, P46, UM248 (PD)

"There's a Song in the Air" (Matt)
C159, UM249 (PD)

"Now the Silence" (Matt, Communion)
C415, E333, L205, R221, UM619, VU475, W668

"Rise Up, Shepherd, and Follow" (Matt)
P50, S2096, SF2096, VU70

Additional Contemporary Suggestions

"Shine, Jesus, Shine" (Epiphany)
B579, R247, S2173, SF2173, SP142

"Shine on Us" (Isa, Epiphany)
M19

"Let it Rise" (Isa)
M4

"Here I Am to Worship" (Isa, Epiphany)
M116

"Famous One" (Isa, Matt, Epiphany)
M126

"Arise, Shine" (Isa)
R123, SP176

"Grace Alone" (Eph)
M100, S2162, SF2162

"The Virgin Mary Had a Baby Boy" (Matt)
S2098, VU73

"We Worship and Adore You" (Matt)
SP103

"Famous One" (Matt)
M126

"O Praise Him" ("All This for a King") (Matt)
M133

"Alleluia" (Matt, Communion)
B223, C106, F361, N765, R136, SP108, UM186

Vocal Solos

"The People That Walked in Darkness" (Isa)
V-2

"The Kings" (Matt, Epiphany)
V-9 p. 13

"Fit for a King" (Matt)
V-10 p. 32

Anthems

"Desert Rose" (Matt)
Drew Collins; Curtis Music Press C9306
SATB divisi a cappella

What Child is This" (Matt)
Arr. Jameson Marvin; Curtis Music Press C9304
TTBB a cappella

Other Suggestions

Visuals:
- **O** Light/dark, nations, kings, dawn, babes in arms, gold/incense
- **P** Scales, mountains/hills, poor, sun/moon, rain, grass, king
- **E** Writing, Christ, all nations
- **G** Wise men, star, Bethlehem, infant, Mary, gifts, escape

Opening Prayer: N826 (Isa, Epiphany)
Prayer of Confession: N838 (Pss)
Prayer: UM255 or C19 (Epiphany)
Prayer: N858. Providence of God (Eph)

Isaiah 43:1-7

1But now thus says the LORD, he who created you, O Jacob, he who formed you, O Israel: Do not fear, for I have redeemed you; I have called you by name, you are mine. 2When you pass through the waters, I will be with you; and through the rivers, they shall not overwhelm you; when you walk through fire you shall not be burned, and the flame shall not consume you. 3For I am the LORD your God, the Holy One of Israel, your Savior. I give Egypt as your ransom, Ethiopia and Seba in exchange for you. 4Because you are precious in my sight, and honored, and I love you, I give people in return for you, nations in exchange for your life. 5Do not fear, for I am with you; I will bring your offspring from the east, and from the west I will gather you; 6I will say to the north, "Give them up," and to the south, "Do not withhold; bring my sons from far away and my daughters from the end of the earth— 7everyone who is called by my name, whom I created for my glory, whom I formed and made."

Psalm 29

1Ascribe to the LORD, O heavenly beings, ascribe to the LORD glory and strength. 2Ascribe to the LORD the glory of his name; worship the LORD in holy splendor. 3The voice of the LORD is over the waters; the God of glory thunders, the Lord, over mighty waters. 4The voice of the LORD is powerful; the voice of the LORD is full of majesty. 5The voice of the LORD breaks the cedars; the LORD breaks the cedars of Lebanon. 6He makes Lebanon skip like a calf, and Sirion like a young wild ox. 7The voice of the LORD flashes forth flames of fire. 8The voice of the LORD shakes the wilderness; the LORD shakes the wilderness of Kadesh. 9The voice of the LORD causes the oaks to whirl, and strips the forest bare; and in his temple all say, "Glory!" 10The LORD sits enthroned over the flood; the LORD sits enthroned as king forever. 11May the LORD give strength to his people! May the LORD bless his people with peace!

Acts 8:14-17

14Now when the apostles at Jerusalem heard that Samaria had accepted the word of God, they sent Peter and John to them. 15The two went down and prayed for them that they might receive the Holy Spirit 16(for as yet the Spirit had not come upon any of them; they had only been baptized in the name of the Lord Jesus). 17Then Peter and John laid their hands on them, and they received the Holy Spirit.

Luke 3:15-17, 21-22

15As the people were filled with expectation, and all were questioning in their hearts concerning John, whether he might be the Messiah, 16John answered all of them by saying, "I baptize you with water; but one who is more powerful than I is coming; I am not worthy to untie the thong of his sandals. He will baptize you with the Holy Spirit and fire. 17His winnowing fork is in his hand, to clear his threshing floor and to gather the wheat into his granary; but the chaff he will burn with unquenchable fire."

21Now when all the people were baptized, and when Jesus also had been baptized and was praying, the heaven was opened, 22and the Holy Spirit descended upon him in bodily form like a dove. And a voice came from heaven, "You are my Son, the Beloved; with you I am well pleased."

Notes

Primary Hymns and Songs for the Day

"Praise to the Lord, the Almighty" (Pss) (O)
B14 (PD), C25, E390, F337, L543, N22, P482, R57, UM139, VU220 (Fr.) and VU221, W547
H-3 Hbl-89; Chr-163; Desc-69; Org-79
S-1 #218-222. Various treatments
"When Jesus Came to Jordan" (Luke)
UM252
"Spirit Song" (Luke)
C352, R248, SP134, UM347
"Stand By Me" (Isa)
C629, UM512
H-3 Chr-177
"How Firm a Foundation" (Isa) (C)
B338, C618, E636, F32, L507, N407, P361, UM529 (PD), VU660, W585
H-3 Hbl-27, 69; Chr-102; Desc-41; Org-41
S-1 #133. Harmonization
#134. Performance note

Additional Hymn Suggestions

"I Was There to Hear Your Borning Cry" (Isa, Luke)
C75, N351, S2051, SF2051, VU644
"The Lily of the Valley" (Isa, Luke)
B189, S2062, SF2062
"O Worship the King" (Pss)
B16, C17, E388, F336, L548 (PD), N26, P476, UM73, VU235
"God of the Sparrow, God of the Whale" (Pss)
C70, N32, P272, UM122, VU229
"We Meet You, O Christ" (Acts, Luke)
C183, P311, UM257, VU183
"Breathe on Me, Breath of God" (Acts, Luke, Baptism)
B241, C254, E508, F161, L488, N292, P316, UM420 (PD), VU382 (Fr.), W725
"Wonder of Wonders" (Acts, Luke, Baptism)
C378, N328, P499, S2247
"Baptized in Water" (Acts, Luke, Baptism)
B362, E294, P492, S2248, W720
"We Were Baptized in Christ Jesus" (Acts, Luke, Baptism)
S2251, SF2251
"At the Name of Jesus" (Luke)
B198, E435, F351, L179, P148, R133 and R279, UM168, VU335, W499
"Praise and Thanksgiving Be to God" (Luke, Baptism)
L191, UM604, VU441
"Wash, O God, Our Sons and Daughters" (Luke, Baptism)
C365, UM605, VU442
'This Is the Spirit's Entry Now" (Luke, Baptism)
L195, UM608. VU451, W722
"We Know That Christ Is Raised" (Luke, Baptism)
E296, L189, P495, UM610, VU448, W721
"Child of Blessing, Child of Promise" (Luke, Baptism)
N325, UM611, VU444, P498
"Wild and Lone the Prophet's Voice" (Luke)
P409, S2089, SF2089
"Loving Spirit" (Luke)
C244, P323, S2123, SF2123, VU387

Additional Contemporary Suggestions

"Lord God Almighty" (Isa)
R40, S2006, SF2006
"Wade in the Water" (Acts, Luke, Baptism)
C371, S2107, SF2107
"I've Just Come from the Fountain" (Acts, Luke)
S2250, SF2250
"Water, River, Spirit, Grace" (Luke, Baptism)
C66, S2253, SF2253
"Jesus, Name Above All Names" (Luke)
R26, SP76, S2071, SF2071
"I Know the Lord's Laid His Hands on Me" (Luke)
S2139, SF2139
"I Will Never Be" (the Same Again) (Luke)
M34
"Famous One" (Luke)
M126
"Great and Mighty Is He" (Luke)
M11, SP4

Vocal Solos

"Spirit of Faith Come Down" (Luke)
V-1 p. 43
"Consume Me" (Luke)
V-3 p. 148
"This is De Healin' Water" (Acts, Luke)
V-7 p. 52

Anthems

"Stand By Me" (Isa)
arr. Larry Shackley; Hope C-5343
SATB with piano and opt. rhythm

"At the Name of Jesus" (Luke)
Stan Pethel; Abingdon Press 9780687648702
SATB with keyboard

Other Suggestions

Visuals:
O Clay, water (baptism), fire
P Nature images as described
E Water, symbols of the Holy Spirit
G Water, Holy Spirit, praying hands, dove, flames
Introit: S2118, SF2118, W473. "Holy Spirit, Come to Us" (Luke)
Opening Prayer: N831 (Isa)
Prayer: UM253. Baptism of the Lord (Baptism, Luke)
Prayer: C364. Blessing of Children (Baptism)
Reading: C369. Welcome after Baptism (Baptism)
For additional ideas, see *The Abingdon Worship Annual 2010.*

Isaiah 62:1-5

1For Zion's sake I will not keep silent, and for Jerusalem's sake I will not rest, until her vindication shines out like the dawn, and her salvation like a burning torch. 2The nations shall see your vindication, and all the kings your glory; and you shall be called by a new name that the mouth of the LORD will give. 3You shall be a crown of beauty in the hand of the LORD, and a royal diadem in the hand of your God. 4You shall no more be termed Forsaken, and your land shall no more be termed Desolate; but you shall be called My Delight Is in Her, and your land Married; for the LORD delights in you, and your land shall be married. 5For as a young man marries a young woman, so shall your builder marry you, and as the bridegroom rejoices over the bride, so shall your God rejoice over you.

Psalm 36:5-10

5Your steadfast love, O LORD, extends to the heavens, your faithfulness to the clouds. 6Your righteousness is like the mighty mountains, your judgments are like the great deep; you save humans and animals alike, O LORD. 7How precious is your steadfast love, O God! All people may take refuge in the shadow of your wings. 8They feast on the abundance of your house, and you give them drink from the river of your delights. 9For with you is the fountain of life; in your light we see light. 10O continue your steadfast love to those who know you, and your salvation to the upright of heart!

1 Corinthians 12:1-11

1Now concerning spiritual gifts, brothers and sisters, I do not want you to be uninformed. 2You know that when you were pagans, you were enticed and led astray to idols that could not speak. 3Therefore I want you to understand that no one speaking by the Spirit of God ever says "Let Jesus be cursed!" and no one can say "Jesus is Lord" except by the Holy Spirit.

4Now there are varieties of gifts, but the same Spirit; 5and there are varieties of services, but the same Lord; 6and there are varieties of activities, but it is the same God who activates all of them in everyone. 7To each is given the manifestation of the Spirit for the common good. 8To one is given through the Spirit the utterance of wisdom, and to another the utterance of knowledge according to the same Spirit, 9to another faith by the same Spirit, to another gifts of healing by the one Spirit, 10to another the working of miracles, to another prophecy, to another the discernment of spirits, to another various kinds of tongues, to another the interpretation of tongues. 11All these are activated by one and the same Spirit, who allots to each one individually just as the Spirit chooses.

John 2:1-11

1On the third day there was a wedding in Cana of Galilee, and the mother of Jesus was there. 2Jesus and his disciples had also been invited to the wedding. 3When the wine gave out, the mother of Jesus said to him, "They have no wine." 4And Jesus said to her, "Woman, what concern is that to you and to me? My hour has not yet come." 5His mother said to the servants, "Do whatever he tells you." 6Now standing there were six stone water jars for the Jewish rites of purification, each holding twenty or thirty gallons. 7Jesus said to them, "Fill the jars with water." And they filled them up to the brim. 8He said to them, "Now draw some out, and take it to the chief steward." So they took it. 9When the steward tasted the water that had become wine, and did not know where it came from (though the servants who had drawn the water knew), the steward called the bridegroom 10and said to him, "Everyone serves the good wine first, and then the inferior wine after the guests have become drunk. But you have kept the good wine until now." 11Jesus did this, the first of his signs, in Cana of Galilee, and revealed his glory; and his disciples believed in him.

Notes

Primary Hymns and Songs for the Day
"Many Gifts, One Spirit" (1 Cor) (O)
N177, UM114
"We Are the Body of Christ" (1 Cor)
S2227, SF2227
"One Bread, One Body" (1 Cor, Comm.)
C393, UM620, VU467
"Forward Through the Ages" (1 Cor) (C)
N355, UM555 (PD)
H-3 Hbl-59; Chr-156; Org-140

Additional Hymn Suggestions
"Lift Every Voice and Sing" (Isa)
B627, C631, E599, L562, N593, P563, UM519, W641
"Are Ye Able" (Isa, Human Relations)
C621, UM530 (PD)
"We've a Story to Tell to the Nations" (Isa)
B586, C484, F659, UM569 (PD)
"I Know Whom I Have Believed" (Isa)
B337, F631, UM714 (PD)
"The Battle Hymn of the Republic" (Isa)
B633, C705, F692, L332, N610, UM717 (PD), W686
"My Lord, What a Morning" (Isa, MLK Day)
C708, P449, UM719, VU708
"God of Many Names" (Isa, Pss)
C13, UM105
"How Like a Gentle Spirit" (Pss)
C69, N443, UM115
"The Lily of the Valley" (Isa, Pss)
B189, S2062, SF2062
"O God in Heaven" (Pss)
N279, UM119
"O Love, How Deep" (Pss)
E449, L88, N209, P83, UM267 (PD), VU348
"Love Divine, All Loves Excelling" (Pss)
B208, C517, F21, N43, UM384 (PD)
E657, L315, P376, R196, VU333, W588 (PD)
"Come, Thou Fount of Every Blessing" (Pss)
B15, C16, E686, F318, L499, N459, P356, UM400 (PD), VU559
"We Sing to You, O God" (Pss)
N9, S2001, SF2001
"Awake, O Sleeper" (1 Cor)
E547, UM551, VU566, W586
"Help Us Accept Each Other" (1 Cor, MLK Day)
C487, N388, P358, UM560, W656
"As a Fire Is Meant for Burning" (1 Cor)
S2237, SF2237, VU578
"We All Are One in Mission" (1 Cor, MLK Day)
P435, S2243, SF2243
"Within the Day-to-Day" (1 Cor)
S2245, SF2245
"We Meet You, O Christ" (John, MLK Day)
C183, P311, UM257, VU183
"Blessed Jesus, at Thy Word" (John)
E440, N74, P454, R93, UM596 (PD), VU500
"Jesus, Joy of Our Desiring" (John)
UM644 (PD), VU328
"Lord, We Come to Ask Your Blessing" (John)
S2230, SF2230

Additional Contemporary Suggestions
"I Could Sing of Your Love Forever" (Pss)
M63; V-3 p. 22 Vocal Solo
"The Steadfast Love of the Lord" (Pss)
R23, SP185
"Shine, Jesus, Shine" (Pss)
B579, R247, S2173, SF2173, SP142
"On Eagle's Wings" (Pss)
B71, C77, N775, R112, UM143, VU807 and VU808
"There Is Joy in the Lord" (Pss)
M74
"Eagle's Wings" (Pss)
M158
"Holy Spirit, Come to Us" (1 Cor)
S2118, SF2118, W473
"We Are One in Christ Jesus" (1 Cor)
C493, S2229, SF2229

Vocal Solos
"Spirit of Faith Come Down" (1 Cor)
V-1 p. 43
"He Turned the Water into Wine" (John)
V-8 p. 76

Anthems
"And the Father Will Dance" (Isa)
Mark Hayes; Hinshaw HMC637
SATB with piano

"Many Gifts, One Spirit" (1 Cor)
Allen Pote; Theodore Presser 392-41388
SATB with keyboard (SSA, SAB, and SB available)

Other Suggestions
Visuals:
O Crown, bride and groom, invitation, torch, sunrise
P Sky, clouds, mountains, wings, banquet, fountain
E "Many gifts, one spirit", ministries, unity
G Large clay water jars, water/wine/bread, wedding
You may wish to include some reference to Martin Luther King, Jr. (MLK) Day, Jan. 15.
Introit: E487, L513, N331, UM164 (PD), VU628, W569. "Come, My Way, My Truth, My Life" (John)
Opening Prayer: N826 (Pss, Epiphany)
Litany: C451. Litany of Ministry (1 Cor)
Prayer: N851 or N861 (1 Cor)
Litany: C488. A Litany of the Saints (MLK Day)
Litany: UM556. Litany for Christian Unity (1 Cor)

JANUARY 24, 2010

Nehemiah 8:1-3, 5-6, 8-10

[1]All the people gathered together into the square before the Water Gate. They told the scribe Ezra to bring the book of the law of Moses, which the LORD had given to Israel. [2]Accordingly, the priest Ezra brought the law before the assembly, both men and women and all who could hear with understanding. This was on the first day of the seventh month. [3]He read from it facing the square before the Water Gate from early morning until midday, in the presence of the men and the women and those who could understand; and the ears of all the people were attentive to the book of the law.

[5]And Ezra opened the book in the sight of all the people, for he was standing above all the people; and when he opened it, all the people stood up. [6]Then Ezra blessed the LORD, the great God, and all the people answered, "Amen, Amen," lifting up their hands. Then they bowed their heads and worshiped the LORD with their faces to the ground.

[8]So they read from the book, from the law of God, with interpretation. They gave the sense, so that the people understood the reading.

[9]And Nehemiah, who was the governor, and Ezra the priest and scribe, and the Levites who taught the people said to all the people, "This day is holy to the LORD your God; do not mourn or weep." For all the people wept when they heard the words of the law. [10]Then he said to them, "Go your way, eat the fat and drink sweet wine and send portions of them to those for whom nothing is prepared, for this day is holy to our LORD; and do not be grieved, for the joy of the LORD is your strength."

Psalm 19

[1]The heavens are telling the glory of God; and the firmament proclaims his handiwork. [2]Day to day pours forth speech, and night to night declares knowledge. [3]There is no speech, nor are there words; their voice is not heard; [4]yet their voice goes out through all the earth, and their words to the end of the world. In the heavens he has set a tent for the sun, [5]which comes out like a bridegroom from his wedding canopy, and like a strong man runs its course with joy. [6]Its rising is from the end of the heavens, and its circuit to the end of them; and nothing is hid from its heat. [7]The law of the LORD is perfect, reviving the soul; the decrees of the LORD are sure, making wise the simple; [8]the precepts of the LORD are right, rejoicing the heart; the commandment of the LORD is clear, enlightening the eyes; [9]the fear of the LORD is pure, enduring forever; the ordinances of the LORD are true and righteous altogether. [10]More to be desired are they than gold, even much fine gold; sweeter also than honey, and drippings of the honeycomb. [11]Moreover by them is your servant warned; in keeping them there is great reward. [12]But who can detect their errors? Clear me from hidden faults. [13]Keep back your servant also from the insolent; do not let them have dominion over me. Then I shall be blameless, and innocent of great transgression. [14]Let the words of my mouth and the meditation of my heart be acceptable to you, O LORD, my rock and my redeemer.

1 Corinthians 12:12-31*a*

[12]For just as the body is one and has many members, and all the members of the body, though many, are one body, so it is with Christ. [13]For in the one Spirit we were all baptized into one body—Jews or Greeks, slaves or free—and we were all made to drink of one Spirit.

[14]Indeed, the body does not consist of one member but of many. [15]If the foot would say, "Because I am not a hand, I do not belong to the body," that would not make it any less a part of the body. [16]And if the ear would say, "Because I am not an eye, I do not belong to the body," that would not make it any less a part of the body. [17]If the whole body were an eye, where would the hearing be? If the whole body were hearing, where would the sense of smell be? [18]But as it is, God arranged the members in the body, each one of them, as he chose. [19]If all were a single member, where would the body be? [20]As it is, there are many members, yet one body. [21] The eye cannot say to the hand, "I have no need of you," nor again the head to the feet, "I have no need of you." [22]On the contrary, the members of the body that seem to be weaker are indispensable, [23]and those members of the body that we think less honorable we clothe with greater honor, and our less respectable members are treated with greater respect; [24]whereas our more respectable members do not need this. But God has so arranged the body, giving the greater honor to the inferior member, [25]that there may be no dissension within the body, but the members may have the same care for one another. [26]If one member suffers, all suffer together with it; if one member is honored, all rejoice together with it.

[27]Now you are the body of Christ and individually members of it. [28]And God has appointed in the church first apostles, second prophets, third teachers; then deeds of power, then gifts of healing, forms of assistance, forms of leadership, various kinds of tongues. [29]Are all apostles? Are all prophets? Are all teachers? Do all work miracles? [30]Do all possess gifts of healing? Do all speak in tongues? Do all interpret? [31]But strive for the greater gifts.

Luke 4:14-21

[14]Then Jesus, filled with the power of the Spirit, returned to Galilee, and a report about him spread through all the surrounding country. [15]He began to teach in their synagogues and was praised by everyone.

[16]When he came to Nazareth, where he had been brought up, he went to the synagogue on the sabbath day, as was his custom. He stood up to read, [17]and the scroll of the prophet Isaiah was given to him. He unrolled the scroll and found the place where it was written: [18]"The Spirit of the Lord is upon me, because he has anointed me to bring good news to the poor. He has sent me to proclaim release to the captives and recovery of sight to the blind, to let the oppressed go free, [19]to proclaim the year of the Lord's favor." [20]And he rolled up the scroll, gave it back to the attendant, and sat down. The eyes of all in the synagogue were fixed on him. [21]Then he began to say to them, "Today this scripture has been fulfilled in your hearing."

Primary Hymns and Songs for the Day
"Stand Up and Bless the Lord" (Neh) (O)
B30, UM662 (PD)
H-3 Hbl-79; Chr-141; Desc-95; Org-143
S-1 #306-308. Various treatments
P491
"How Great Thou Art" (Pss)
B10, C33, F2, L532, N35, P467, R250, UM77, VU238 (Fr.)
H-3 Chr-103; Org-105
S-1 #163. Harmonization
"One Bread, One Body" (1 Cor, Communion)
C393, UM620, VU467
H-3 Chr-156
"They'll Know We Are Christians" (1 Cor)
C494, S2223, SF2223
"Gather Us In" (1 Cor, Luke)
C284, S2236, SF2236, W665
"O for a Thousand Tongues to Sing" (Luke) (C)
B216, C5, E493, F349, L559, N42, P466, R32, UM57 (PD), VU326
H-3 Hbl-79; Chr-142; Desc-17; Org-12
S-1 #33-38. Various Treatments

Additional Hymn Suggestions
"Wonderful Words of Life" (Neh)
B261, C323, F29, N319, UM600 (PD)
"God Is Here" (Neh)
C280, N70, P461, UM660, VU389, W667
"All Who Hunger" (Neh)
C419, S2126, SF2126, VU460
"God Who Stretched the Spangled Heavens" (Pss)
B47, C651, E580, L463, N556, P268, UM150, W648
"In Christ There Is No East or West" (1 Cor)
B385, C687, F685, N394, P439
E529, L359, N394, P440, UM548, VU606, W659
"We Are God's People" (1 Cor)
B383, F546, S2220, SF2220
"Who Is My Mother, Who Is My Brother"
C486, S2225, SF2225
"As a Fire Is Meant for Burning" (1 Cor)
S2237, SF2237, VU578
"One God and Father of Us All" (1 Cor)
S2240, SF2240
"We All Are One in Mission" (1 Cor)
P435, S2243, SF2243
"When Jesus the Healer Passed Through Galilee" (Luke)
UM263, VU358
"Come, Ye Sinners, Poor and Needy" (Luke)
B323 (PD), R141, UM340, W756
"Christ for the World We Sing" (Luke)
E537, F686, R299, UM568 (PD)
"Lord, Whose Love Through Humble Service" (Luke)
C461, L423, UM581, R286
"The Spirit Sends Us Forth to Serve" (Luke) (C)
S2241, SF2241

Additional Contemporary Suggestions
"Let My Words Be Few" (Neh)
M105
"All Heaven Declares" (Pss)
M58, R163
"God of Wonders" (Pss)
M80; V-3 p. 184 Vocal Solo
"The Heavens Shall Declare" (Pss)
M111
"I Will Call Upon the Lord" (Pss)
R15, S2002, SF2002, SP224
"Make Us One" (1 Cor)
S2224, SF2224, SP137
"We Are One in Christ Jesus" (1 Cor)
C493, S2229, SF2229
"Let Us Be Bread" (1 Cor, Communion)
S2260, SF2260
"Holy Spirit, Come to Us" (Luke)
S2118, SF2118, W473
"Days of Elijah" (Luke)
M139
"Let the River Flow" (Luke)
M142

Vocal Solos
"The Body of the Lord" (1 Cor, Communion)
V-8 p. 344
"O For a Thousand Tongues to Sing" (Luke)
V-1 p. 32
V-6 p. 28

Anthems
"Sing Praise to the Mighty God" (Pss)
Bach, arr. Hopson; Choristers Guild CGA-942
Unison with keyboard

"The Spirit of the Lord Is Upon Me" (Luke)
Edward Elgar; Novello 29-0219
SATB with organ

Other Suggestions
Visuals:
O Open Bible, scroll, morning, assembly, weeping/joy
P Gold, honey comb, runner, groom
E Teamwork, body, health, harmony, gifts
G Images of poor/captives/blind/freedom, Jubilee
Greeting: N824 (Pss)
Prayer of Confession: N838 (Luke)
Prayer: F561 or N860 (1 Cor)
Prayer: C52. Fire of the Spirit (Luke)
Reading: B259, C325 or C57 (Neh, Pss)
Response: C327. "Write These Words" (Neh, Pss)
Litany: C451. Litany of Ministry (1 Cor)
Prayers: F549, N855 (1 Cor)

Jeremiah 1:4-10

[4]Now the word of the LORD came to me saying, [5]"Before
I formed you in the womb I knew you, and before you
were born I consecrated you; I appointed you a prophet
to the nations." [6]Then I said, "Ah, Lord GOD! Truly I do
not know how to speak, for I am only a boy." [7]But the
LORD said to me, "Do not say, 'I am only a boy'; for you
shall go to all to whom I send you, and you shall speak
whatever I command you, [8]Do not be afraid of them, for
I am with you to deliver you, says the LORD." [9]Then the
LORD put out his hand and touched my mouth; and the
LORD said to me, "Now I have put my words in your
mouth. [10]See, today I appoint you over nations and over
kingdoms, to pluck up and to pull down, to destroy and to
overthrow, to build and to plant."

Psalm 71:1-6

[1]In you, O LORD, I take refuge; let me never be put to
shame. [2]In your righteousness deliver me and rescue me;
incline your ear to me and save me. [3]Be to me a rock of
refuge, a strong fortress, to save me, for you are my rock
and my fortress. [4]Rescue me, O my God, from the hand of
the wicked, from the grasp of the unjust and cruel. [5]For
you, O Lord, are my hope, my trust, O LORD, from my
youth. [6]Upon you I have leaned from my birth; it was you
who took me from my mother's womb. My praise is continually of you.

1 Corinthians 13:1-13

[1]If I speak in the tongues of mortals and of angels, but
do not have love, I am a noisy gong or a clanging cymbal.
[2]And if I have prophetic powers, and understand all mys-
teries and all knowledge, and if I have all faith, so as to
remove mountains, but do not have love, I am nothing.
[3]If I give away all my possessions, and if I hand over
my body so that I may boast, but do not have love, I
gain nothing.

[4]Love is patient; love is kind; love is not envious or
boastful or arrogant [5]or rude. It does not insist on its own
way; it is not irritable or resentful; [6]it does not rejoice in
wrongdoing, but rejoices in the truth. [7]It bears all things,
believes all things, hopes all things, endures all things.

[8]Love never ends. But as for prophecies, they will come
to an end; as for tongues, they will cease; as for knowledge, it will come to an end. [9]For we know only in part,
and we prophesy only in part; [10]but when the complete
comes, the partial will come to an end. [11]When I was a
child, I spoke like a child, I thought like a child, I rea-
soned like a child; when I became an adult, I put an end
to childish ways. [12]For now we see in a mirror, dimly, but
then we will see face to face. Now I know only in part;
then I will know fully, even as I have been fully known.
[13]And now faith, hope, and love abide, these three; and
the greatest of these is love.

Luke 4:21-30

[21]Then he began to say to them, "Today this scripture
has been fulfilled in your hearing." [22]All spoke well of him
and were amazed at the gracious words that came from
his mouth. They said, "Is not this Joseph's son?" [23]He said
to them, "Doubtless you will quote to me this proverb,
'Doctor, cure yourself!' And you will say, 'Do here also in
your hometown the things that we have heard you did at
Capernaum.' " [24]And he said, "Truly I tell you, no prophet
is accepted in the prophet's hometown. [25]But the truth is,
there were many widows in Israel in the time of Elijah,
when the heaven was shut up three years and six months,
and there was a severe famine over all the land; [26]yet
Elijah was sent to none of them except to a widow at
Zarephath in Sidon. [27]There were also many lepers in
Israel in the time of the prophet Elisha, and none of them
was cleansed except Naaman the Syrian." [28]When they
heard this, all in the synagogue were filled with rage.
[29]They got up, drove him out of the town, and led him to
the brow of the hill on which their town was built, so that
they might hurl him off the cliff. [30]But he passed through
the midst of them and went on his way.

Notes

Primary Hymns and Songs for the Day

"A Mighty Fortress Is Our God" (Pss, 1 Cor) (O)
B8, C65, E687 or E688, F118, L228 or L229, N439 or N440, P259 or P260, UM110 (PD), VU261 (Fr.) or VU262 or VU263, W575 or W576
"God of Love and God of Power" (Jer, Luke) (O)
UM578 (PD)
"My Life Is in You, Lord" (Pss)
S2032, SF2032, SP204
"The Gift of Love" (1 Cor)
B423, C526, P335, R155, UM408, VU372
H-3 Chr-200; Org-45
"O Young and Fearless Prophet" (Luke)
UM444 (PD)
S-2 #27. Descant
C669
"Here I Am, Lord" (Jer, Luke) (C)
C452, P525, R149, UM593, VU509
H-3 Chr-97; Org-54

Additional Hymn Suggestions

"Womb of Life" (Jer)
C14, N274, S2046, SF2046
"Mothering God, You Gave Me Birth" (Jer, 1 Cor)
C83, N467, S2050, SF2050, VU320
"I Was There to Hear Your Borning Cry" (Jer, Baptism)
C75, N351, S2051, SF2051, VU644
"Morning Glory, Starlit Sky" (Jer, 1 Cor)
E585, UM194, W587
"Of All the Spirit's Gifts to Me" (Jer, 1 Cor)
B442, C270, UM336
"This Little Light of Mine" (Jer, Luke)
N525, UM585
"We'll Understand It Better By and By" (Pss, 1 Cor)
N444, UM525 (PD)
"Where Charity and Love Prevail" (1 Cor)
E581, L126, N396, UM549
"Draw Us in the Spirit's Tether" (1 Cor, Comm.)
C392, N337, P504, UM632, VU479, W731
"When Love Is Found" (1 Cor, Communion)
C499, N362, UM643, VU489, W745
"O Perfect Love" (1 Cor, Communion)
B512, F530, L287, P533, UM645, VU491
"Your Love, O God, Has Called Us Here" (1 Cor)
B509, E353, N361, UM647
"Healer of Our Every Ill" (1 Cor)
C506, S2213, SF2213, VU619
"Sacred the Body" (1 Cor)
S2228
"Let Us Be Bread" (1 Cor, Communion)
S2260, SF2260
"Spirit, Spirit of Gentleness" (Luke)
C249, N286, P319, S2120, VU375 (Fr.)
"We Are Called" (Luke)
S2172, SF2172
"Gather Us In" (Luke)
C284, S2236, SF2236, W665 .

Additional Contemporary Suggestions

"I Know the Lord's Laid His Hands on Me" (Jer)
S2139, SF2139
"Ah, Lord God" (Jer)
R254, SP2
"I Will Call Upon the Lord" (Pss)
R15, S2002, SF2002, SP224
"Praise the Name of Jesus" (Pss)
R7, S2066, SF2066, SP87
"Rock of Ages" (Pss)
M93
"Live in Charity" ("Ubi Caritas") (1 Cor)
C523, R226, S2179, SF2179, W604
"There's a Song" (1 Cor)
S2141, SF2141
"He Came Down" (1 Cor)
S2085, SF2085

Vocal Solos

"Jesus, Lover of My Soul" (Pss)
V-1 p. 37
"Prayer" (Pss)
V-9 p. 32
"The Gift of Love" (1 Cor)
V-8 p. 120
"Of Love I Sing" (1 Cor)
V-8 p. 106

Anthems

"Love Never Ends" (1 Cor)
Mark Burrows: Abingdon Press 9780687648207
SATB with piano

"Love Never Ends" (1 Cor)
Gradley Ellingboe; Kjos 9064
SATB, solo, and piano

Other Suggestions

Visuals:
O Pregnancy, boy, Jer 1:7b or 9b, hand/mouth, nations
P Ear, Ps 71:3 or 5a, rock, fortress, rescue, youth
E Speak, cymbals, remove mts., love, child/adult, mirror
G Bible, Jesus speaking/walking, widows, famine, leper
Greeting: N820 (1 Cor)
Opening Prayer: N827 (1 Cor)
Canticle: C525, UM646. "Canticle of Love" (1 Cor)
Reading: C525 or F683 (1 Cor)
Prayer: C178. You Were Like Me, Jesus (Luke)
Call to Communion: C412. The Miracle of Communion (Luke)

Isaiah 6:1-8 (9-13)
1In the year that King Uzziah died, I saw the Lord sitting on a throne, high and lofty; and the hem of his robe
filled the temple. 2Seraphs were in attendance above him;
each had six wings: with two they covered their faces, and
with two they covered their feet, and with two they flew.
3And one called to another and said: "Holy, holy, holy is
the LORD of hosts; the whole earth is full of his glory."
4The pivots on the thresholds shook at the voices of those
who called, and the house filled with smoke. 5And I said:
"Woe is me! I am lost, for I am a man of unclean lips, and
I live among a people of unclean lips; yet my eyes have
seen the King, the LORD of hosts!"
6Then one of the seraphs flew to me, holding a live coal
that had been taken from the altar with a pair of tongs.
7The seraph touched my mouth with it and said: "Now that
this has touched your lips, your guilt has departed and
your sin is blotted out." 8Then I heard the voice of the
Lord saying, "Whom shall I send, and who will go for us?"
And I said, "Here am I; send me!" 9And he said, "Go and
say to this people: 'Keep listening, but do not comprehend;
keep looking, but do not understand.' 10Make the mind of
this people dull, and stop their ears, and shut their eyes, so
that they may not look with their eyes, and listen with their
ears, and comprehend with their minds, and turn and be
healed." 11Then I said, "How long, O Lord?" And he said:
"Until cities lie waste without inhabitant, and houses without people, and the land is utterly desolate; 12until the
LORD sends everyone far away, and vast is the emptiness in
the midst of the land. 13Even if a tenth part remain in it, it
will be burned again, like a terebinth or an oak whose
stump remains standing when it is felled." The holy seed
is its stump.

Psalm 138
1I give you thanks, O LORD, with my whole heart; before
the gods I sing your praise; 2I bow down toward your holy
temple and give thanks to your name for your steadfast
love and your faithfulness; for you have exalted your
name and your word above everything. 3On the day I
called, you answered me, you increased my strength of
soul. 4All the kings of the earth shall praise you, O LORD,
for they have heard the words of your mouth. 5They shall
sing of the ways of the LORD, for great is the glory of the
LORD. 6For though the LORD is high, he regards the lowly;
but the haughty he perceives from far away. 7Though I
walk in the midst of trouble, you preserve me against the
wrath of my enemies; you stretch out your hand, and your
right hand delivers me. 8The LORD will fulfill his purpose
for me; your steadfast love, O LORD, endures forever. Do
not forsake the work of your hands.

1 Corinthians 15:1-11
1Now I would remind you, brothers and sisters, of the
good news that I proclaimed to you, which you in turn
received, in which also you stand, 2through which also
you are being saved, if you hold firmly to the message that
I proclaimed to you—unless you have come to believe
in vain.
3For I handed on to you as of first importance what I in
turn had received: that Christ died for our sins in accordance with the scriptures, 4and that he was buried, and that
he was raised on the third day in accordance with the scriptures, 5and that he appeared to Cephas, then to the twelve.
6Then he appeared to more than five hundred brothers
and sisters at one time, most of whom are still alive, though
some have died. 7Then he appeared to James, then to all
the apostles. 8Last of all, as to one untimely born, he
appeared also to me. 9For I am the least of the apostles,
unfit to be called an apostle, because I persecuted the
church of God. 10But by the grace of God I am what I am,
and his grace toward me has not been in vain. On the contrary, I worked harder than any of them—though it was not
I, but the grace of God that is with me. 11Whether then it
was I or they, so we proclaim and so you have come
to believe.

Luke 5:1-11
1Once while Jesus was standing beside the lake of
Gennesaret, and the crowd was pressing in on him to
hear the word of God, 2he saw two boats there at the
shore of the lake; the fishermen had gone out of them
and were washing their nets. 3He got into one of the
boats, the one belonging to Simon, and asked him to put
out a little way from the shore. Then he sat down and
taught the crowds from the boat. 4When he had finished
speaking, he said to Simon, "Put out into the deep water
and let down your nets for a catch." 5Simon answered,
"Master, we have worked all night long but have caught
nothing. Yet if you say so, I will let down the nets." 6When
they had done this, they caught so many fish that their
nets were beginning to break. 7So they signaled their partners in the other boat to come and help them. And they
came and filled both boats, so that they began to sink.
8But when Simon Peter saw it, he fell down at Jesus'
knees, saying, "Go away from me, Lord, for I am a sinful
man!" 9For he and all who were with him were amazed at
the catch of fish that they had taken; 10and so also were
James and John, sons of Zebedee, who were partners with
Simon. Then Jesus said to Simon, "Do not be afraid; from
now on you will be catching people." 11When they had
brought their boats to shore, they left everything and followed him.

Primary Hymns and Songs for the Day

"Holy, Holy, Holy! Lord God Almighty" (Isa) (O)
B2, C4, E362, F323, L165, N277, P138, R204, UM64 and UM65, VU315, W485
H-3 Hbl-68; Chr-99; Desc-80; Org-97
S-1 #245-248. Various treatments.
"Send Me, Lord" (Isa, Luke, Black History)
C447, N360, R308, UM497, VU572
S-2 #173. Percussion arrangement
"Tu Has Venido a la Orilla" ("Lord, You Have Come to the Lakeshore") (Luke)
C342, N173, P377, UM344, VU563
"The Voice of God Is Calling" (Isa, 1 Cor)
C666, UM436 (PD)
S-2 #119-120. Descant and harmonization
"Jesus Calls Us" (Luke) (C)
B293, C337, F399, L494, N172, UM398 (PD), VU562
H-3 Chr-115
S-2 #65. Harmonization
E550, E549, N171

Additional Hymn Suggestions

"Holy God, We Praise Thy Name" (Isa)
E366 (PD), F385, L535, N276, P460, UM79, VU894 (Fr.), W524
"Ye Watchers and Ye Holy Ones" (Isa)
E618, L175, P451, UM90, W707
"Faith, While Trees Are Still in Blossom" (Isa, Luke)
C535, UM508, VU643
"Here I Am, Lord" (Isa, Luke)
C452, P525, R149, UM593, VU509
"Stand Up and Bless the Lord" (Isa)
B30, UM662 (PD), P491
"The Lord's My Shepherd, I'll Not Want" (Pss)
F40, C78, P170, UM136, VU747
"O God Beyond All Praising" (Pss)
S2009, SF2009, VU256, W541
"O How I Love Jesus" (1 Cor)
B217, C99, F634, N52, UM170 (PD)
"Ah, Holy Jesus" (1 Cor)
C210, E158, L123, N218, P93, R183, UM289 (PD), VU138
"Christ Is Risen" (1 Cor)
C222, P104, UM307
"Cristo Vive" ("Christ Is Risen") (1 Cor)
B167, N235, P109, UM313
"You Satisfy the Hungry Heart" (Luke, Communion)
C429, P521, UM629, R217, VU478, W736
"Where He Leads Me" (Luke)
B288, C346, F607, UM338 (PD)
"Rise Up, Shepherd, and Follow" (Luke)
P50, S2096, SF2096, VU70
"Two Fishermen" (Luke)
S2101, SF2101, W633
"The Summons" (Luke)
S2130, SF2130, VU567

Additional Contemporary Suggestions

"Holy, Holy, Holy" ("Santo, Santo, Santo") (Isa)
C111, N793, S2007, SF2007
"Holy, Holy" (Isa)
B254, F149, P140, R206, S2039, SF2039, SP141
"Offering" (Isa)
M130
"Holy Is the Lord" (Isa)
M131
"Forever" (Pss)
M68
"Thank You, Lord" (Pss)
C531, UM84
"Give Thanks" (Pss)
C528, R266, S2036, SF2036, SP170
"Lord, I Lift Your Name on High" (1 Cor)
M2, R4, S2088, SF2088
"Grace Alone" (1 Cor)
M100, S2162, SF2162
"I Have Decided to Follow Jesus" (Luke)
B305, C344, S2129, SF2129
"Amen, Amen" (Luke, Black History)
N161, P299, S2072
"Breathe" (Luke)
M61; V-3 p. 42 Vocal Solo
"In Christ Alone" ("My Hope Is Found") (Luke)
M138
"Everyday" (Luke)
M150

Vocal Solos

"Here I Am" (Isa, Luke)
V-11 p. 19
"Jesus, My All to Heaven Is Gone" (Luke, Black History)
V-9 p. 39

Anthem

"Holy, Holy, Holy!" (Isa)
arr. Robert C. Clatterbuck; Hope C5470
SATB with keyboard

"I Will Praise You, O Lord" (Pss)
Mark Patterson; Choristers Guild CGA867
Unison with keyboard

Other Suggestions

Visuals:
O Burning coals, tongs, stump
P Thanks, heart, bowing, glory, singing, danger, hand
E Phoenix or peacock, resurrection
G Net, fish, people
Greeting: N821 or N822 (Pss)
Reading: F448. In the Year that King Uzziah Died (Isa)
Prayer: C89. Christ Comes as One Unknown (Luke)
Prayer: C443. Joy Through Involvement (Luke, Black History)

Exodus 34:29-35

29Moses came down from Mount Sinai. As he came down from the mountain with the two tablets of the covenant in his hand, Moses did not know that the skin of his face shone because he had been talking with God. 30When Aaron and all the Israelites saw Moses, the skin of his face was shining, and they were afraid to come near him. 31But Moses called to them; and Aaron and all the leaders of the congregation returned to him, and Moses spoke with them. 32Afterward all the Israelites came near, and he gave them in commandment all that the LORD had spoken with him on Mount Sinai. 33When Moses had finished speaking with them, he put a veil on his face; 34but whenever Moses went in before the LORD to speak with him, he would take the veil off, until he came out; and when he came out, and told the Israelites what he had been commanded, 35the Israelites would see the face of Moses, that the skin of his face was shining; and Moses would put the veil on his face again, until he went in to speak with him.

Psalm 99

1The LORD is king; let the peoples tremble! He sits enthroned upon the cherubim; let the earth quake! 2The LORD is great in Zion; he is exalted over all the peoples. 3Let them praise your great and awesome name. Holy is he! 4Mighty King, lover of justice, you have established equity; you have executed justice and righteousness in Jacob. 5Extol the LORD our God; worship at his footstool. Holy is he! 6Moses and Aaron were among his priests, Samuel also was among those who called on his name. They cried to the LORD, and he answered them. 7He spoke to them in the pillar of cloud; they kept his decrees, and the statutes that he gave them. 8O LORD our God, you answered them; you were a forgiving God to them, but an avenger of their wrongdoings. 9Extol the LORD our God, and worship at his holy mountain; for the LORD our God is holy.

---

2 Corinthians 3:12–4:2

12Since, then, we have such a hope, we act with great boldness, 13not like Moses, who put a veil over his face to keep the people of Israel from gazing at the end of the glory that was being set aside. 14But their minds were hardened. Indeed, to this very day, when they hear the reading of the old covenant, that same veil is still there, since only in Christ is it set aside. 15Indeed, to this very day whenever Moses is read, a veil lies over their minds; 16but when one turns to the Lord, the veil is removed. 17Now the Lord is the Spirit, and where the Spirit of the Lord is, there is freedom. 18And all of us, with unveiled faces, seeing the glory of the Lord as though reflected in a mirror, are being transformed into the same image from one degree of glory to another; for this comes from the Lord, the Spirit.

1Therefore, since it is by God's mercy that we are engaged in this ministry, we do not lose heart. 2We have renounced the shameful things that one hides; we refuse to practice cunning or to falsify God's word; but by the open statement of the truth we commend ourselves to the conscience of everyone in the sight of God.

Luke 9:28-36 (37-43*a*)

28Now about eight days after these sayings Jesus took with him Peter and John and James, and went up on the mountain to pray. 29And while he was praying, the appearance of his face changed, and his clothes became dazzling white. 30Suddenly they saw two men, Moses and Elijah, talking to him. 31They appeared in glory and were speaking of his departure, which he was about to accomplish at Jerusalem. 32Now Peter and his companions were weighed down with sleep; but since they had stayed awake, they saw his glory and the two men who stood with him. 33Just as they were leaving him, Peter said to Jesus, "Master, it is good for us to be here; let us make three dwellings, one for you, one for Moses, and one for Elijah"—not knowing what he said. 34While he was saying this, a cloud came and overshadowed them; and they were terrified as they entered the cloud. 35Then from the cloud came a voice that said, "This is my Son, my Chosen; listen to him!" 36When the voice had spoken, Jesus was found alone. And they kept silent and in those days told no one any of the things they had seen.

37On the next day, when they had come down from the mountain, a great crowd met him. 38Just then a man from the crowd shouted, "Teacher, I beg you to look at my son; he is my only child. 39Suddenly a spirit seizes him, and all at once he shrieks. It convulses him until he foams at the mouth; it mauls him and will scarcely leave him. 40I begged your disciples to cast it out, but they could not." 41Jesus answered, "You faithless and perverse generation, how much longer must I be with you and bear with you? Bring your son here." 42While he was coming, the demon dashed him to the ground in convulsions. But Jesus rebuked the unclean spirit, healed the boy, and gave him back to his father. 43aAnd all were astounded at the greatness of God.

Notes

Primary Hymns and Songs for the Day

"When Morning Gilds the Skies" (Exod, Luke) (O)
B221, C100, E427, F322, L546, N86, P487, UM185, VU339 (Fr.), W675
H-3 Hbl-103; Chr-126, 216; Desc-68; Org-76
S-1 #208. Introduction and interlude
S-2 #107. Trumpet descant
#108-109. Harmonization with descant

"Holy Ground" (Exod, Luke)
B224, C112, S2272, SF2272, SP86

"Shine, Jesus, Shine" (2 Cor, Transfiguration)
B579, R247, S2173, SF2173, SP142

"Christ, Whose Glory Fills the Skies" (Luke)
E7, L265, P462, UM173 (PD), VU336
H-3 Hbl-51; Chr-206; Desc-89; Org-120
S-1 #278-279. Harmonizations

"O Wondrous Sight! O Vision Fair" (Luke)
E137, UM258 (PD)
H-3 Hbl-47; Chr-32; Desc-102; Org-175
S-2 #191. Harmonization
L80, N184, P75
H-3 Org-145
S-1 #82-84. Various treatments

"Take Time to Be Holy" (2 Cor, Luke)
B446, C572, F457, UM395 (PD), VU672
H-3 Chr-178
S-1 #159. Harmonization

"Be Thou My Vision" (Luke) (C)
B60, C595, E488, F468, N451, P339, R151, UM451, VU642
H-3 Hbl-15, 48; Chr-36; Org-153
S-1 #319. Arr. for organ and voices in canon

Additional Hymn Suggestions

"Immortal, Invisible, God Only Wise" (Exod)
B6, C66, E423, F319, L526, N1, P263, R46, UM103 (PD), VU264, W512

"God the Spirit, Guide and Guardian" (Exod)
C450, P523, N355, UM648, VU514

"Love Divine, All Loves Excelling" (2 Cor)
B208, C517, F21, N43, UM384 (PD)
E657, L315, P376, R196, VU333, W588 (PD)

"O Jesus, I Have Promised" (2 Cor, Luke)
B276, C612, F402, N493, P388, UM396 (PD)
E655, L503 (PD), P389, VU120

"Christ, Upon the Mountain Peak" (Luke)
E129, P74, UM260, VU102, W701

"O Christ, the Healer" (Luke)
C503, L360, N175, P380, R191, UM265, W747

"I Come With Joy" (Luke, Communion)
B371, C420, E304, N349, P607, R195, UM617, VU477 W726

"Here, O My Lord, I See Thee" (Luke, Communion)
C416, E318, F567, L211, P520, UM623 (PD), VU459

"Swiftly Pass the Clouds of Glory" (Luke)
P73, S2102

"We Have Come at Christ's Own Bidding" (Luke) (O)
N182, S2103, SF2103. VU104

Additional Contemporary Suggestions

"Arise, Shine" (Exod, Luke, Transfig.)
S2005, SF2005

"Famous One" (Pss)
M126

"Where the Spirit of the Lord Is" (2 Cor)
C264, S2119, SF2119

"Shine on Us" (2 Cor, Transfiguration)
M19

"Let it Rise" (2 Cor)
M4

"In Christ Alone" ("My Hope Is Found") (2 Cor)
M138

"Turn Your Eyes upon Jesus" (Luke)
B320, F621, SP218, UM349

"Awesome In This Place" (Luke)
M36

"He Is Exalted" (Luke)
R238, S2070, SF2070, SP66

"Honor and Praise" (Luke)
S2018, SF2018

"All Hail King Jesus" (Transfig.)
S2069, SF2069, SP63

"How Great Is Our God" (Luke, Transfiguration)
M117

Vocal Solos

"Be Thou My Vision" (Exod, Luke)
V-6 p. 13
V-5 p. 13

"Show Me Your Glory" (Luke, Transfiguration)
V-3 p. 178

Anthems

"Shine on Us" (2 Cor, Transfiguration)
arr. Jack Schrader; Hope C5481
SATB with piano

"Spirit, Shine on Us" (2 Cor, Transfiguration)
arr. Lloyd Larson; Daybreak Muisc 08744589
SATB with keyboard

Other Suggestions

Visuals:
O Mountain, tablets, veil
P Throne, earthquake, footstool, cloud, mountain
E Veil, glory, mirror, transformer, Bible, 2 Cor 3:17b
G Mountain, prayer, dazzling light, 3 booths, cloud

Greeting: N819 (Exod, Luke)
Opening Prayer: N826 (Luke)
Prayer: C332. God of Wondrous Darkness (Exod, Black History)
Blessing: C268. Sarum Blessing (Exod)

Joel 2:1-2, 12-17

[1]Blow the trumpet in Zion; sound the alarm on my holy mountain! Let all the inhabitants of the land tremble, for the day of the LORD is coming, it is near— [2]a day of darkness and gloom, a day of clouds and thick darkness! Like blackness spread upon the mountains a great and powerful army comes; their like has never been from of old, nor will be again after them in ages to come.

[12]Yet even now, says the LORD, return to me with all your heart, with fasting, with weeping, and with mourning; [13]rend your hearts and not your clothing. Return to the LORD, your God, for he is gracious and merciful, slow to anger, and abounding in steadfast love, and relents from punishing. [14]Who knows whether he will not turn and relent, and leave a blessing behind him, a grain offering and a drink offering for the LORD, your God? [15]Blow the trumpet in Zion; sanctify a fast; call a solemn assembly; [16]gather the people. Sanctify the congregation; assemble the aged; gather the children, even infants at the breast. Let the bridegroom leave his room, and the bride her canopy. [17]Between the vestibule and the altar let the priests, the ministers of the LORD, weep. Let them say, "Spare your people, O LORD, and do not make your heritage a mockery, a byword among the nations. Why should it be said among the peoples, 'Where is their God?' "

Psalm 51:1-17

[1]Have mercy on me, O God, according to your steadfast love; according to your abundant mercy blot out my transgressions. [2]Wash me thoroughly from my iniquity, and cleanse me from my sin. [3]For I know my transgressions, and my sin is ever before me. [4]Against you, you alone, have I sinned, and done what is evil in your sight, so that you are justified in your sentence and blameless when you pass judgment. [5]Indeed, I was born guilty, a sinner when my mother conceived me. [6]You desire truth in the inward being; therefore teach me wisdom in my secret heart. [7]Purge me with hyssop, and I shall be clean; wash me, and I shall be whiter than snow. [8]Let me hear joy and gladness; let the bones that you have crushed rejoice. [9]Hide your face from my sins, and blot out all my iniquities. [10]Create in me a clean heart, O God, and put a new and right spirit within me. [11]Do not cast me away from your presence, and do not take your holy spirit from me. [12]Restore to me the joy of your salvation, and sustain in me a willing spirit. [13]Then I will teach transgressors your ways, and sinners will return to you. [14]Deliver me from bloodshed, O God, O God of my salvation, and my tongue will sing aloud of your deliverance. [15]O Lord, open my lips, and my mouth will declare your praise. [16]For you have no delight in sacrifice; if I were to give a burnt offering, you would not be pleased. [17]The sacrifice acceptable to God is a broken spirit; a broken and contrite heart, O God, you will not despise.

2 Corinthians 5:20*b*–6:10

[20b]We entreat you on behalf of Christ, be reconciled to God. [21]For our sake he made him to be sin who knew no sin, so that in him we might become the righteousness of God.

[1]As we work together with him, we urge you also not to accept the grace of God in vain. [2]For he says, "At an acceptable time I have listened to you, and on a day of salvation I have helped you." See, now is the acceptable time; see, now is the day of salvation! [3]We are putting no obstacle in anyone's way, so that no fault may be found with our ministry, [4]but as servants of God we have commended ourselves in every way: through great endurance, in afflictions, hardships, calamities, [5]beatings, imprisonments, riots, labors, sleepless nights, hunger; [6]by purity, knowledge, patience, kindness, holiness of spirit, genuine love, [7]truthful speech, and the power of God; with the weapons of righteousness for the right hand and for the left; [8]in honor and dishonor, in ill repute and good repute. We are treated as impostors, and yet are true; [9]as unknown, and yet are well known; as dying, and see—we are alive; as punished, and yet not killed; [10]as sorrowful, yet always rejoicing; as poor, yet making many rich; as having nothing, and yet possessing everything.

Matthew 6:1-6, 16-21

[1]"Beware of practicing your piety before others in order to be seen by them; for then you have no reward from your Father in heaven.

[2]"So whenever you give alms, do not sound a trumpet before you, as the hypocrites do in the synagogues and in the streets, so that they may be praised by others. Truly I tell you, they have received their reward. [3]But when you give alms, do not let your left hand know what your right hand is doing, [4]so that your alms may be done in secret; and your Father who sees in secret will reward you.

[5]"And whenever you pray, do not be like the hypocrites; for they love to stand and pray in the synagogues and at the street corners, so that they may be seen by others. Truly I tell you, they have received their reward. [6]But whenever you pray, go into your room and shut the door and pray to your Father who is in secret; and your Father who sees in secret will reward you.

[16]"And whenever you fast, do not look dismal, like the hypocrites, for they disfigure their faces so as to show others that they are fasting. Truly I tell you, they have received their reward. [17]But when you fast, put oil on your head and wash your face, [18]so that your fasting may be seen not by others but by your Father who is in secret; and your Father who sees in secret will reward you.

[19]"Do not store up for yourselves treasures on earth, where moth and rust consume and where thieves break in and steal; [20]but store up for yourselves treasures in heaven, where neither moth nor rust consumes and where thieves do not break in and steal. [21]For where your treasure is, there your heart will be also."

Primary Hymns and Songs for the Day

"Lord, Who Throughout These Forty Days" (Luke, Lent) (O)
C180, E142, N211, P81, W417 (PD)
H-3 Chr-36, 132; Desc-94; Org-137
UM269
H-3 Hbl-129; Chr-106; Desc-65; Org-72
S-2 #105. Flute/violin descant
#106. Harmonization
"More Love to Thee, O Christ" (Matt)
B473, C527, F476, N456, P359, UM453 (PD)
H-3 Org-94
"Come and Find the Quiet Center" (Matt)
C575, S2128, SF2128, VU374
"Sunday's Palms Are Wednesday's Ashes" (Pss)
S2138, SF2138, VU107
H-3 Hbl-14, 64; Chr-132, 203
S-2 #22. Descant
"Lord, I Want to Be a Christian" (Joel, Matt) (C)
B489, C589, F421, N454, P372 (PD), R145, UM402
H-3 Chr-130

Additional Hymn Suggestions

"There's a Wideness in God's Mercy" (Joel)
B25, C73, E469 and E470, F115, L290, N23, P298, UM121, VU271, W595 and W596
"Have Thine Own Way, Lord" (Pss)
B294, C588, F400, UM382 (PD)
"Alas! And Did My Savior Bleed" (2 Cor)
B145, F274, L98, N200, P78, UM294 (PD)
B139, C204, N199, UM359 (PD)
"Close to Thee" (2 Cor)
B464, F405, UM407 (PD)
"I Love Thy Kingdom, Lord" (2 Cor)
B354, C274, E524, F545, L368, N312, P441, UM540
"Lead On, O King Eternal" (2 Cor)
B621, C632, E555, F595, L495, N573, P447 and P448, R298, UM580
"Lead On, O Cloud of Presence" (2 Cor, Lent)
C633, S2234, SF2234, VU421
"Love Divine, All Loves Excelling" (2 Cor, Matt) (O)
B208, C517, F21, N43, UM384 (PD)
E657, L315, P376, R196, VU333, W588 (PD)
"What Wondrous Love Is This" (2 Cor) (C)
B143 (PD), C200, E439, F283, L385, N223, P85, R277, UM292, VU147 (Fr.), W600
"It's Me, It's Me, O Lord" (Matt, Black History)
C579, N519, UM352
"Just as I Am, Without One Plea" (Matt)
B307, C339, E693, F417, L296, N207, P370, R140, UM357 (PD), VU508
"Take Time to Be Holy" (Matt)
B446, C572, F457, UM395 (PD), VU672
"Near to the Heart of God" (Matt)
B295, C581, F35, P527, UM472 (PD)
"Prayer is the Soul's Sincere Desire" (Matt)
F446 (PD), N508, UM492
"Sweet Hour of Prayer" (Matt)
B445, C570, F439, N505, UM496 (PD)

Additional Contemporary Suggestions

"Refiner's Fire" (Pss)
M50
"Purify My Heart" (Pss)
M90
"Lord You Have My Heart" (Pss)
M151
"Give Me a Clean Heart" (Pss)
C515, N188, S2133, SF2133
"Come and Fill Our Hearts" (Pss)
S2157, SF2157, W561
"Change My Heart, O God" (Pss)
R143, SP195, S2152, SF2152
"You Are My Hiding Place" (Pss, Matt)
C554, S2055, SF2055
"Open Our Eyes, Lord" (Pss, Matt)
B499, R91, S2086, SF2086, SP199
"You Are My All in All" (Matt Lent)
SP220

Vocal Solos

"A Contrite Heart" (Pss)
V-4 p. 10
"Clean Before My Lord" (Pss)
V-8 p. 233

Anthems

"Return to God" (Joel)
Marty Haugen; GIA G-3537
SATB with keyboard and opt. C instrument

"Have Mercy on Me, O God" (Pss)
Carl Schalk; Augsburg 11-10937
SATB a cappella

Other Suggestions

Visuals:
O Trumpet, alarm, dark, cloud, weeping, heart
P Blot, wash, heart, hyssop, snow, Ps 51:10, joy, sing
E Christ, cross, clock, suffer, serve, weep/joy
G Hands, prayer, closed door, oil/basin, moth/rust, treasure/heart

Introit: S2138, SF2138, VU107. "Sunday's Palms Are Wednesday's Ashes," stanza 1 (Pss)
Sung Prayer: S2134, SF2134. "Forgive Us, Lord" (Pss)
Prayer: C456 or C574 (Matt) or N846 (Pss)
Words of Assurance: N840 (Joel)
Readings: C219 (Matt) and F426. (Pss)
Response: S2205, SF2205. "The Fragrance of Christ" (Matt)

Deuteronomy 26:1-11

[1]When you have come into the land that the LORD your
God is giving you as an inheritance to possess, and you possess it, and settle in it, [2]you shall take some of the first of all
the fruit of the ground, which you harvest from the land
that the LORD your God is giving you, and you shall put it
in a basket and go to the place that the LORD your God will
choose as a dwelling for his name. [3]You shall go to the
priest who is in office at that time, and say to him, "Today
I declare to the LORD your God that I have come into the
land that the LORD swore to our ancestors to give us."
[4]When the priest takes the basket from your hand and sets
it down before the altar of the LORD your God, [5]you shall
make this response before the LORD your God: "A wandering Aramean was my ancestor; he went down into Egypt
and lived there as an alien, few in number, and there he
became a great nation, mighty and populous. [6]When the
Egyptians treated us harshly and afflicted us, by imposing
hard labor on us, [7]we cried to the LORD, the God of our
ancestors; the LORD heard our voice and saw our affliction,
our toil, and our oppression. [8]The LORD brought us out of
Egypt with a mighty hand and an outstretched arm, with a
terrifying display of power, and with signs and wonders;
[9]and he brought us into this place and gave us this land,
a land flowing with milk and honey. [10]So now I bring the
first of the fruit of the ground that you, O LORD, have
given me." You shall set it down before the LORD your
God and bow down before the LORD your God. [11]Then
you, together with the Levites and the aliens who reside
among you, shall celebrate with all the bounty that the
LORD your God has given to you and to your house.

Psalm 91:1-2, 9-16

[1]You who live in the shelter of the Most High, who
abide in the shadow of the Almighty, [2]will say to the LORD,
"My refuge and my fortress; my God, in whom I trust."

[9]Because you have made the LORD your refuge, the
Most High your dwelling place, [10]no evil shall befall you,
no scourge come near your tent. [11]For he will command
his angels concerning you to guard you in all your ways.
[12]On their hands they will bear you up, so that you will
not dash your foot against a stone. [13]You will tread on the
lion and the adder, the young lion and the serpent you
will trample under foot. [14]Those who love me, I will deliver; I will protect those who know my name. [15]When they
call to me, I will answer them; I will be with them in trouble, I will rescue them and honor them. [16]With long life I
will satisfy them, and show them my salvation.

Romans 10:8*b*-13

[8b]"The word is near you, on your lips and in your heart"
(that is, the word of faith that we proclaim); [9]because if
you confess with your lips that Jesus is Lord and believe in
your heart that God raised him from the dead, you will be
saved. [10]For one believes with the heart and so is justified,
and one confesses with the mouth and so is saved. [11]The
scripture says, "No one who believes in him will be put to
shame." [12]For there is no distinction between Jew and
Greek; the same Lord is Lord of all and is generous to all
who call on him. [13]For, "Everyone who calls on the name
of the Lord shall be saved."

Luke 4:1-13

[1]Jesus, full of the Holy Spirit, returned from the Jordan
and was led by the Spirit in the wilderness, [2]where for
forty days he was tempted by the devil. He ate nothing at
all during those days, and when they were over, he was
famished. [3]The devil said to him, "If you are the Son of
God, command this stone to become a loaf of bread."
[4]Jesus answered him, "It is written, 'One does not live by
bread alone.' "

[5]Then the devil led him up and showed him in an
instant all the kingdoms of the world. [6]And the devil said
to him, "To you I will give their glory and all this authority;
for it has been given over to me, and I give it to anyone I
please. [7]If you, then, will worship me, it will all be yours."
[8]Jesus answered him, "It is written, 'Worship the Lord
your God, and serve only him.' "

[9]Then the devil took him to Jerusalem, and placed him
on the pinnacle of the temple, saying to him, "If you are
the Son of God, throw yourself down from here, [10]for it is
written, 'He will command his angels concerning you, to
protect you,' [11]and 'On their hands they will bear you up,
so that you will not dash your foot against a stone.' "
[12]Jesus answered him, "It is said, 'Do not put the Lord your
God to the test.' " [13]When the devil had finished every test,
he departed from him until an opportune time.

Notes

Primary Hymns and Songs for the Day

"The God of Abraham Praise" (Deut) (O)
B34, C24, E401, F332, L544, N24, P488, R51, UM116 (PD), VU255, W537
H-3 Hbl-62, 95; Chr-59; Org-77
S-1 #211. Harmonization

"A Mighty Fortress Is Our God" (Pss) (O)
B8, C65, E687 or E688, F118, L228 or L229, N439 or N440, P259 or P260, UM110 (PD), VU261 (Fr.) or VU262 or VU263, W575 or W576
H-3 Chr-19; Desc-35; Org-34
S-1 #111-113. Various treatments

"On Eagle's Wings" (Pss)
B71, C77, N775, R112, UM143, VU807 and VU808

"He Is Lord" (Rom)
B178, C117, F234, R29, SP122, UM177

"Jesus, Tempted in the Desert" (Luke)
S2105, SF2105
H-3 Chr-53; Org-33
S-1 #109-10. Descant and harmonization
VU115
H-3 Hbl-14, 64; Chr-132, 203
S-2 #22. Descant

"Lord, Who Throughout These Forty Days" (Luke, Lent) (C)
C180, E142, N211, P81, W417 (PD)
H-3 Chr-36, 132; Desc-94; Org-137
UM269
H-3 Hbl-129; Chr-106; Desc-65; Org-72
S-2 #105. Flute/violin descant
#106. Harmonization
L99

"Jesus Walked This Lonesome Valley" (Luke, Lent) (C)
C211, F217, P80, S2112, W427

"Into My Heart" (Rom)
C304, S2160, SF2160

"I Love to Tell the Story" (Rom)
B572, C480, F619, L390, N522, UM156 (PD), VU343

"We Walk by Faith" (Rom, Luke)
E209, N256, P399, S2196, SF2196, W572

"Hope of the World" (Luke)
C538, E472, L493, N46, P360, UM178, VU215, W565

"O Love, How Deep" (Luke, Communion)
E449, L88, N209, P83, UM267 (PD), VU348

"Take Time to Be Holy" (Luke)
B446, C572, F457, UM395 (PD), VU672

"Loving Spirit" (Luke)
C244, P323, S2123, SF2123, VU387

Additional Hymn Suggestions

"Praise, My Soul, the King of Heaven" (Deut) (O)
B32, C23, E410, F339, L549, P478 or 479, R53, UM66 (PD), VU240, W530

"Lead On, O Cloud of Presence" (Deut) (O)
C633, S2234, SF2234, VU421

"In the Midst of New Dimensions" (Deut)
N391, S2238, SF2238

"For the Fruits of This Creation" (Deut)
B643, C714, E424, L563, N425, P553, UM97, VU227

"Praise to the Lord, the Almighty" (Deut)
B14 (PD), C25, E390, F337, L543, N22, P482, R57, UM139, VU220 (Fr.) and VU221, W547

"O God, Our Help in Ages Past" (Pss)
B74, C67, E680, F370, L320, N25, P210, UM117 (PD), VU806, W579

"God Will Take Care of You" (Pss)
B64, F56, N460, UM130 (PD)

"Children of the Heavenly Father" (Pss)
B55, F89, L474, N487, UM141

"It is Well with My Soul" (Pss)
B410, C561, F495, L346, N438, UM377 (PD)

"Since Jesus Came into My Heart" (Rom)
B441, F639, S2140, SF2140

Additional Contemporary Suggestions

"The Power of Your Love" (Pss, Lent)
M26

"I Stand Amazed" (Pss, Lent)
M79

"Eagle's Wings" (Pss)
M158

"Made Me Glad" (Pss, Luke)
M123

"God Is So Good" (Rom)
B23, S2056, SF2056

"Come, Now Is the Time to Worship" (Rom)
M56; V-3 p. 114Vocal Solo

"That's Why We Praise Him" (Luke, Lent)
M94

Vocal Solo

"Grace Greater Than Our Sin" (Rom)
V-8 p. 180

"Courage, My Heart" (Luke, Lent)
V-9 p. 20

Anthem

"I Wonder As I Wander" (Luke)
arr. Keith Christopher; Hal Leonard HL50482417
SATB with flute and piano

Other Suggestions

Visuals:
O Basket with food/produce, hand, arm, wrapped gift
P Angels, stone, lion, snake, "deliverance"
E Faces, professing, multi-racial, all ages, Christ
G Loaf bread, stone (also arranged as a wall), angels

Introit: S2138, SF2138, VU107. "Sunday's Palms Are Wednesday's Ashes," stanza 1 (Lent)
Greeting: N821 (Deut)
Prayer: UM268. Lent (Deut)
Prayer: C178 or F218 (Luke, Lent)

FEBRUARY 28, 2010

Genesis 15:1-12, 17-18
[1]After these things the word of the LORD came to Abram
in a vision, "Do not be afraid, Abram, I am your shield;
your reward shall be very great." [2]But Abram said, "O Lord
GOD, what will you give me, for I continue childless, and
the heir of my house is Eliezer of Damascus?" [3]And Abram
said, "You have given me no offspring, and so a slave born
in my house is to be my heir." [4]But the word of the LORD
came to him, "This man shall not be your heir; no one but
your very own issue shall be your heir." [5]He brought him
outside and said, "Look toward heaven and count the stars,
if you are able to count them." Then he said to him, "So
shall your descendants be." [6]And he believed the LORD; and
the LORD reckoned it to him as righteousness.
[7]Then he said to him, "I am the LORD who brought you
from Ur of the Chaldeans, to give you this land to possess." [8]But he said, "O Lord GOD, how am I to know that I
shall possess it?" [9]He said to him, "Bring me a heifer three
years old, a female goat three years old, a ram three years
old, a turtledove, and a young pigeon." [10]He brought him
all these and cut them in two, laying each half over
against the other; but he did not cut the birds in two.
[11]And when birds of prey came down on the carcasses,
Abram drove them away.
[12]As the sun was going down, a deep sleep fell upon
Abram, and a deep and terrifying darkness descended
upon him.
[17]When the sun had gone down and it was dark, a smok-
ing fire pot and a flaming torch passed between these
pieces. [18]On that day the LORD made a covenant with
Abram, saying, "To your descendants I give this land, from
the river of Egypt to the great river, the river Euphrates."

Psalm 27
[1]The LORD is my light and my salvation; whom shall I
fear? The LORD is the stronghold of my life; of whom shall
I be afraid? [2]When evildoers assail me to devour my
flesh—my adversaries and foes—they shall stumble and
fall. [3]Though an army encamp against me, my heart shall
not fear; though war rise up against me, yet I will be confident. [4]One thing I asked of the LORD, that will I seek after:
to live in the house of the LORD all the days of my life, to
behold the beauty of the LORD, and to inquire in his temple. [5]For he will hide me in his shelter in the day of trouble; he will conceal me under the cover of his tent; he will
set me high on a rock. [6]Now my head is lifted up above my
enemies all around me, and I will offer in his tent sacrifices with shouts of joy; I will sing and make melody to the
LORD. [7]Hear, O LORD, when I cry aloud, be gracious to me
and answer me! [8]"Come," my heart says, "seek his face!"
Your face, LORD, do I seek. [9]Do not hide your face from
me. Do not turn your servant away in anger, you who have
been my help. Do not cast me off, do not forsake me, O
God of my salvation! [10]If my father and mother forsake
me, the LORD will take me up. [11]Teach me your way, O
LORD, and lead me on a level path because of my enemies.
[12]Do not give me up to the will of my adversaries, for false
witnesses have risen against me, and they are breathing
out violence. [13]I believe that I shall see the goodness of
the LORD in the land of the living. [14]Wait for the LORD; be
strong, and let your heart take courage; wait for the LORD!

Philippians 3:17–4:1
[17]Brothers and sisters, join in imitating me, and observe
those who live according to the example you have in us.
[18]For many live as enemies of the cross of Christ; I have
often told you of them, and now I tell you even with tears.
[19]Their end is destruction; their god is the belly; and their
glory is in their shame; their minds are set on earthly
things. [20]But our citizenship is in heaven, and it is from
there that we are expecting a Savior, the Lord Jesus
Christ. [21]He will transform the body of our humiliation
that it may be conformed to the body of his glory, by the
power that also enables him to make all things subject
to himself.
[1]Therefore, my brothers and sisters, whom I love and
long for, my joy and crown, stand firm in the Lord in this
way, my beloved.

Luke 13:31-35
[31]At that very hour some Pharisees came and said to
him, "Get away from here, for Herod wants to kill you."
[32]He said to them, "Go and tell that fox for me, 'Listen, I
am casting out demons and performing cures today and
tomorrow, and on the third day I finish my work. [33]Yet
today, tomorrow, and the next day I must be on my way,
because it is impossible for a prophet to be killed outside
of Jerusalem.' [34]Jerusalem, Jerusalem, the city that kills the
prophets and stones those who are sent to it! How often
have I desired to gather your children together as a hen
gathers her brood under her wings, and you were not willing! [35]See, your house is left to you. And I tell you, you will
not see me until the time comes when you say, 'Blessed is
the one who comes in the name of the Lord.' "

Notes

Primary Hymns and Songs for the Day

"The God of Abraham Praise" (Gen) (O)
B34, C24, E401, F332, L544, N24, P488, R51, UM116 (PD), VU255, W537
H-3 Hbl-62, 95; Chr-59; Org-77
S-1 #211. Harmonization

"Great is Thy Faithfulness" (Gen) (O)
B54, C86, F98, N423, P276, R249, UM140, VU288
H-3 Chr-87; Desc-39; Org-39
S-2 #59. Piano arrangement

"O Lord, You're Beautiful" (Pss)
S2064, SF2064

"In the Cross of Christ I Glory" (Phil) (C)
B554, C207, E441, F251, L104, N193, P84, UM295 (PD)
H-3 Hbl-72; Chr-113; Desc-89; Org-119
S-1 #276-277. Harmonization with descant

"O Jesus I Have Promised" (Phil) (C)
B276, C612, F402, N493, P388, UM396 (PD)
S-2 #9. Descant
E655, L503 (PD), P389, VU120

"Lord Christ, When First You Came to Earth" (Luke)
E598, L421, P7, W438
H-3 Hbl-92; Chr-22, 126; Desc-76; Org-91
S-1 #237. Descant

Additional Hymn Suggestions

"All My Hope Is Firmly Grounded" (Gen)
C88, E665, N408, UM132, VU654 and VU655

"If Thou But Suffer God to Guide Thee" (Gen)
B57, C565, E635, L453, N410, P282, UM142 (PD), VU285 (Fr.) and VU286

"Be Thou My Vision" (Gen)
B60, C595, E488, F468, N451, P339, R151, UM451, VU642

"Jesus, Lover of My Soul" (Pss)
C542, E699, F222, P303, UM479 (PD), VU669
B180 (PD), N546

"Lead On, O King Eternal" (Pss, Phil)
B621, C632, E555, F595, L495, N573, P447 and P448, R298, UM580

"Lead Me, Guide Me" (Pss)
C583, R176, S2214, SF2214

"Fairest Lord Jesus" (Phil)
B176, C97, E383, F240, L518, N44, P306, R166, UM189 (PD), VU341

"O Sacred Head, Now Wounded" (Phil)
B137, C202, E168 or E169, F284, L116 or L117, N226, P98, R235, UM286, VU145 (Fr.), W434

"I Am Thine, O Lord" (Phil)
B290, C601, F455, N455, UM419 (PD)

"By Gracious Powers" (Phil, Luke)
E695 and E696, N413, P342, UM517, W577

"How Like a Gentle Spirit" (Luke)
C69, N443, UM115

"The Care the Eagle Gives Her Young" (Luke)
C76, N468, UM118, VU269

"O Love, How Deep" (Luke, Communion)
E449, L88, N209, P83, UM267 (PD), VU348

"Jesus Walked This Lonesome Valley" (Luke, Lent)
C211, F217, P80, S2112, W427

"Loving Spirit" (Luke)
C244, P323, S2123, SF2123, VU387

"We Sing to You, O God" (Luke) (C)
S2001, SF2001
N9 (alternate tune)

Additional Contemporary Suggestions

"El Shaddai" (Gen)
UM123

"Nothing Can Trouble" ("Nada Te Turbe") (Pss)
S2054, SF2054, VU290

"Someone Asked the Question" (Pss)
N523, S2144

"The Lord Is My Light" (Pss)
R102, SDP209

"All Things Are Possible" (Pss)
M92

"Just Let Me Say" (Pss, Phil)
M83

"In Christ Alone" (Pss, Phil, Luke)
M138

"Lord of the Dance" (Luke)
P302, UM261, VU352, W636

Vocal Solos

"Patiently Have I Waited for the Lord" (Pss)
V-4 p. 24

"The Lord Is My Light" (Pss)
V-8 p. 57

Anthem

"O Jesus I Have Promised" (Phil)
arr. Evelyn R. Larter; Abingdon Press 9780687648801
SATB with piano and opt. violin

"Kyrie" (Luke)
Gabriel Faure; Warner Brothers BSC9821
Two-part with keyboard

Other Suggestions

Visuals:
O Shield, stars, heifer, goat, ram, pigeon, fire, torch
P Light, army/war, sanctuary, tent, rock, singing, path
E Cross, "citizens", Christ, love, crown, Phil 4:1c
G Jerusalem, hen/chicks, Luke 13:35c

Prayer of Confession: N865. Endeavors of the Day (Phil)
Prayer: C103. Prayer of St. Anselm (Luke)
Response: C299, S2277, SF2277. "Lord, Have Mercy" (Lent)
Litany: C11. Names of God Litany (Gen, Luke)
Call to Communion: C418. Behold These Emblems (Luke)
Blessing: N873 (Gen, Luke)

Isaiah 55:1-9

1Ho, everyone who thirsts, come to the waters; and you that have no money, come, buy and eat! Come, buy wine and milk without money and without price. 2Why do you spend your money for that which is not bread, and your labor for that which does not satisfy? Listen carefully to me, and eat what is good, and delight yourselves in rich food. 3Incline your ear, and come to me; listen, so that you may live. I will make with you an everlasting covenant, my steadfast, sure love for David. 4See, I made him a witness to the peoples, a leader and commander for the peoples. 5See, you shall call nations that you do not know, and nations that do not know you shall run to you, because of the LORD your God, the Holy One of Israel, for he has glorified you. 6Seek the LORD while he may be found, call upon him while he is near; 7let the wicked forsake their way, and the unrighteous their thoughts; let them return to the LORD, that he may have mercy on them, and to our God, for he will abundantly pardon. 8For my thoughts are not your thoughts, nor are your ways my ways, says the LORD. 9For as the heavens are higher than the earth, so are my ways higher than your ways and my thoughts than your thoughts.

Psalm 63:1-8

1O God, you are my God, I seek you, my soul thirsts for you; my flesh faints for you, as in a dry and weary land where there is no water. 2So I have looked upon you in the sanctuary, beholding your power and glory. 3Because your steadfast love is better than life, my lips will praise you. 4So I will bless you as long as I live; I will lift up my hands and call on your name. 5My soul is satisfied as with a rich feast, and my mouth praises you with joyful lips 6when I think of you on my bed, and meditate on you in the watches of the night; 7for you have been my help, and in the shadow of your wings I sing for joy. 8My soul clings to you; your right hand upholds me.

---

1 Corinthians 10:1-13

1I do not want you to be unaware, brothers and sisters, that our ancestors were all under the cloud, and all passed through the sea, 2and all were baptized into Moses in the cloud and in the sea, 3and all ate the same spiritual food, 4and all drank the same spiritual drink. For they drank from the spiritual rock that followed them, and the rock was Christ. 5Nevertheless, God was not pleased with most of them, and they were struck down in the wilderness.

6Now these things occurred as examples for us, so that we might not desire evil as they did. 7Do not become idolaters as some of them did; as it is written, "The people sat down to eat and drink, and they rose up to play." 8We must not indulge in sexual immorality as some of them did, and twenty-three thousand fell in a single day. 9We must not put Christ to the test, as some of them did, and were destroyed by serpents. 10And do not complain as some of them did, and were destroyed by the destroyer. 11These things happened to them to serve as an example, and they were written down to instruct us, on whom the ends of the ages have come. 12So if you think you are standing, watch out that you do not fall. 13No testing has overtaken you that is not common to everyone. God is faithful, and he will not let you be tested beyond your strength, but with the testing he will also provide the way out so that you may be able to endure it.

Luke 13:1-9

1At that very time there were some present who told him about the Galileans whose blood Pilate had mingled with their sacrifices. 2He asked them, "Do you think that because these Galileans suffered in this way they were worse sinners than all other Galileans? 3No, I tell you; but unless you repent, you will all perish as they did. 4Or those eighteen who were killed when the tower of Siloam fell on them—do you think that they were worse offenders than all the others living in Jerusalem? 5No, I tell you; but unless you repent, you will all perish just as they did."

6Then he told this parable: "A man had a fig tree planted in his vineyard; and he came looking for fruit on it and found none. 7So he said to the gardener, 'See here! For three years I have come looking for fruit on this fig tree, and still I find none. Cut it down! Why should it be wasting the soil?' 8He replied, 'Sir, let it alone for one more year, until I dig around it and put manure on it. 9If it bears fruit next year, well and good; but if not, you can cut it down.' "

Notes

Primary Hymns and Songs for the Day
"There's a Wideness in God's Mercy" (Isa) (O)
B25, C73, F115, UM121
H-3 Chr-195; Desc-102; Org-179
E470
H-3 Chr-134; Desc-18; Org-13
S-1 #41-42. Descant and harmonization
N23, P298, W595
H-3 Chr-90; Desc-54; Org-60
S-1 #178-179. Harmonizations
E469, L290, VU271, W596
"You Who Are Thirsty" (Isa)
S2132, SF2132
"We Walk by Faith" (Isa)
N256, P399, W572
H-3 Chr-67
S2196, SF2196
H-3 Chr-21
E209
"O Jesus I Have Promised" (1 Cor)
B276, C612, F402, N493, P388, UM396 (PD)
S-2 #9. Descant
E655, L503 (PD), P389, VU120
"Guide Me, O Thou Great Jehovah" (Isa, 1 Cor) (C)
B56, C622, E690, F608, L343, N18, P281, UM127 (PD), VU651 (Fr.)
H-3 Hbl-25, 51, 58; Chr-89; Desc-26; Org-23
S-1 #76-77. Descant and harmonization
N19

Additional Hymn Suggestions
"Come, Ye Sinners, Poor and Needy" (Isa)
B323 (PD), R141, UM340, W756
"Come, Ye Disconsolate" (Isa)
B67, C502, SF2132, UM510 (PD)
"You Satisfy the Hungry Heart" (Isa)
C429, P521, UM629, R217, VU478, W736
"I'll Fly Away" (Isa)
N595, S2282, SF2282
"Savior, Like a Shepherd Lead Us" (Pss)
B61, C558, E708, F601, L481, N252, P387, UM381 (PD)
"Come Down, O Love Divine" (Pss)
C582, E516, L508, N289, P313, UM475 (PD), VU367, W472
"Wellspring of Wisdom" (Pss, 1 Cor, Luke)
C596, UM506, VU287
"We Sing to You, O God" (Pss, 1 Cor)
N9, S2001, SF2001
"O God, What You Ordain Is Right" (1 Cor)
L446, N415, P284
"How Shall They Hear the Word of God" (1 Cor)
UM649, W629
"Lift Every Voice and Sing" (1 Cor, Luke)
B627, C631, E599, L562, N593, P563, UM519, W641
"Forth in Thy Name, O Lord" (Luke)
L505, UM438 (PD), VU416
"God the Sculptor of the Mountains" (Luke)
S2060, SF2060

Additional Contemporary Suggestions
"Holy and Anointed One" (Isa, Lent)
M32
"Step By Step" (Isa, Pss, Lent)
M51
"All Who Are Thirsty" (Isa)
M159
M155 "Hungry" ("Falling on My Knees")
M155
"Your Love, Oh Lord" (Isa, Pss)
M189
"Draw Me Close" (Pss)
M29
"Jesus, Draw Me Close" (Pss)
M48, S2159, SF2159
"Eagle's Wings" (Pss)
M158
"As the Deer" (Pss)
R9, S2025, SF2025, SP200, VU766
"On Eagle's Wings" (Pss)
B71, C77, N775, R112, UM143, VU807 and VU808
"Praise the Name of Jesus" (1 Cor)
R7, S2066, SF2066, SP87

Vocal Solos
"For Those Tears I Died" (Isa, Lent)
V-8 p. 242
"Wondrous Love" (Lent)
V-6 p. 47

Anthems
"A Rose Touched by the Sun's Warm Rays" (Isa)
Jean Berger; Augsburg 11-953
SATB a cappella

"You Shall Go Out in Joy" (Isa)
Leland Sateren; Augsburg 11-0576
SATB a cappella

Other Suggestions
Visuals:
O Water, wine/milk/honey, money, listen, Isa 55:6a
P Desert, lifted hands, food, bed, Ps 63:7b, wings
E Water/food, larger rock, bread/wine, baptism
G Fig branch or tree, figs, axe, cross
Greeting: N819 or N822 (Pss)
Canticle: N734. "Second Canticle of Isaiah" (Isa)
Prayer: C524, UM423. Prayer of the Restless Heart (Pss)
Prayer: N855. For the Church (Pss).

Joshua 5:9-12

[9]The LORD said to Joshua, "Today I have rolled away from you the disgrace of Egypt." And so that place is called Gilgal to this day.

[10]While the Israelites were camped in Gilgal they kept the passover in the evening on the fourteenth day of the month in the plains of Jericho. [11]On the day after the passover, on that very day, they ate the produce of the land, unleavened cakes and parched grain. [12]The manna ceased on the day they ate the produce of the land, and the Israelites no longer had manna; they ate the crops of the land of Canaan that year.

Psalm 32

[1]Happy are those whose transgression is forgiven, whose sin is covered. [2]Happy are those to whom the LORD imputes no iniquity, and in whose spirit there is no deceit. [3]While I kept silence, my body wasted away through my groaning all day long. [4]For day and night your hand was heavy upon me; my strength was dried up as by the heat of summer. [5]Then I acknowledged my sin to you, and I did not hide my iniquity; I said, "I will confess my transgressions to the LORD," and you forgave the guilt of my sin. [6]Therefore let all who are faithful offer prayer to you; at a time of distress, the rush of mighty waters shall not reach them. [7]You are a hiding place for me; you preserve me from trouble; you surround me with glad cries of deliverance. [8]I will instruct you and teach you the way you should go; I will counsel you with my eye upon you. [9]Do not be like a horse or a mule, without understanding, whose temper must be curbed with bit and bridle, else it will not stay near you. [10]Many are the torments of the wicked, but steadfast love surrounds those who trust in the LORD. [11]Be glad in the LORD and rejoice, O righteous, and shout for joy, all you upright in heart.

---

2 Corinthians 5:16-21

[16]From now on, therefore, we regard no one from a human point of view; even though we once knew Christ from a human point of view, we know him no longer in that way. [17]So if anyone is in Christ, there is a new creation: everything old has passed away; see, everything has become new! [18]All this is from God, who reconciled us to himself through Christ, and has given us the ministry of reconciliation; [19]that is, in Christ God was reconciling the world to himself, not counting their trespasses against them, and entrusting the message of reconciliation to us. [20]So we are ambassadors for Christ, since God is making his appeal through us; we entreat you on behalf of Christ, be reconciled to God. [21]For our sake he made him to be sin who knew no sin, so that in him we might become the righteousness of God.

Luke 15:1-3, 11*b*-32

[1]Now all the tax collectors and sinners were coming near to listen to him. [2]And the Pharisees and the scribes were grumbling and saying, "This fellow welcomes sinners and eats with them."

[3]So he told them this parable:

[11b] "There was a man who had two sons. [12]The younger of them said to his father, 'Father, give me the share of the property that will belong to me.' So he divided his property between them. [13]A few days later the younger son gathered all he had and traveled to a distant country, and there he squandered his property in dissolute living. [14]When he had spent everything, a severe famine took place throughout that country, and he began to be in need. [15]So he went and hired himself out to one of the citizens of that country, who sent him to his fields to feed the pigs. [16]He would gladly have filled himself with the pods that the pigs were eating; and no one gave him anything. [17]But when he came to himself he said, 'How many of my father's hired hands have bread enough and to spare, but here I am dying of hunger! [18]I will get up and go to my father, and I will say to him, "Father, I have sinned against heaven and before you; [19]I am no longer worthy to be called your son; treat me like one of your hired hands." ' [20]So he set off and went to his father. But while he was still far off, his father saw him and was filled with compassion; he ran and put his arms around him and kissed him. [21]Then the son said to him, 'Father, I have sinned against heaven and before you; I am no longer worthy to be called your son.' [22]But the father said to his slaves, 'Quickly, bring out a robe—the best one—and put it on him; put a ring on his finger and sandals on his feet. [23]And get the fatted calf and kill it, and let us eat and celebrate; [24]for this son of mine was dead and is alive again; he was lost and is found!' And they began to celebrate.

[25] "Now his elder son was in the field; and when he came and approached the house, he heard music and dancing. [26]He called one of the slaves and asked what was going on. [27]He replied, 'Your brother has come, and your father has killed the fatted calf, because he has got him back safe and sound.' [28]Then he became angry and refused to go in. His father came out and began to plead with him. [29]But he answered his father, 'Listen! For all these years I have been working like a slave for you, and I have never disobeyed your command; yet you have never given me even a young goat so that I might celebrate with my friends. [30]But when this son of yours came back, who has devoured your property with prostitutes, you killed the fatted calf for him!' [31]Then the father said to him, 'Son, you are always with me, and all that is mine is yours. [32]But we had to celebrate and rejoice, because this brother of yours was dead and has come to life; he was lost and has been found.' "

Primary Hymns and Songs for the Day

"All My Hope Is Firmly Grounded" (Josh) (O)
E665, N408, UM132, VU654 and VU655
H-3 Chr-23, 78
C88
H-3 Chr-108; Desc-79; Org-96
S-1 #338 and 341. Descants
"You Are My Hiding Place" (Pss, Luke)
C554, S2055, SF2055
"Great Is Thy Faithfulness" (Luke)
B54, C86, F98, N423, P276, R249, UM140, VU288
H-3 Chr-87; Desc-39; Org-39
S-2 #59. Piano arrangement
"This Is a Day of New Beginnings" (2 Cor, Luke) (C)
B370, C518, N417, UM383
H-3 Chr-196
"Love Divine, All Loves Excelling" (2 Cor, Luke) (C)
B208, C517, F21, N43, UM384 (PD)
H-3 Chr-134; Desc-18; Org-13
S-1 #41-42. Descant and harmonization
E657, L315, P376, R196, VU333, W588 (PD)
H-3 Hbl-46; Chr-26, 134; Desc-53; Org-56
S-1 #168-171. Various treatments

Additional Hymn Suggestions

"For the Fruits of This Creation" (Josh)
B643, C714, E424, L563, N425, P553, UM97, VU227, W562
"The King of Love My Shepherd Is" (Josh)
E645 and E646, L456, P171, R106, N248, UM138 (PD), VU273, W609
"The Trees of the Field" (Pss)
R302, S2279, SF2279, SP128, VU884
"Lord God, Your Love Has Called Us Here" (2 Cor) (O)
P353, UM579 (different tunes)
"What Wondrous Love Is This" (2 Cor)
B143 (PD), C200, E439, F283, L385, N223, P85, R277, UM292, VU147 (Fr.), W600
"Alas! And Did My Savior Bleed" (2 Cor)
B145, F274, L98, N200, P78, UM294 (PD)
B139, C204, N199, UM359 (PD)
"The Church's One Foundation" (2 Cor)
B350, C272, E525, F547, L369, N386, P442, UM545 (PD), VU332 (Fr.)
"My Song Is Love Unknown" (2 Cor)
E458, P76, VU143, W439
L94, N222, S2083, SF2083 (alternate tune)
"How Like a Gentle Spirit" (Luke)
C69, N443, UM115
"Your Love, O God" (Luke)
C71, UM120
"Come, Ye Sinners, Poor and Needy" (Luke)
B323 (PD), R141, UM340, W756
"Come Back Quickly to the Lord" (Luke)
P381, UM343
"Softly and Tenderly Jesus Is Calling" (Luke)
B312, C340, F432, N449, R147, UM348
"Cuando El Pobre" ("When the Poor Ones") (Luke)
C662, P407, UM434, VU702

"Lord of All Hopefulness" (Luke)
E482, L469, R174, S2197, SF2197, W568
"Living for Jesus" (Luke) (C)
B282, C610, F462, S2149, SF2149

Additional Contemporary Suggestions

"Holy Ground" (Josh)
B224, C112, S2272, SF2272, SP86
"Through It All" (Pss, Luke)
C555, F43, UM507
"My Life Is in You, Lord" (Pss)
S2032, SF2032, SP204
"My Redeemer Lives" (Pss, Lent)
M73
"Refresh My Heart" (2 Cor)
M49
"He Knows My Name" (Luke)
M109
"I Come to the Cross" (Luke, Lent)
M106
"Let the River Flow" (Luke)
M142
"Hungry" ("Falling on My Knees") (Luke)
M155
"I'm So Glad Jesus Lifted Me" (Luke)
C529, N474, S2151, SF2151

Vocal Solos

"So Art Thou with Me" (Luke, Lent)
V-9 p. 34
"My Shepherd Will Supply My Need"
V-10 p. 4

Anthems

"Rejoice! I Found the Lost" (Luke)
arr. Wayne L. Wold; Augsburg 11-10463
Unison or two-part with keyboard

"And the Father Will Dance" (Luke)
Mark Hayes; Hinshaw HMC637
SATB with piano

Other Suggestions

Visuals:
O Fruit, vegetable, grain, unleavened bread
P Praying hands, embracing arms, bridle/bit
E Butterfly/chrysalis, flowering bulbs, Spring flowers
G Rembrandt "Return of the Prodigal," embrace, lost/found, robe, ring, sandals, goat, calf
Affirmation of Faith: N887, UM883 (2 Cor)
Prayer: C653, UM639 or C660, UM446 (Luke)
Readings: F116 (Pss) and F673 (Luke)

Isaiah 43:16-21

16 Thus says the LORD, who makes a way in the sea, a path in the mighty waters, 17 who brings out chariot and horse, army and warrior; they lie down, they cannot rise, they are extinguished, quenched like a wick: 18 Do not remember the former things, or consider the things of old. 19 I am about to do a new thing; now it springs forth, do you not perceive it? I will make a way in the wilderness and rivers in the desert. 20 The wild animals will honor me, the jackals and the ostriches; for I give water in the wilderness, rivers in the desert, to give drink to my chosen people, 21 the people whom I formed for myself so that they might declare my praise.

Psalm 126

1 When the LORD restored the fortunes of Zion, we were like those who dream. 2 Then our mouth was filled with laughter, and our tongue with shouts of joy; then it was said among the nations, "The LORD has done great things for them." 3 The LORD has done great things for us, and we rejoiced. 4 Restore our fortunes, O LORD, like the watercourses in the Negeb. 5 May those who sow in tears reap with shouts of joy. 6 Those who go out weeping, bearing the seed for sowing, shall come home with shouts of joy, carrying their sheaves.

Philippians 3:4*b*-14

4b If anyone else has reason to be confident in the flesh, I have more: 5 circumcised on the eighth day, a member of the people of Israel, of the tribe of Benjamin, a Hebrew born of Hebrews; as to the law, a Pharisee; 6 as to zeal, a persecutor of the church; as to righteousness under the law, blameless.

7 Yet whatever gains I had, these I have come to regard as loss because of Christ. 8 More than that, I regard everything as loss because of the surpassing value of knowing Christ Jesus my Lord. For his sake I have suffered the loss of all things, and I regard them as rubbish, in order that I may gain Christ 9 and be found in him, not having a righteousness of my own that comes from the law, but one that comes through faith in Christ, the righteousness from God based on faith. 10 I want to know Christ and the power of his resurrection and the sharing of his sufferings by becoming like him in his death, 11 if somehow I may attain the resurrection from the dead.

12 Not that I have already obtained this or have already reached the goal; but I press on to make it my own, because Christ Jesus has made me his own. 13 Beloved, I do not consider that I have made it my own; but this one thing I do: forgetting what lies behind and straining forward to what lies ahead, 14 I press on toward the goal for the prize of the heavenly call of God in Christ Jesus.

John 12:1-8

1 Six days before the Passover Jesus came to Bethany, the home of Lazarus, whom he had raised from the dead. 2 There they gave a dinner for him. Martha served, and Lazarus was one of those at the table with him. 3 Mary took a pound of costly perfume made of pure nard, anointed Jesus' feet, and wiped them with her hair. The house was filled with the fragrance of the perfume. 4 But Judas Iscariot, one of his disciples (the one who was about to betray him), said, 5 "Why was this perfume not sold for three hundred denarii and the money given to the poor?" 6 (He said this not because he cared about the poor, but because he was a thief; he kept the common purse and used to steal what was put into it.) 7 Jesus said, "Leave her alone. She bought it so that she might keep it for the day of my burial. 8 You always have the poor with you, but you do not always have me."

Notes

Primary Hymns and Songs for the Day

"Sing Praise to God Who Reigns Above" (Isa) (O)
B20, C6, E408, F343, N6, P483, R52, UM126 (PD), VU216, W528
H-3 Hbl-92; Chr-173; Desc-76; Org-91
S-1 #237. Descant
"When God Restored Our Common Life" (Pss)
S2182, SF2182
H-3 Chr-139; Desc-90; Org-123
"When I Survey the Wondrous Cross" (Phil)
B144, C195, F258, N224, P101, R236, UM298 (PD)
H-3 Hbl-6, 102; Chr-213; Desc-49; Org-49
S-1 #155. Descant
"When I Survey the Wondrous Cross" (Phil)
E474, L482, P100, UM299 (PD), VU149 (Fr.), W433
H-3 Hbl-47; Chr-214; Desc-90; Org-127
S-1 #288. Transposition to E-flat major
"To Know You More" (Phil)
S2161, SF2161
"More Love to Thee, O Christ" (John) (C)
B473, C527, F476, N456, P359, UM453 (PD)
H-3 Org-94

Additional Hymn Suggestions

"Cantemos al Señor" ("Let's Sing") (Isa, Pss)
B38, C60, N39, R11, UM149
"This Is a Day of New Beginnings" (Isa, Phil)
B370, C518, N417, UM383
"Go Down, Moses" (Isa, Phil)
C663, E648, N572, P334, UM448, W508
"Hail to the Lord's Anointed" (Pss)
C140, E616 (PD), L87, N104, P205, UM203 (PD), VU30
"Come, Ye Disconsolate" (Pss)
B67, C502, SF2132, UM510 (PD)
"Joy Comes with the Dawn" (Pss)
S2210, SF2210, VU166
"The Trees of the Field" (Pss) (C)
R302, S2279, SF2279, SP128, VU884
"And Can It Be That I Should Gain" (Phil)
B147, F260, R193, UM363 (PD)
"When Our Confidence Is Shaken" (Phil)
C534, UM505
"When We All Get to Heaven" (Phil)
B514, F123, UM701 (PD)
"Guide My Feet" (Phil)
N497, P354, S2208
"Healer of Our Every Ill" (Phil)
C506, S2213, SF2213, VU619
"O How I Love Jesus" (John)
B217, C99, F634, N52, UM170 (PD)
"My Jesus, I Love Thee" (John)
B210, C349, F456, R275, UM172 (PD)
"Jesus, the Very Thought of Thee" (John)
B225, C102, F465, L316, N507, P310, UM175 (PD)
"Morning Glory, Starlit Sky" (John, Lent)
E585, UM194, W587
"Woman in the Night" (John)
C188, UM274

Additional Contemporary Suggestions

"Refresh My Heart" (Isa)
M49
"Trading My Sorrows" (Pss)
M75
"Something Beautiful" (Phil)
F656, UM394
"More Like You" (Phil)
S2167, SF2167
"Sanctuary" (Phil)
M52, R185, S2164, SF2164
"He Who Began a Good Work in You" (Phil)
S2163, SF2163, SP180, R134
"The Wonderful Cross" (Phil)
M76
"In the Secret" ("I Want to Know You") (Phil)
M38; V-3 p. 36 Vocal Solo
"Knowing You" ("All I Once Held Dear") (Phil)
M30

Vocal Solos

"For Those Tears I Died" (Isa, Lent)
V-8 p. 242
"Christ Living Within You" (Phil)
V-8 p. 177
"And Can It Be That I Should Gain" (Phil)
V-1 p. 29

Anthems

"Take My Life and Let It Be" (Phil)
Ruth W. Henderson; Gordon Thompson Music VTS-4064
SATB with keyboard

"Jesus, the Very Thought of You" (John)
arr. Jerry Gunderson; Concordia 98-3477
SSAA a cappella

Other Suggestions

Visuals:
O Sand, water, horse/chariot, wick, river, animals
P Laughter, joy, sheaves of wheat, water, baptism
E Trash can with "things," baptism, cross /black drape
G Perfume bottle, leather bag, anointing, baptism
Opening Prayer: N847 (Luke)
Call to Confession: N833 (Lent)
Prayer of Confession: N834 (Lent) or N871 (Luke)
Response: S2113, SF2113. "Lamb of God" (Lent)
Response: C299, S2277, SF2277. "Lord, Have Mercy" (Lent)
Litany: F583. God's Power in Our Weakness (Phil)
Reading: F615. The Temptation to Quit (Phil)

Luke 19:28-40 (Palms)

28 After he had said this, he went on ahead, going up to Jerusalem.

29 When he had come near Bethphage and Bethany, at the place called the Mount of Olives, he sent two of the disciples, 30 saying, "Go into the village ahead of you, and as you enter it you will find tied there a colt that has never been ridden. Untie it and bring it here. 31 If anyone asks you, 'Why are you untying it?' just say this, 'The Lord needs it.' " 32 So those who were sent departed and found it as he had told them. 33 As they were untying the colt, its owners asked them, "Why are you untying the colt?" 34 They said, "The Lord needs it." 35 Then they brought it to Jesus; and after throwing their cloaks on the colt, they set Jesus on it. 36 As he rode along, people kept spreading their cloaks on the road. 37 As he was now approaching the path down from the Mount of Olives, the whole multitude of the disciples began to praise God joyfully with a loud voice for all the deeds of power that they had seen, 38 saying, "Blessed is the king who comes in the name of the Lord! Peace in heaven, and glory in the highest heaven!" 39 Some of the Pharisees in the crowd said to him, "Teacher, order your disciples to stop." 40 He answered, "I tell you, if these were silent, the stones would shout out."

Psalm 118:1-2, 19-29 (Palms)

1 O give thanks to the LORD, for he is good; his steadfast love endures forever! 2 Let Israel say, "His steadfast love endures forever."

19 Open to me the gates of righteousness, that I may enter through them and give thanks to the LORD. 20 This is the gate of the LORD; the righteous shall enter through it. 21 I thank you that you have answered me and have become my salvation. 22 The stone that the builders rejected has become the chief cornerstone. 23 This is the LORD's doing; it is marvelous in our eyes. 24 This is the day that the LORD has made; let us rejoice and be glad in it. 25 Save us, we beseech you, O LORD! O LORD, we beseech you, give us success! 26 Blessed is the one who comes in the name of the LORD. We bless you from the house of the LORD. 27 The LORD is God, and he has given us light. Bind the festal procession with branches, up to the horns of the altar. 28 You are my God, and I will give thanks to you; you are my God, I will extol you. 29 O give thanks to the LORD, for he is good, for his steadfast love endures forever.

Isaiah 50:4-9*a* (Passion)

4 The Lord GOD has given me the tongue of a teacher, that I may know how to sustain the weary with a word. Morning by morning he wakens—wakens my ear to listen as those who are taught. 5 The Lord GOD has opened my ear, and I was not rebellious, I did not turn backward. 6 I gave my back to those who struck me, and my cheeks to those who pulled out the beard; I did not hide my face from insult and spitting. 7 The Lord GOD helps me; therefore I have not been disgraced; therefore I have set my face like flint, and I know that I shall not be put to shame; 8 he who vindicates me is near. Who will contend with me? Let us stand up together. Who are my adversaries? Let them confront me. 9a It is the Lord GOD who helps me.

Psalm 31:9-16 (Passion)

9 Be gracious to me, O LORD, for I am in distress; my eye wastes away from grief, my soul and body also. 10 For my life is spent with sorrow, and my years with sighing; my strength fails because of my misery, and my bones waste away. 11 I am the scorn of all my adversaries, a horror to my neighbors, an object of dread to my acquaintances; those who see me in the street flee from me. 12 I have passed out of mind like one who is dead; I have become like a broken vessel. 13 For I hear the whispering of many—terror all around!—as they scheme together against me, as they plot to take my life. 14 But I trust in you, O LORD; I say, "You are my God." 15 My times are in your hand; deliver me from the hand of my enemies and persecutors. 16 Let your face shine upon your servant; save me in your steadfast love.

Philippians 2:5-11

5 Let the same mind be in you that was in Christ Jesus, 6 who, though he was in the form of God, did not regard equality with God as something to be exploited, 7 but emptied himself, taking the form of a slave, being born in human likeness. And being found in human form, 8 he humbled himself and became obedient to the point of death—even death on a cross. 9 Therefore God also highly exalted him and gave him the name that is above every name, 10 so that at the name of Jesus every knee should bend, in heaven and on earth and under the earth, 11 and every tongue should confess that Jesus Christ is Lord, to the glory of God the Father.

Luke 22:14–23:56
or Luke 23:1-49

14 When the hour came, he took his place at the table, and the apostles with him. 15 He said to them, "I have eagerly desired to eat this Passover with you before I suffer; 16 for I tell you, I will not eat it until it is fulfilled in the kingdom of God." 17 Then he took a cup, and after giving thanks he said, "Take this and divide it among yourselves; 18 for I tell you that from now on I will not drink of the fruit of the vine until the kingdom of God comes." 19 Then he took a loaf of bread, and when he had given thanks, he broke it and gave it to them, saying, "This is my body, which is given for you. Do this in remembrance of me." 20 And he did the same with the cup after supper, saying, "This cup that is poured out for you is the new covenant in my blood. 21 But see, the one who betrays me is with me, and his hand is on the table. 22 For the Son of Man is going as it has been determined, but woe to that one by

whom he is betrayed!" 23Then they began to ask one
another which one of them it could be who would do this.
24A dispute also arose among them as to which one of
them was to be regarded as the greatest. 25But he said to
them, "The kings of the Gentiles lord it over them; and
those in authority over them are called benefactors. 26But
not so with you; rather the greatest among you must
become like the youngest, and the leader like one who
serves. 27For who is greater, the one who is at the table or
the one who serves? Is it not the one at the table? But I
am among you as one who serves.
28"You are those who have stood by me in my trials;
29and I confer on you, just as my Father has conferred on
me, a kingdom, 30so that you may eat and drink at my
table in my kingdom, and you will sit on thrones judging
the twelve tribes of Israel.
31"Simon, Simon, listen! Satan has demanded to sift all
of you like wheat, 32 but I have prayed for you that your
own faith may not fail; and you, when once you have
turned back, strengthen your brothers." 33And he said to
him, "Lord, I am ready to go with you to prison and to
death!" 34Jesus said, "I tell you, Peter, the cock will not
crow this day, until you have denied three times that you
know me."
35He said to them, "When I sent you out without a
purse, bag, or sandals, did you lack anything?" They said,
"No, not a thing." 36He said to them, "But now, the one
who has a purse must take it, and likewise a bag. And the
one who has no sword must sell his cloak and buy one.
37For I tell you, this scripture must be fulfilled in me, 'And
he was counted among the lawless'; and indeed what is
written about me is being fulfilled." 38They said, "Lord,
look, here are two swords." He replied, "It is enough."
39He came out and went, as was his custom, to the
Mount of Olives; and the disciples followed him. 40When
he reached the place, he said to them, "Pray that you may
not come into the time of trial." 41Then he withdrew from
them about a stone's throw, knelt down, and prayed,
42"Father, if you are willing, remove this cup from me; yet,
not my will but yours be done." 43Then an angel from
heaven appeared to him and gave him strength. 44In his
anguish he prayed more earnestly, and his sweat became
like great drops of blood falling down on the ground.
45When he got up from prayer, he came to the disciples
and found them sleeping because of grief, 46and he said
to them, "Why are you sleeping? Get up and pray that you
may not come into the time of trial."
47While he was still speaking, suddenly a crowd came,
and the one called Judas, one of the twelve, was leading
them. He approached Jesus to kiss him; 48but Jesus said to
him, "Judas, is it with a kiss that you are betraying the Son
of Man?" 49When those who were around him saw what
was coming, they asked, "Lord, should we strike with the
sword?" 50Then one of them struck the slave of the high
priest and cut off his right ear. 51But Jesus said, "No more
of this!" And he touched his ear and healed him. 52Then
Jesus said to the chief priests, the officers of the temple
police, and the elders who had come for him, "Have you
come out with swords and clubs as if I were a bandit?
53When I was with you day after day in the temple, you did
not lay hands on me. But this is your hour, and the power
of darkness!"
54Then they seized him and led him away, bringing him
into the high priest's house. But Peter was following at a
distance. 55When they had kindled a fire in the middle of
the courtyard and sat down together, Peter sat among
them. 56Then a servant-girl, seeing him in the firelight,
stared at him and said, "This man also was with him." 57But
he denied it, saying, "Woman, I do not know him." 58A little later someone else, on seeing him, said, "You also are
one of them." But Peter said, "Man, I am not!" 59Then
about an hour later still another kept insisting, "Surely this
man also was with him; for he is a Galilean." 60But Peter
said, "Man, I do not know what you are talking about!" At
that moment, while he was still speaking, the cock crowed.
61The Lord turned and looked at Peter. Then Peter
remembered the word of the Lord, how he had said to
him, "Before the cock crows today, you will deny me three
times." 62And he went out and wept bitterly.
63Now the men who were holding Jesus began to mock
him and beat him; 64they also blindfolded him and kept
asking him, "Prophesy! Who is it that struck you?" 65They
kept heaping many other insults on him.
66When day came, the assembly of the elders of the people, both chief priests and scribes, gathered together, and
they brought him to their council. 67They said, "If you are
the Messiah, tell us." He replied, "If I tell you, you will not
believe; 68and if I question you, you will not answer. 69 But
from now on the Son of Man will be seated at the right
hand of the power of God." 70All of them asked, "Are you,
then, the Son of God?" He said to them, "You say that I
am." 71Then they said, "What further testimony do we
need? We have heard it ourselves from his own lips!"
1Then the assembly rose as a body and brought Jesus
before Pilate. 2They began to accuse him, saying, "We
found this man perverting our nation, forbidding us to
pay taxes to the emperor, and saying that he himself is the
Messiah, a king." 3Then Pilate asked him, "Are you the
king of the Jews?" He answered, "You say so." 4Then Pilate
said to the chief priests and the crowds, "I find no basis
for an accusation against this man." 5But they were insis-
tent and said, "He stirs up the people by teaching
throughout all Judea, from Galilee where he began even
to this place."
6When Pilate heard this, he asked whether the man was
a Galilean. 7And when he learned that he was under
Herod's jurisdiction, he sent him off to Herod, who was
himself in Jerusalem at that time. 8 When Herod saw Jesus,

he was very glad, for he had been wanting to see him for a long time, because he had heard about him and was hoping to see him perform some sign. [9]He questioned him at some length, but Jesus gave him no answer. [10]The chief priests and the scribes stood by, vehemently accusing him. [11]Even Herod with his soldiers treated him with contempt and mocked him; then he put an elegant robe on him, and sent him back to Pilate. [12]That same day Herod and Pilate became friends with each other; before this they had been enemies.

[13]Pilate then called together the chief priests, the leaders, and the people, [14]and said to them, "You brought me this man as one who was perverting the people; and here I have examined him in your presence and have not found this man guilty of any of your charges against him. [15]Neither has Herod, for he sent him back to us. Indeed, he has done nothing to deserve death. [16]I will therefore have him flogged and release him."

[18]Then they all shouted out together, "Away with this fellow! Release Barabbas for us!" [19](This was a man who had been put in prison for an insurrection that had taken place in the city, and for murder.) [20]Pilate, wanting to release Jesus, addressed them again; [21]but they kept shouting, "Crucify, crucify him!" [22]A third time he said to them, "Why, what evil has he done? I have found in him no ground for the sentence of death; I will therefore have him flogged and then release him." [23]But they kept urgently demanding with loud shouts that he should be crucified; and their voices prevailed. [24]So Pilate gave his verdict that their demand should be granted. [25]He released the man they asked for, the one who had been put in prison for insurrection and murder, and he handed Jesus over as they wished.

[26]As they led him away, they seized a man, Simon of Cyrene, who was coming from the country, and they laid the cross on him, and made him carry it behind Jesus. [27]A great number of the people followed him, and among them were women who were beating their breasts and wailing for him. [28]But Jesus turned to them and said, "Daughters of Jerusalem, do not weep for me, but weep for yourselves and for your children. [29]For the days are surely coming when they will say, 'Blessed are the barren, and the wombs that never bore, and the breasts that never nursed.' [30]Then they will begin to say to the mountains, 'Fall on us'; and to the hills, 'Cover us.' [31]For if they do this when the wood is green, what will happen when it is dry?"

[32] Two others also, who were criminals, were led away to be put to death with him. [33]When they came to the place that is called The Skull, they crucified Jesus there with the criminals, one on his right and one on his left. [34]Then Jesus said, "Father, forgive them; for they do not know what they are doing." And they cast lots to divide his clothing. [35]And the people stood by, watching; but the leaders scoffed at him, saying, "He saved others; let him save himself if he is the Messiah of God, his chosen one!" [36]The soldiers also mocked him, coming up and offering him sour wine, [37]and saying, "If you are the King of the Jews, save yourself!" [38]There was also an inscription over him, "This is the King of the Jews."

[39]One of the criminals who were hanged there kept deriding him and saying, "Are you not the Messiah? Save yourself and us!" [40]But the other rebuked him, saying, "Do you not fear God, since you are under the same sentence of condemnation? [41]And we indeed have been condemned justly, for we are getting what we deserve for our deeds, but this man has done nothing wrong." [42]Then he said, "Jesus, remember me when you come into your kingdom." [43]He replied, "Truly I tell you, today you will be with me in Paradise."

[44]It was now about noon, and darkness came over the whole land until three in the afternoon, [45]while the sun's light failed; and the curtain of the temple was torn in two. [46]Then Jesus, crying with a loud voice, said, "Father, into your hands I commend my spirit." Having said this, he breathed his last. [47]When the centurion saw what had taken place, he praised God and said, "Certainly this man was innocent." [48]And when all the crowds who had gathered there for this spectacle saw what had taken place, they returned home, beating their breasts. [49]But all his acquaintances, including the women who had followed him from Galilee, stood at a distance, watching these things.

[50]Now there was a good and righteous man named Joseph, who, though a member of the council, [51]had not agreed to their plan and action. He came from the Jewish town of Arimathea, and he was waiting expectantly for the kingdom of God. [52]This man went to Pilate and asked for the body of Jesus. [53]Then he took it down, wrapped it in a linen cloth, and laid it in a rock-hewn tomb where no one had ever been laid. [54]It was the day of Preparation, and the sabbath was beginning. [55]The women who had come with him from Galilee followed, and they saw the tomb and how his body was laid. [56]Then they returned, and prepared spices and ointments.

On the sabbath they rested according to the commandment.

Primary Hymns and Songs for the Day

"All Glory, Laud, and Honor" (Palms Gospel) (O)
B126, C192, E154, F249, L108, N216, P88, UM280 (PD), VU122, W428
H-3 Hbl-45; Chr-22; Desc-96; Org-144
S-1 #309-310. Harmonization with descant
N217, E155, W805
"Hosanna, Loud Hosanna" (Palms Gospel)
B130, F248, N213, P89, UM278 (PD), VU123
H-3 Hbl-16, 22, 68; Chr-101; Desc-37
S-1 #115. Harmonization
"He Never Said a Mumbalin' Word" (Isa)
C208, P95 (PD), UM291, VU141
"O Sacred Head, Now Wounded" (Passion, Communion)
B137, C202, E168 or E169, F284, L116 or L117, N226, P98, R235, UM286, VU145 (Fr.), W434
H-3 Hbl-82; Chr-148; Desc-86; Org-111
"We Sang Our Glad Hosannas" (Palms/Passion)
S2111, SF2111
"My Song Is Love Unknown" (Palms/Passion) (C)
E458, P76, VU143, W439
H-3 Chr-139
L94, N222, S2083, SF2083
H-3 Chr-139, 158; Desc-90; Org-126
S-1 #284-285. Descant and harmonization

Additional Hymn Suggestions

"Tell Me the Stories of Jesus" (Palms)
B129, C190, F212, UM277 (PD), VU357
"This Is the Day the Lord Hath Made" (Pss 118)
B358 (PD), E50 (PD), P230, UM658 (PD)
"Rejoice Ye Pure in Heart" (Phil) (O)
B39, C15, E556, F394, N55, P145, UM160 (PD)
"Thou Didst Leave Thy Throne" (Phil, Passion Gospel)
B121, F170, S2100, SF2100
"What Wondrous Love Is This" (Passion)
B143 (PD), C200, E439, F283, L385, N223, P85, R277, UM292, VU147 (Fr.), W600
"Lord, Whose Love Through Humble Service" (Passion)
C461, E610, L423, P427, UM581, W630
"For the Bread Which You Have Broken" (Passion, Communion)
C411, E341, L200, P508 and P509, UM614, VU470
"The Bread of Life for All is Broken" (Passion, Communion)
E342, N333, UM633
"When Jesus Wept" (Passion Gospel)
C199, E715, P312, S2106, SF2106, VU146
"In Remembrance of Me" (Passion Gospel, Communion)
B365, C403, S2254
"Broken for Me (Passion Gospel, Communion)
S2263, SF2263
"Life-Giving Bread" (Passion Gospel, Communion)
S2261, SF2261

Additional Contemporary Suggestions

"I Will Enter His Gates" (Pss 118)
S2270, SF2270, SP168
"Forever" (Pss 118)
M68
"Sing to the King" (Palms Gospel)
M141
"Hosanna" (Palms Gospel)
R71, SP82
S2109, SF2109 (alternate tune)
"All Hail King Jesus" (Palms Gospel)
S2069, SF2069, SP63
"The King of Glory Comes" (Palms Gospel)
B127, R267, S2091, SF2091, W501
"The Power of Your Love" (Isa)
M26
"How Majestic Is Your Name" (Phil)
C63, R98, S2023, SF2023, SP14
"He Is Exalted" (Phil)
R238, S2070, SF2070, SP66
"Jesus, Name Above All Names" (Phil)
R26, SP76, S2071, SF2071
"Come, Now Is the Time to Worship" (Phil)
M56; V-3 p. 114Vocal Solo
"Lamb of God" (Passion Gospel)
S2113, SF2113
"Eat This Bread" (Passion Gospel, Communion)
C414, N788, R228, UM628, VU466, W734
"Above All" (Passion Gospel)
M77 or V-3 p. 17 Vocal Solo
"Surrender" (Passion Gospel, Holy Week)
M157

Vocal Solos

"Ride On, Jesus" (Palms Gospel)
V-7 p. 8
"The Shepherd Became a Lamb" (Palms, Passion)
V-10 p. 48

Anthems

"Ride On!" (Palms Gospel)
Taylor Davis; Choristers Guild CGA1116
SATB with piano

"Bring Palm Branches" (Palms Gospel)
Cindy Berry; Choristers Guild CGA1113
Unison/Two-part with piano

Other Suggestions

Visuals:

Palms Gospel	Palms, cloaks, colt, crowd, Jesus, stones
Ps 118	Gates, cornerstone, joy, light
O	teacher, morning, cheek/beard, spitting,
Ps 31	Grief, starvation, broken jar, whispering
E	Jesus, manacles, crucifixion, knees bent
Passion Gospel	rooster, 2 swords, pray, kiss, robe, whip

Greeting: N821 or N822 (Pss)
Canticle: C96, UM167. Song of Christ's Obedience (Phil)
Prayer: F286. If We Had Been There (Passion Gospel)

Exodus 12:1-4 (5-10), 11-14

1The LORD said to Moses and Aaron in the land of Egypt: 2This month shall mark for you the beginning of months; it shall be the first month of the year for you. 3Tell the whole congregation of Israel that on the tenth of this month they are to take a lamb for each family, a lamb for each household. 4If a household is too small for a whole lamb, it shall join its closest neighbor in obtaining one; the lamb shall be divided in proportion to the number of people who eat of it. 5Your lamb shall be without blemish, a year-old male; you may take it from the sheep or from the goats. 6You shall keep it until the fourteenth day of this month; then the whole assembled congregation of Israel shall slaughter it at twilight. 7They shall take some of the blood and put it on the two doorposts and the lintel of the houses in which they eat it. 8They shall eat the lamb that same night; they shall eat it roasted over the fire with unleavened bread and bitter herbs. 9Do not eat any of it raw or boiled in water, but roasted over the fire, with its head, legs, and inner organs. 10You shall let none of it remain until the morning; anything that remains until the morning you shall burn. 11This is how you shall eat it: your loins girded, your sandals on your feet, and your staff in your hand; and you shall eat it hurriedly. It is the passover of the LORD. 12For I will pass through the land of Egypt that night, and I will strike down every firstborn in the land of Egypt, both human beings and animals; on all the gods of Egypt I will execute judgments: I am the LORD. 13The blood shall be a sign for you on the houses where you live: when I see the blood, I will pass over you, and no plague shall destroy you when I strike the land of Egypt.

14This day shall be a day of remembrance for you. You shall celebrate it as a festival to the LORD; throughout your generations you shall observe it as a perpetual ordinance.

Psalm 116:1-4, 12-19

1I love the LORD, because he has heard my voice and my supplications. 2Because he inclined his ear to me, therefore I will call on him as long as I live. 3The snares of death encompassed me; the pangs of Sheol laid hold on me; I suffered distress and anguish. 4Then I called on the name of the LORD: "O LORD, I pray, save my life!"

12What shall I return to the LORD for all his bounty to me? 13I will lift up the cup of salvation and call on the name of the LORD, 14I will pay my vows to the LORD in the presence of all his people. 15Precious in the sight of the LORD is the death of his faithful ones. 16O LORD, I am your servant; I am your servant, the child of your serving girl. You have loosed my bonds. 17I will offer to you a thanksgiving sacrifice and call on the name of the LORD. 18I will pay my vows to the LORD in the presence of all his people, 19in the courts of the house of the LORD, in your midst, O Jerusalem. Praise the LORD!

1 Corinthians 11:23-26

23For I received from the Lord what I also handed on to you, that the Lord Jesus on the night when he was betrayed took a loaf of bread, 24 and when he had given thanks, he broke it and said, "This is my body that is for you. Do this in remembrance of me." 25In the same way he took the cup also, after supper, saying, "This cup is the new covenant in my blood. Do this, as often as you drink it, in remembrance of me." 26 For as often as you eat this bread and drink the cup, you proclaim the Lord's death until he comes.

John 13:1-17, 31*b*-35

1Now before the festival of the Passover, Jesus knew that his hour had come to depart from this world and go to the Father. Having loved his own who were in the world, he loved them to the end. 2The devil had already put it into the heart of Judas son of Simon Iscariot to betray him. And during supper 3Jesus, knowing that the Father had given all things into his hands, and that he had come from God and was going to God, 4got up from the table, took off his outer robe, and tied a towel around himself. 5Then he poured water into a basin and began to wash the disciples' feet and to wipe them with the towel that was tied around him. 6He came to Simon Peter, who said to him, "Lord, are you going to wash my feet?" 7Jesus answered, "You do not know now what I am doing, but later you will understand." 8Peter said to him, "You will never wash my feet." Jesus answered, "Unless I wash you, you have no share with me." 9Simon Peter said to him, "Lord, not my feet only but also my hands and my head!" 10Jesus said to him, "One who has bathed does not need to wash, except for the feet, but is entirely clean. And you are clean, though not all of you." 11For he knew who was to betray him; for this reason he said, "Not all of you are clean."

12After he had washed their feet, had put on his robe, and had returned to the table, he said to them, "Do you know what I have done to you? 13You call me Teacher and Lord—and you are right, for that is what I am. 14So if I, your Lord and Teacher, have washed your feet, you also ought to wash one another's feet. 15For I have set you an example, that you also should do as I have done to you. 16Very truly, I tell you, servants are not greater than their master, nor are messengers greater than the one who sent them. 17If you know these things, you are blessed if you do them.

31b"Now the Son of Man has been glorified, and God has been glorified in him. 32If God has been glorified in him, God will also glorify him in himself and will glorify him at once. 33Little children, I am with you only a little longer. You will look for me; and as I said to the Jews so now I say to you, 'Where I am going, you cannot come.' 34 I give you a new commandment, that you love one another. Just as I have loved you, you also should love one another. 35By this everyone will know that you are my disciples, if you have love for one another."

Primary Hymns and Songs for the Day

"Lord God, Your Love Has Called Us Here" (John) (O)
P353
H-3 Chr-85
UM579
S-1 #57-61. Various treatments
"Here, O My Lord, I See Thee" (Exod, Communion)
F567, UM623 (PD)
S-1 #265. Descant
P520
H-3 Hbl-97; Chr-63
C416, E318, L211, VU459
Jesu, Jesu" (John, Footwashing)
B501, C600, E602, N498, P367, R289, UM432, VU593, W431
H-3 Chr-114; Org-19
S-1 #63. Vocal part
"In Remembrance of Me" (1 Cor, Communion)
B365, C403, S2254
"Ah, Holy Jesus" (John) (C)
C210, E158, L123, N218, P93, R183, UM289 (PD), VU138
H-3 Chr-20; Desc-51
S-2 #81-85. Harmonizations
#86. Instrumental descant
"What Wondrous Love Is This" (John) (C)
B143 (PD), C200, E439, F283, L385, N223, P85, R277, UM292, VU147 (Fr.), W600
H-3 Hbl-102; Chr-212; Org-185
S-1 #347. Harmonization

Additional Hymn Suggestions

"Deep in the Shadows of the Past" (Exod)
N320, P330, S2246
"For the Bread Which You Have Broken" (1 Cor, Comm.)
C411, E341, L200, P508 and P509, UM614, VU470
E340, UM615
"Let Us Break Bread Together" (1 Cor, Communion)
B366, C425, E325 (PD), F564, L212, N330, P513, UM618, VU480, W727
"The Bread of Life for All Is Broken" (1 Cor, Communion)
E342, N333, UM633
"In the Singing" (1 Cor, Communion)
S2255, SF2255
"Broken for Me" (1 Cor, Communion)
S2263, SF2263
"Who Is He in Yonder Stall" (John)
B124, UM190 (PD)
"Jesus' Hands Were Kind Hands" (John)
B477, UM273, VU570
"Were You There" (John)
B156, C198, E172, F287, L92, N230, P102, UM288, VU144, W436
"By Gracious Powers" (John)
E695 and E696, N413, P342, UM517, W577
"We Sang Our Glad Hosannas" (John, Holy Thursday)
S2111, SF2111
"Let Us Be Bread" (John, Communion)
S2260, SF2260
"Healer of Our Every Ill" (John)
C506, S2213, SF2213, VU619
"As We Gather at Your Table" (John, Communion)
N332, S2268, SF2268, VU457

Additional Contemporary Suggestions

"We Bring the Sacrifice of Praise" (Pss)
R3, S2031, SF2031, SP1
"I Will Call Upon the Lord" (Pss)
R15, S2002, SF2002, SP224
"I Love You, Lord" (Pss)
B212, R36, S2068, SF2068, SP72
"I Stand Amazed" (Pss)
M79
"Eat This Bread" (1 Cor, Communion)
C414, N788, R228, UM628, VU466, W734
Take Our Bread" (1 Cor, Communion)
C413, UM640
"Make Me a Servant" (John)
S2176, SF2176, SP193
"Make Us One" (John)
S2224, SF2224, SP137
"They'll Know We Are Christians" (John)
C494, S2223, SF2223
"Live in Charity" ("Ubi Caritas") (John)
C523, R226, S2179, SF2179, W604
"Bind Us Together" (John)
R292, S2226, SF2226, SP140

Vocal Solos

"King of Glory, King of Peace" (Pss, Lent)
V-9 p. 24
"He Breaks the Bread, He Pours the Wine" (John, Comm.)
V-10 p. 43

Anthems

"Holy Jesus" (John)
Dana Mengel; Abingdon Press 9780687648009
SATB with piano

"Ah, Holy Jesus" (John)
arr. John Ferguson; Augsburg 11-10572
SATB with organ

Other Suggestions

Visuals:
O Lamb/blood/doorpost, sandals, staff, Exod 12:14
P Ear, snare, cup, open shackles, Ps 116:4b, 12, 13, 15
E Broken loaf, cup, 1 Cor 11:24b, 25b
G Robe, towel/basin, footwashing, disciples, love
Opening Prayer: N827 (John)
Prayer: C332. God of Wondrous Darkness (Exod)
Readings: C189, F562, F566 (2 Cor, John, Lent)

Isaiah 52:13–53:12

[13]See, my servant shall prosper; he shall be exalted and lifted up, and shall be very high. [14]Just as there were many who were astonished at him—so marred was his appearance, beyond human semblance, and his form beyond that of mortals— [15]so he shall startle many nations; kings shall shut their mouths because of him; for that which had not been told them they shall see, and that which they had not heard they shall contemplate.

[1]Who has believed what we have heard? And to whom has the arm of the LORD been revealed? [2]For he grew up before him like a young plant, and like a root out of dry ground; he had no form or majesty that we should look at him, nothing in his appearance that we should desire him. [3]He was despised and rejected by others; a man of suffering and acquainted with infirmity; and as one from whom others hide their faces he was despised, and we held him of no account. [4]Surely he has borne our infirmities and carried our diseases; yet we accounted him stricken, struck down by God, and afflicted. [5]But he was wounded for our transgressions, crushed for our iniquities; upon him was the punishment that made us whole, and by his bruises we are healed. [6]All we like sheep have gone astray; we have all turned to our own way, and the LORD has laid on him the iniquity of us all. [7]He was oppressed, and he was afflicted, yet he did not open his mouth; like a lamb that is led to the slaughter, and like a sheep that before its shearers is silent, so he did not open his mouth. [8]By a perversion of justice he was taken away. Who could have imagined his future? For he was cut off from the land of the living, stricken for the transgression of my people. [9]They made his grave with the wicked and his tomb with the rich, although he had done no violence, and there was no deceit in his mouth. [10]Yet it was the will of the LORD to crush him with pain. When you make his life an offering for sin, he shall see his offspring, and shall prolong his days; through him the will of the LORD shall prosper. [11]Out of his anguish he shall see light; he shall find satisfaction through his knowledge. The righteous one, my servant, shall make many righteous, and he shall bear their iniquities. [12]Therefore I will allot him a portion with the great, and he shall divide the spoil with the strong; because he poured out himself to death, and was numbered with the transgressors; yet he bore the sin of many, and made intercession for the transgressors.

Psalm 22

[1]My God, my God, why have you forsaken me? Why are you so far from helping me, from the words of my groaning? [2]O my God, I cry by day, but you do not answer; and by night, but find no rest. [3]Yet you are holy, enthroned on the praises of Israel. [4]In you our ancestors trusted; they trusted, and you delivered them. [5]To you they cried, and were saved; in you they trusted, and were not put to shame. [6]But I am a worm, and not human; scorned by others, and despised by the people. [7]All who see me mock at me; they make mouths at me, they shake their heads; [8]"Commit your cause to the LORD; let him deliver—let him rescue the one in whom he delights!" [9]Yet it was you who took me from the womb; you kept me safe on my mother's breast.
[10]On you I was cast from my birth, and since my mother bore me you have been my God. [11]Do not be far from me, for trouble is near and there is no one to help. [12]Many bulls encircle me, strong bulls of Bashan surround me; [13]they open wide their mouths at me, like a ravening and roaring lion. [14]I am poured out like water, and all my bones are out of joint; my heart is like wax; it is melted within my breast; [15]my mouth is dried up like a potsherd, and my tongue sticks to my jaws; you lay me in the dust of death. [16]For dogs are all around me; a company of evildoers encircles me. My hands and feet have shriveled; [17]I can count all my bones. They stare and gloat over me; [18]they divide my clothes among themselves, and for my clothing they cast lots. [19]But you, O LORD, do not be far away! O my help, come quickly to my aid! [20]Deliver my soul from the sword, my life from the power of the dog! [21]Save me from the mouth of the lion! From the horns of the wild oxen you have rescued me. [22]I will tell of your name to my brothers and sisters; in the midst of the congregation I will praise you: [23]You who fear the LORD, praise him! All you offspring of Jacob, glorify him; stand in awe of him, all you offspring of Israel! [24]For he did not despise or abhor the affliction of the afflicted; he did not hide his face from me, but heard when I cried to him. [25]From you comes my praise in the great congregation; my vows I will pay before those who fear him. [26]The poor shall eat and be satisfied; those who seek him shall praise the LORD. May your hearts live forever! [27]All the ends of the earth shall remember and turn to the LORD; and all the families of the nations shall worship before him. [28]For dominion belongs to the LORD, and he rules over the nations. [29]To him, indeed, shall all who sleep in the earth bow down; before him shall bow all who go down to the dust, and I shall live for him. [30]Posterity will serve him; future generations will be told about the Lord, [31]and proclaim his deliverance to a people yet unborn, saying that he has done it.

Hebrews 10:16-25

[16]"This is the covenant that I will make with them after those days, says the Lord: I will put my laws in their hearts, and I will write them on their minds," [17]he also adds, "I will remember their sins and their lawless deeds no more." [18]Where there is forgiveness of these, there is no longer any offering for sin.

[19]Therefore, my friends, since we have confidence to enter the sanctuary by the blood of Jesus, [20]by the new and living way that he opened for us through the curtain (that is, through his flesh), [21]and since we have a great priest

over the house of God, 22let us approach with a true heart
in full assurance of faith, with our hearts sprinkled clean
from an evil conscience and our bodies washed with pure
water. 23Let us hold fast to the confession of our hope without wavering, for he who has promised is faithful.
24And let us consider how to provoke one another to love
and good deeds, 25not neglecting to meet together, as is
the habit of some, but encouraging one another, and all
the more as you see the Day approaching.

John 18:1–19:42

1After Jesus had spoken these words, he went out with
his disciples across the Kidron valley to a place where
there was a garden, which he and his disciples entered.
2Now Judas, who betrayed him, also knew the place,
because Jesus often met there with his disciples. 3So Judas
brought a detachment of soldiers together with police
from the chief priests and the Pharisees, and they came
there with lanterns and torches and weapons. 4Then Jesus,
knowing all that was to happen to him, came forward and
asked them, "Whom are you looking for?" 5They
answered, "Jesus of Nazareth." Jesus replied, "I am he."
Judas, who betrayed him, was standing with them. 6When
Jesus said to them, "I am he," they stepped back and fell
to the ground. 7Again he asked them, "Whom are you
looking for?" And they said, "Jesus of Nazareth." 8Jesus
answered, "I told you that I am he. So if you are looking
for me, let these men go." 9This was to fulfill the word that
he had spoken, "I did not lose a single one of those whom
you gave me." 10Then Simon Peter, who had a sword, drew
it, struck the high priest's slave, and cut off his right ear.
The slave's name was Malchus. 11Jesus said to Peter, "Put
your sword back into its sheath. Am I not to drink the cup
that the Father has given me?"

12 So the soldiers, their officer, and the Jewish police
arrested Jesus and bound him. 13First they took him to
Annas, who was the father-in-law of Caiaphas, the high
priest that year. 14Caiaphas was the one who had advised
the Jews that it was better to have one person die for
the people.

15 Simon Peter and another disciple followed Jesus.
Since that disciple was known to the high priest, he went
with Jesus into the courtyard of the high priest, 16but Peter
was standing outside at the gate. So the other disciple,
who was known to the high priest, went out, spoke to the
woman who guarded the gate, and brought Peter in.
17The woman said to Peter, "You are not also one of this
man's disciples, are you?" He said, "I am not." 18Now the
slaves and the police had made a charcoal fire because it
was cold, and they were standing around it and warming
themselves. Peter also was standing with them and warming himself.

19Then the high priest questioned Jesus about his disciples and about his teaching. 20Jesus answered, "I have spoken openly to the world; I have always taught in synagogues and in the temple, where all the Jews come together. I have said nothing in secret. 21Why do you ask me? Ask
those who heard what I said to them; they know what I
said." 22When he had said this, one of the police standing
nearby struck Jesus on the face, saying, "Is that how you
answer the high priest?" 23Jesus answered, "If I have spoken wrongly, testify to the wrong. But if I have spoken
rightly, why do you strike me?" 24Then Annas sent him
bound to Caiaphas the high priest.

25Now Simon Peter was standing and warming himself.
They asked him, "You are not also one of his disciples, are
you?" He denied it and said, "I am not." 26One of the
slaves of the high priest, a relative of the man whose ear
Peter had cut off, asked, "Did I not see you in the garden
with him?" 27Again Peter denied it, and at that moment
the cock crowed.

28Then they took Jesus from Caiaphas to Pilate's headquarters. It was early in the morning. They themselves did
not enter the headquarters, so as to avoid ritual defile-
ment and to be able to eat the Passover. 29So Pilate went
out to them and said, "What accusation do you bring
against this man?" 30They answered, "If this man were not
a criminal, we would not have handed him over to you."
31Pilate said to them, "Take him yourselves and judge him
according to your law." The Jews replied, "We are not per-
mitted to put anyone to death." 32(This was to fulfill what
Jesus had said when he indicated the kind of death he was
to die.)

33Then Pilate entered the headquarters again, summoned Jesus, and asked him, "Are you the King of the
Jews?" 34Jesus answered, "Do you ask this on your own, or
did others tell you about me?" 35 Pilate replied, "I am not
a Jew, am I? Your own nation and the chief priests have
handed you over to me. What have you done?" 36 Jesus
answered, "My kingdom is not from this world. If my kingdom were from this world, my followers would be fighting
to keep me from being handed over to the Jews. But as it
is, my kingdom is not from here." 37Pilate asked him, "So
you are a king?" Jesus answered, "You say that I am a king.
For this I was born, and for this I came into the world, to
testify to the truth. Everyone who belongs to the truth listens to my voice." 38Pilate asked him, "What is truth?"

After he had said this, he went out to the Jews again and
told them, "I find no case against him. 39But you have a
custom that I release someone for you at the Passover. Do
you want me to release for you the King of the Jews?"
40They shouted in reply, "Not this man, but Barabbas!"
Now Barabbas was a bandit.

1Then Pilate took Jesus and had him flogged. 2And the
soldiers wove a crown of thorns and put it on his head,
and they dressed him in a purple robe. 3They kept coming
up to him, saying, "Hail, King of the Jews!" and striking
him on the face. 4Pilate went out again and said to them,
"Look, I am bringing him out to you to let you know that I

find no case against him." 5So Jesus came out, wearing the crown of thorns and the purple robe. Pilate said to them, "Here is the man!" 6When the chief priests and the police saw him, they shouted, "Crucify him! Crucify him!" Pilate said to them, "Take him yourselves and crucify him; I find no case against him." 7The Jews answered him, "We have a law, and according to that law he ought to die because he has claimed to be the Son of God."

8 Now when Pilate heard this, he was more afraid than ever. 9He entered his headquarters again and asked Jesus, "Where are you from?" But Jesus gave him no answer. 10Pilate therefore said to him, "Do you refuse to speak to me? Do you not know that I have power to release you, and power to crucify you?" 11Jesus answered him, "You would have no power over me unless it had been given you from above; therefore the one who handed me over to you is guilty of a greater sin." 12From then on Pilate tried to release him, but the Jews cried out, "If you release this man, you are no friend of the emperor. Everyone who claims to be a king sets himself against the emperor."

13When Pilate heard these words, he brought Jesus outside and sat on the judge's bench at a place called The Stone Pavement, or in Hebrew Gabbatha. 14Now it was the day of Preparation for the Passover; and it was about noon. He said to the Jews, "Here is your King!" 15They cried out, "Away with him! Away with him! Crucify him!" Pilate asked them, "Shall I crucify your King?" The chief priests answered, "We have no king but the emperor." 16Then he handed him over to them to be crucified.

So they took Jesus; 17and carrying the cross by himself, he went out to what is called The Place of the Skull, which in Hebrew is called Golgotha. 18There they crucified him, and with him two others, one on either side, with Jesus between them. 19Pilate also had an inscription written and put on the cross. It read, "Jesus of Nazareth, the King of the Jews." 20Many of the Jews read this inscription, because the place where Jesus was crucified was near the city; and it was written in Hebrew, in Latin, and in Greek. 21Then the chief priests of the Jews said to Pilate, "Do not write, 'The King of the Jews,' but, 'This man said, I am King of the Jews.' " 22Pilate answered, "What I have written I have written." 23When the soldiers had crucified Jesus, they took his clothes and divided them into four parts, one for each soldier. They also took his tunic; now the tunic was seamless, woven in one piece from the top. 24So they said to one another, "Let us not tear it, but cast lots for it to see who will get it." This was to fulfill what the scripture says, "They divided my clothes among themselves, and for my clothing they cast lots." 25And that is what the soldiers did.

Meanwhile, standing near the cross of Jesus were his mother, and his mother's sister, Mary the wife of Clopas, and Mary Magdalene. 26When Jesus saw his mother and the disciple whom he loved standing beside her, he said to his mother, "Woman, here is your son." 27Then he said to the disciple, "Here is your mother." And from that hour the disciple took her into his own home.

28After this, when Jesus knew that all was now finished, he said (in order to fulfill the scripture), "I am thirsty." 29A jar full of sour wine was standing there. So they put a sponge full of the wine on a branch of hyssop and held it to his mouth. 30When Jesus had received the wine, he said, "It is finished." Then he bowed his head and gave up his spirit.

31Since it was the day of Preparation, the Jews did not want the bodies left on the cross during the sabbath, especially because that sabbath was a day of great solemnity. So they asked Pilate to have the legs of the crucified men broken and the bodies removed. 32Then the soldiers came and broke the legs of the first and of the other who had been crucified with him. 33But when they came to Jesus and saw that he was already dead, they did not break his legs. 34Instead, one of the soldiers pierced his side with a spear, and at once blood and water came out. 35(He who saw this has testified so that you also may believe. His testimony is true, and he knows that he tells the truth.) 36These things occurred so that the scripture might be fulfilled, "None of his bones shall be broken." 37And again another passage of scripture says, "They will look on the one whom they have pierced."

38After these things, Joseph of Arimathea, who was a disciple of Jesus, though a secret one because of his fear of the Jews, asked Pilate to let him take away the body of Jesus. Pilate gave him permission; so he came and removed his body. 39Nicodemus, who had at first come to Jesus by night, also came, bringing a mixture of myrrh and aloes, weighing about a hundred pounds. 40They took the body of Jesus and wrapped it with the spices in linen cloths, according to the burial custom of the Jews. 41Now there was a garden in the place where he was crucified, and in the garden there was a new tomb in which no one had ever been laid. 42And so, because it was the Jewish day of Preparation, and the tomb was nearby, they laid Jesus there.

Notes

Primary Hymns and Songs for the Day

"Ah, Holy Jesus" (John) (O)
C210, E158, L123, N218, P93, R183, UM289 (PD), VU138
H-3 Chr-20; Desc-51
S-2 #81-86. Harmonizations & Descant

"Go to Dark Gethsemane" (John) (O)
C196, E171, F281, L109, N219, P97, UM290 (PD), VU133
H-3 Hbl-18; Chr-74; Desc-89; Org-121
S-2 #150. Harmonization

"Alas! And Did My Savior Bleed" (Isa, John)
B145, F274, L98, N200, P78, UM294 (PD)
H-3 Chr-21
B139, C204, N199, UM359 (PD)

"Why Stand So Far Away, My God?" (Pss)
C671, S2180, SF2180
H-3 Chr-139, 145; Desc-77
S-1 #241-242. Orff arrangement and descant

"Were You There" (John)
B156, C198, E172, F287, L92, N230, P102, UM288, VU144, W436

"We Sang Our Glad Hosannas" (John, Good Friday) (C)
S2111, SF2111

"When Jesus Wept" (John)
C199, E715, P312, S2106, SF2106, VU146

"Why Has God Forsaken Me?" (Good Friday)
P406, S2110, VU154

"Living for Jesus" (John)
B282, C610, F462, S2149, SF2149

Additional Hymn Suggestions

"Hallelujah! What a Savior" (Isa)
B175, F246, UM165 (PD)

"He Never Said a Mumbalin' Word" (Isa)
C208, P95 (PD), UM291, VU141

"I Am Thine, O Lord" (Heb)
B290, C601, F455, N455, UM419 (PD)

"Near to the Heart of God" (Heb)
B295, C581, F35, P527, UM472 (PD)

"Since Jesus Came into My Heart" (Heb)
B441, F639, S2140, SF2140

"Victim Divine" (Heb, John)
L202, S2259, SF2259

"O Love, How Deep" (John)
E449, L88, N209, P83, UM267 (PD), VU348

"Woman in the Night" (John)
C188, UM274

"'Tis Finished! The Messiah Dies" (John)
B148, UM282 (PD)

"To Mock Your Reign, O Dearest Lord" (John)
E170, UM285

"O Sacred Head, Now Wounded" (John)
B137, C202, E168 or E169, F284, L116 or L117, N226, P98, R235, UM286, VU145 (Fr.), W434

"When I Survey the Wondrous Cross" (John)
B144, C195, F258, N224, P101, R236, UM298 (PD)

"And Can It Be That I Should Gain" (John)
B147, F260, R193, UM363 (PD)

"The Bread of Life for All Is Broken" (John, Communion)
E342, N333, UM633

"My Song Is Love Unknown" (Good Friday)
E458, L94, N222, P76, S2083, SF2083, VU143, W439

"Thou Didst Leave Thy Throne" (John)
B121, F170, S2100, SF2100

"Swiftly Pass the Clouds of Glory" (John)
P73, S2102

Additional Contemporary Suggestions

"Our God Reigns" (Isa)
SP64

"Jesus, Remember Me" (John)
C569, P599, R227, UM488, VU148, W423

"Jesus, We Crown You with Praise" (John, Good Friday)
M24

"Above All" (John, Good Friday)
M77; V-3 p. 17 p. 18 Vocal Solo

"The Wonderful Cross" (John, Good Friday)
M76

"There Is a Redeemer" (Good Friday)
R232, SP111

"Amazing Love" (Good Friday)
R272, M81

Vocal Solos

"Were You There?" (John, Good Friday)
V-7 p. 60

"O Love Divine, What hast Thou Done!" (John)
V-1 p. 17

Anthems

"The Earth Did Tremble" (John)
Peter Niedmann; Augsburg 11-10922
SATB with organ

"Go to Dark Gethsemane" (John)
Hal H. Hopson; GIA G-2169
SATB a cappella

Other Suggestions

Visuals: Cross draped in black, altar stripped
O Crucifixion, root, Isa 53:3, lamb, shears, grave, light
P Worm, mock, nursing child, spilled water, melted wax, dice
E Open Bible, heart, crucifixion, water, Heb 10:23a
G Torch, sword, fire, cock crowing, robe, INRI, wine, branch, spear, linen cloth, tomb

Call and Prayer of Confession: N833, N834 (Good Friday)
Words of Assurance: N841 (Good Friday)
Prayer: F257 or UM284 (Good Friday, John)
Prayer: C332. God of Wondrous Darkness (John)
Litany: C201 or F286 (John)
Readings: F245, F272, F356, UM293 (Isa, John)
Prayer: N859. Thankfulness and Hope (Pss)

Acts 10:34-43

[34]Then Peter began to speak to them: “I truly understand that God shows no partiality, [35]but in every nation anyone who fears him and does what is right is acceptable to him. [36]You know the message he sent to the people of Israel, preaching peace by Jesus Christ—he is Lord of all. [37]That message spread throughout Judea, beginning in Galilee after the baptism that John announced: [38]how God anointed Jesus of Nazareth with the Holy Spirit and with power; how he went about doing good and healing all who were oppressed by the devil, for God was with him. [39]We are witnesses to all that he did both in Judea and in Jerusalem. They put him to death by hanging him on a tree; [40]but God raised him on the third day and allowed him to appear, [41]not to all the people but to us who were chosen by God as witnesses, and who ate and drank with him after he rose from the dead. [42]He commanded us to preach to the people and to testify that he is the one ordained by God as judge of the living and the dead. [43]All the prophets testify about him that everyone who believes in him receives forgiveness of sins through his name.”

Psalm 118:1-2, 14-24

[1]O give thanks to the LORD, for he is good; his steadfast love endures forever! [2]Let Israel say, “His steadfast love endures forever.”

[14]The LORD is my strength and my might; he has become my salvation. [15]There are glad songs of victory in the tents of the righteous: “The right hand of the LORD does valiantly; [16]the right hand of the LORD is exalted; the right hand of the LORD does valiantly.” [17]I shall not die, but I shall live, and recount the deeds of the LORD. [18]The LORD has punished me severely, but he did not give me over to death. [19]Open to me the gates of righteousness, that I may enter through them and give thanks to the LORD. [20]This is the gate of the LORD; the righteous shall enter through it. [21]I thank you that you have answered me and have become my salvation. [22]The stone that the builders rejected has become the chief cornerstone. [23]This is the LORD’s doing; it is marvelous in our eyes. [24]This is the day that the LORD has made; let us rejoice and be glad in it.

1 Corinthians 15:19-26

[19]If for this life only we have hoped in Christ, we are of all people most to be pitied.

[20]But in fact Christ has been raised from the dead, the first fruits of those who have died. [21]For since death came through a human being, the resurrection of the dead has also come through a human being; [22]for as all die in Adam, so all will be made alive in Christ. [23]But each in his own order: Christ the first fruits, then at his coming those who belong to Christ. [24]Then comes the end, when he hands over the kingdom to God the Father, after he has destroyed every ruler and every authority and power. [25]For he must reign until he has put all his enemies under his feet. [26]The last enemy to be destroyed is death.

John 20:1-18 (or Luke 24:1-12)

[1]Early on the first day of the week, while it was still dark, Mary Magdalene came to the tomb and saw that the stone had been removed from the tomb. [2] So she ran and went to Simon Peter and the other disciple, the one whom Jesus loved, and said to them, “They have taken the Lord out of the tomb, and we do not know where they have laid him.” [3]Then Peter and the other disciple set out and went toward the tomb. [4]The two were running together, but the other disciple outran Peter and reached the tomb first. [5]He bent down to look in and saw the linen wrappings lying there, but he did not go in. [6]Then Simon Peter came, following him, and went into the tomb. He saw the linen wrappings lying there, [7]and the cloth that had been on Jesus’ head, not lying with the linen wrappings but rolled up in a place by itself. [8]Then the other disciple, who reached the tomb first, also went in, and he saw and believed; [9]for as yet they did not understand the scripture, that he must rise from the dead. [10]Then the disciples returned to their homes.

[11]But Mary stood weeping outside the tomb. As she wept, she bent over to look into the tomb; [12]and she saw two angels in white, sitting where the body of Jesus had been lying, one at the head and the other at the feet. [13]They said to her, “Woman, why are you weeping?” She said to them, “They have taken away my Lord, and I do not know where they have laid him.” [14]When she had said this, she turned around and saw Jesus standing there, but she did not know that it was Jesus. [15]Jesus said to her, “Woman, why are you weeping? Whom are you looking for?” Supposing him to be the gardener, she said to him, “Sir, if you have carried him away, tell me where you have laid him, and I will take him away.” [16]Jesus said to her, “Mary!” She turned and said to him in Hebrew, “Rabbouni!” (which means Teacher). [17]Jesus said to her, “Do not hold on to me, because I have not yet ascended to the Father. But go to my brothers and say to them, ‘I am ascending to my Father and your Father, to my God and your God.’ ” [18]Mary Magdalene went and announced to the disciples, “I have seen the Lord”; and she told them that he had said these things to her.

Notes

Primary Hymns and Songs for the Day

"Christ the Lord Is Risen Today" (John, Luke) (O)
B159, C216, F289, N233, UM302 (PD), VU155 and VU157,
E207, F297, L151, P123, W442 (PD)
C216 Descant
H-3 Hbl-8, 51; Chr-49; Desc-31; Org-32
S-1 #104-108. Various treatments
"Hail the Day That Sees Him Rise" (1 Cor, John)
E214, UM312, W471 (PD)
H-3 Hbl-72; Chr-50; Desc-69; Org-78
S-1 #213-214. Transposition with descant
B165, N260, VU189
"The Day of Resurrection" (John, Luke) (C)
E210, VU164
H-3 Hbl-16, 22, 68; Chr-101; Desc-37
S-1 #115. Harmonization
B164, C228, N245, P118, UM303 (PD)
H-3 Hbl-74; Chr-123; Desc-64; Org-71
S-1 #9-197. Various treatments

Additional Hymn Suggestions

"At the Font We Start Our Journey" (Acts, Baptism)
N308, S2114, SF2114
"We Meet You, O Christ" (Acts)
C183, P311, UM257, VU183
"Christ Jesus Lay in Death's Strong Bands" (Acts, John)
E186, L134, P110, UM319 (PD)
"Stand Up and Bless the Lord" (Pss)
B30, P491, UM662 (PD)
"Come, Let Us with Our Lord Arise" (Pss, Easter)
E49, R18, S2084, SF2084
"Thine Be the Glory" (1 Cor, John)
B163, C218, F291, L145, N253, P122, UM308, VU173
"Now the Green Blade Riseth" (John, Luke)
C230, E204, L148, N238, UM311, VU186, W453
"In the Garden" (John, Luke)
B187, C227, F588, N237, UM314
"Come, Ye Faithful, Raise the Strain" (John, Luke)
C215, E199, N230, P115, UM315 (PD)
E200, L132, P114 (PD), VU165, W456
"O Sons and Daughters, Let Us Sing" (John)
C220, E203, L139, N244, P116 (PD), UM317, VU170, W447
"Up from the Grave He Arose" (John)
B160, C224, UM322 (PD)
"Hail Thee, Festival Day" (John, Luke)
E175, L142, N262, UM324, VU163, W444
"You Alone Are Holy" ("Solo Tu Eres Santo") (Easter)
S2077, SF2077
"Faith Is Patience in the Night" (Easter)
S2211, SF2211
"Walk with Me" (John)
S2242, SF2242, VU649
"Christ is Alive" (John, Luke)
B173, E182, L363, P108, R300, UM318, VU158

Additional Contemporary Suggestions

"Holy and Anointed One" (Acts)
M32
"Alleluia" (Pss, 1 Cor, Easter)
S2043, SF2043
"I Will Enter His Gates" (Pss)
S2270, SF2270, SP168
"Forever" (Pss)
M68
"Hallelujah" ("Your Love Is Amazing") (Pss)
M118
"You Are My All in All" (Pss, Easter)
SP220
"Lord, I Lift Your Name on High" (1 Cor Easter)
M2, R4, S2088, SF2088
"Christ the Lord Is Risen" (1 Cor, Easter)
S2116, SF2116
"Above All" (John)
M77; V-3 p. 17 Vocal Solo
"In Christ Alone" ("My Hope Is Found") Easter)
M138
"Holy, Holy" (Easter)
B254, F149, P140, R206, S2039, SP141
"Sing Alleluia to the Lord" (Easter, Communion)
B214, C32, S2258, SF2258, R202, SP93

Vocal Solos

"Jesus Christ is Risen Today" (Easter)
V-1 p. 50
"Crown Him, the Risen King"
V-10 p. 55

Anthems

"Christ the Lord is Risen Today!" (John)
Mark L. Williams; Hinshaw HMC1651
SATB with organ and brass

"An Easter Song of Praise" (Easter)
Arr. A. Steven Taranto; Choristers Guild CGA1115
Unison/Two-part with piano

Other Suggestions

Visuals: Flowers, butterfly, peacock
Acts Risen Christ, cross draped in white, all nations
P Right hand, gates, cornerstone, Pss 118:1a, b, 17 or 24
E Resurrection, fruit, empty tomb
G Stone, running feet, shroud, rolled napkin, weep/joy
Greeting: N821 or N822 (Pss)
Canticle: C217. The Easter Affirmations (1 Cor)
Prayers: F294, UM320, or UM360 (1 Cor, Easter)
Response: B120, F208, N51, P308, UM179 (PD), stanza 4.
"O Sing a Song of Bethlehem" (Acts)
Blessing: N872 (John, Easter)

Acts 5:27-32

[27]When they had brought them, they had them stand before the council. The high priest questioned them, [28] saying, "We gave you strict orders not to teach in this name, yet here you have filled Jerusalem with your teaching and you are determined to bring this man's blood on us." [29]But Peter and the apostles answered, "We must obey God rather than any human authority. [30]The God of our ancestors raised up Jesus, whom you had killed by hanging him on a tree. [31]God exalted him at his right hand as Leader and Savior that he might give repentance to Israel and forgiveness of sins. [32]And we are witnesses to these things, and so is the Holy Spirit whom God has given to those who obey him."

Psalm 150

[1]Praise the Lord! Praise God in his sanctuary; praise him in his mighty firmament! [2]Praise him for his mighty deeds; praise him according to his surpassing greatness! [3]Praise him with trumpet sound; praise him with lute and harp! [4]Praise him with tambourine and dance; praise him with strings and pipe! [5]Praise him with clanging cymbals; praise him with loud clashing cymbals! [6]Let everything that breathes praise the Lord! Praise the Lord!

Revelation 1:4-8

[4]John to the seven churches that are in Asia:

Grace to you and peace from him who is and who was and who is to come, and from the seven spirits who are before his throne, [5]and from Jesus Christ, the faithful witness, the firstborn of the dead, and the ruler of the kings of the earth.

To him who loves us and freed us from our sins by his blood, [6]and made us to be a kingdom, priests serving his God and Father, to him be glory and dominion forever and ever. Amen. [7]Look! He is coming with the clouds; every eye will see him, even those who pierced him; and on his account all the tribes of the earth will wail. So it is to be. Amen.

[8]"I am the Alpha and the Omega," says the Lord God, who is and who was and who is to come, the Almighty.

John 20:19-31

[19]When it was evening on that day, the first day of the week, and the doors of the house where the disciples had met were locked for fear of the Jews, Jesus came and stood among them and said, "Peace be with you." [20]After he said this, he showed them his hands and his side. Then the disciples rejoiced when they saw the Lord. [21]Jesus said to them again, "Peace be with you. As the Father has sent me, so I send you." [22]When he had said this, he breathed on them and said to them, "Receive the Holy Spirit. [23]If you forgive the sins of any, they are forgiven them; if you retain the sins of any, they are retained."

[24]But Thomas (who was called the Twin), one of the twelve, was not with them when Jesus came. [25]So the other disciples told him, "We have seen the Lord." But he said to them, "Unless I see the mark of the nails in his hands, and put my finger in the mark of the nails and my hand in his side, I will not believe."

[26]A week later his disciples were again in the house, and Thomas was with them. Although the doors were shut, Jesus came and stood among them and said, "Peace be with you." [27]Then he said to Thomas, "Put your finger here and see my hands. Reach out your hand and put it in my side. Do not doubt but believe." [28]Thomas answered him, "My Lord and my God!" [29]Jesus said to him, "Have you believed because you have seen me? Blessed are those who have not seen and yet have come to believe."

[30]Now Jesus did many other signs in the presence of his disciples, which are not written in this book. [31]But these are written so that you may come to believe that Jesus is the Messiah, the Son of God, and that through believing you may have life in his name.

Notes

Primary Hymns and Songs for the Day

"Come, Ye Faithful, Raise the Strain" (Acts, John)
C215, E199, N230, P115, UM315 (PD)
H-3 Hbl-53; Chr-57; Desc-94; Org-141
S-2 #161. Descant
L132, VU165, W456
"Praise to the Lord, the Almighty" (Pss) (O)
B14 (PD), C25, E390, F337, L543, N22, P482, R57, UM139, VU220 (Fr.) and VU221, W547
H-3 Hbl-89; Chr-163; Desc-69; Org-79
S-1 #218-222. Various treatments
"The Head That Once Was Crowned" (Acts)
E483, L173, P149, UM326 (PD), VU190, W464
H-3 Chr-187, 207; Desc-95; Org-142
S-1 #305. Descant
"Praise Ye the Lord" (Pss)
P258, S2010
"We Walk by Faith" (John)
N256, P399, W572
H-3 Chr-67
S2196, SF2196
H-3 Chr-21
E209
"Without Seeing You" (John)
S2206, SF2206

Additional Hymn Suggestions

"We Meet You, O Christ" (Acts, John)
C183, P311, UM257, VU183
"Let All Things Now Living" (Pss)
B640, C717, F389, L557, P554, R48, S2008, VU242, W559
"Praise to the Lord, the Almighty" (Pss)
B14 (PD), C25, E390, F337, L543, N22, P482, R57, UM139, VU220 (Fr.) and VU221, W547
"Lo, He Comes with Clouds Descending" (Rev)
B199, F306
E57, L27, P6, UM718 (PD), VU25 (alternate tune)
"Love Divine, All Loves Excelling" (Rev)
B208, C517, F21, N43, UM384 (PD)
E657, L315, P376, R196, VU333, W588 (PD)
"Thine Be the Glory" (John)
B163, C218, F291, L145, N253, P122, UM308, VU173
"O Sons and Daughters, Let Us Sing" (John, Easter)
C220, E203, L139, N244, P116 (PD), UM317, VU170, W447
"Breathe on Me, Breath of God" (John)
B241, C254, E508, F161, L488, N292, P316, UM420 (PD), VU382 (Fr.), W725
"Holy Spirit, Truth Divine" (John)
C241, L257, N63, P321, UM465 (PD), VU368
"Come Down, O Love Divine" (John)
C582, E516, L508, N289, P313, UM475 (PD), VU367, W472
"Spirit of God, Descend Upon My Heart" (John)
B245, C265, F147, L486, N290, P326, UM500 (PD), VU378
"When Our Confidence Is Shaken" (John)
C534, UM505
"O Breath of Life" (John)
C250, UM543, VU202
"Christ Has Risen" (John, Easter)
S2115, SF2115

Additional Contemporary Suggestions

"He Is Exalted" (Acts)
R238, S2070, SF2070, SP66
"Jesus, Draw Me Close" (Acts)
S2159, SF2159, M48
"Let Everything That Has Breath" (Pss)
M59
"Turn Your Eyes upon Jesus" (Rev, John)
B320, F621, SP218, UM349
"We Will Glorify" (Rev)
B213, S2087, SF2087, SP68
"Soon and Very Soon" (Rev)
B192, R276, UM706; S-2 #187
"Jesus Is Alive" (Rev, Easter)
M20
"Surely the Presence of the Lord" (Rev)
C263, R167, SP243, UM328; S-2, #200 Stanzas for soloist
"Open Our Eyes, Lord" (John)
B499, R91, S2086, SF2086, SP199

Vocal Solos

"My Father's Heart" (Pss)
V-3 p. 134
"Sing a Song of Joy" (Pss)
V-4 p. 2

Anthems

"Jubilate" (Pss)
Carolee R. Curtright; Choristers Guild CGA582
Two-part with keyboard

"Sound the Trumpet" (Easter)
Mark Patterson; Choristers Guild CGA1117
Two-part with keyboard and opt. trumpet

Other Suggestions

Visuals:
Acts Cross draped in white
P Musical instruments, dancing
E Alpha/Omega, clouds, art-Christ descending, 7 flames
G Risen Christ, Holy Spirit, nails, kneel, closed door
Greeting: N823 (Pss) or N824 (Rev) or F350 (John)
Opening Prayer: N831 (John)
Prayer: UM335 or F146. The Holy Spirit (John)
Prayer: C9. Church Musicians' Prayer (Pss)

Acts 9:1-6 (7-20)

1Meanwhile Saul, still breathing threats and murder against the disciples of the Lord, went to the high priest 2and asked him for letters to the synagogues at Damascus, so that if he found any who belonged to the Way, men or women, he might bring them bound to Jerusalem. 3Now as he was going along and approaching Damascus, suddenly a light from heaven flashed around him. 4He fell to the ground and heard a voice saying to him, "Saul, Saul, why do you persecute me?" 5He asked, "Who are you, Lord?" The reply came, "I am Jesus, whom you are persecuting.
6But get up and enter the city, and you will be told what you are to do." 7The men who were traveling with him stood speechless because they heard the voice but saw no one. 8Saul got up from the ground, and though his eyes were open, he could see nothing; so they led him by the hand and brought him into Damascus. 9For three days he was without sight, and neither ate nor drank.

10Now there was a disciple in Damascus named Ananias. The Lord said to him in a vision, "Ananias." He answered, "Here I am, Lord." 11The Lord said to him, "Get up and go to the street called Straight, and at the house of Judas look for a man of Tarsus named Saul. At this moment he is praying, 12and he has seen in a vision a man named Ananias come in and lay his hands on him so that he might regain his sight." 13But Ananias answered, "Lord, I have heard from many about this man, how much evil he has done to your saints in Jerusalem; 14and here he has authority from the chief priests to bind all who invoke your name." 15But the Lord said to him, "Go, for he is an instrument whom I have chosen to bring my name before Gentiles and kings and before the people of Israel; 16I myself will show him how much he must suffer for the sake of my name." 17So Ananias went and entered the house. He laid his hands on Saul and said, "Brother Saul, the Lord Jesus, who appeared to you on your way here, has sent me so that you may regain your sight and be filled with the Holy Spirit." 18And immediately something like scales fell from his eyes, and his sight was restored. Then he got up and was baptized, 19and after taking some food, he regained his strength.

For several days he was with the disciples in Damascus, 20and immediately he began to proclaim Jesus in the synagogues, saying, "He is the Son of God."

Psalm 30

1I will extol you, O LORD, for you have drawn me up, and did not let my foes rejoice over me. 2O LORD my God, I cried to you for help, and you have healed me. 3O LORD, you brought up my soul from Sheol, restored me to life from among those gone down to the Pit. 4Sing praises to the LORD, O you his faithful ones, and give thanks to his holy name. 5For his anger is but for a moment; his favor is for a lifetime. Weeping may linger for the night, but joy comes with the morning. 6As for me, I said in my prosperity, "I shall never be moved." 7By your favor, O LORD, you had established me as a strong mountain; you hid your face; I was dismayed. 8To you, O LORD, I cried, and to the LORD I made supplication:
9"What profit is there in my death, if I go down to the Pit? Will the dust praise you? Will it tell of your faithfulness? 10Hear, O LORD, and be gracious to me! O LORD, be my helper!" 11You have turned my mourning into dancing; you have taken off my sackcloth and clothed me with joy, 12so that my soul may praise you and not be silent. O LORD my God, I will give thanks to you forever.

Revelation 5:11-14

11Then I looked, and I heard the voice of many angels surrounding the throne and the living creatures and the elders; they numbered myriads of myriads and thousands of thousands,
12singing with full voice, "Worthy is the Lamb that was slaughtered to receive power and wealth and wisdom and might and honor and glory and blessing!" 13Then I heard every creature in heaven and on earth and under the earth and in the sea, and all that is in them, singing, "To the one seated on the throne and to the Lamb be blessing and honor and glory and might forever and ever!" 14And the four living creatures said, "Amen!" And the elders fell down and worshiped.

John 21:1-19

1After these things Jesus showed himself again to the disciples by the Sea of Tiberias; and he showed himself in this way.
2Gathered there together were Simon Peter, Thomas called the Twin, Nathanael of Cana in Galilee, the sons of Zebedee, and two others of his disciples. 3Simon Peter said to them, "I am going fishing." They said to him, "We will go with you." They went out and got into the boat, but that night they caught nothing.

4Just after daybreak, Jesus stood on the beach; but the disciples did not know that it was Jesus. 5Jesus said to them, "Children, you have no fish, have you?" They answered him, "No." 6He said to them, "Cast the net to the right side of the boat, and you will find some." So they cast it, and now they were not able to haul it in because there were so many fish. 7That disciple whom Jesus loved said to Peter, "It is the Lord!" When Simon Peter heard that it was the Lord, he put on some clothes, for he was naked, and jumped into the sea. 8But the other disciples came in the boat, dragging the net full of fish, for they were not far from the land, only about a hundred yards off.

9When they had gone ashore, they saw a charcoal fire there, with fish on it, and bread. 10Jesus said to them, "Bring some of the fish that you have just caught." 11So Simon Peter went aboard and hauled the net ashore, full of large fish, a hundred fifty-three of them; and though there were so many, the net was not torn.
12Jesus said to them, "Come and have breakfast." Now none of the disciples dared to ask him, "Who are you?" because they knew it was the Lord. 13Jesus came and took the bread and gave it to them, and did the same with the fish. 14This was now the third time that Jesus appeared to the disciples after he was raised from the dead.

15When they had finished breakfast, Jesus said to Simon Peter, "Simon son of John, do you love me more than these?" He said to him, "Yes, Lord; you know that I love you." Jesus said to him, "Feed my lambs." 16A second time he said to him, "Simon son of John, do you love me?" He said to him, "Yes, Lord; you know that I love you." Jesus said to him, "Tend my sheep." 17He said to him the third time, "Simon son of John, do you love me?" Peter felt hurt because he said to him the third time, "Do you love me?" And he said to him, "Lord, you know everything; you know that I love you." Jesus said to him, "Feed my sheep. 18Very truly, I tell you, when you were younger, you used to fasten your own belt and to go wherever you wished. But when you grow old, you will stretch out your hands, and someone else will fasten a belt around you and take you where you do not wish to go." 19(He said this to indicate the kind of death by which he would glorify God.) After this he said to him, "Follow me."

Primary Hymns and Songs for the Day

"Christ, Whose Glory Fills the Skies" (Acts, John) (O)
E7, L265, P462, UM173 (PD), VU336
H-3 Hbl-51; Chr-206; Desc-89; Org-120
S-1 #278-279. Harmonizations
"Ye Servants of God" (Rev) (O)
B589, VU342
H-3 Hbl-85; Chr-154; Desc-71; Org-82
S-1 #223-226. Various treatments
C110, F360, N305, P477, UM181 (PD)
C110 Descant
H-3 Hbl-90, 105; Chr-221; Desc-49; Org-51
S-2 #71-74. Introduction and harmonizations
"Amazing Grace" (Acts, Pss)
B330, C546, E671, F107, L448, N547 and N548, P280, R189, UM378 (PD), VU266 (Fr.), W583
H-3 Hbl-14, 46; Chr-27; Desc-14; Org-4
S-2 #5-7. Various treatments
"Open Our Eyes, Lord" (Acts)
B499, R91, S2086, SF2086, SP199
"Joy Comes with the Dawn" (Pss, John)
S2210, SF2210, VU166
"More Love to Thee, O Christ" (John) (C)
B473, C527, F476, N456, P359, UM453 (PD)
H-3 Org-94

Additional Hymn Suggestions

"It Is Well with My Soul" (Acts, Pss)
B410, C561, F495, L346, N438, UM377 (PD)
"And Can It Be That I Should Gain" (Acts)
B147, F260, R193, UM363 (PD)
"Come, Ye Disconsolate" (Acts, Pss)
B67, C502, SF2132, UM510 (PD)
"Baptized in Water" (Acts, Baptism)
B362, E294, P492, S2248, SF2248, W720
"All Hail the Power of Jesus' Name" (Rev) (O)
B202, C91, E450, F325, L328, N304, P142, R45, UM154 (PD), W494
B200, C92, F326, P143, UM155 (PD)
B201, E451, F327, L329 (PD), VU334
"Holy God, We Praise Thy Name" (Rev)
E366 (PD), F385, L535, N276, P460, UM79, VU894 (Fr.), W524
"This Is the Feast of Victory" (Rev, Communion)
E417, P594, R199, UM638, VU904, W458
"My Lord, What a Morning" (Rev)
C708, P449, UM719, VU708
"Christ Is Risen" (John, Communion)
C222, P104, UM307
"Lord, You Have Come to the Lakeshore" (John)
C342, N173, P377, UM344, VU563
"Jesu, Jesu" (John)
B501, C600, E602, N498, P367, R289, UM432, VU593, W431
"In Remembrance of Me" (John, Communion)
B365, C403, S2254

Additional Contemporary Suggestions

"Nobody Fills My Heart Like Jesus" (Acts)
M8
"Word of God, Speak" (Acts, John)
M148
"Trading My Sorrows" (Pss)
M75
"Great Is the Lord" (Rev)
B12, R22, S2022, SF2022, SP30
"Blessing, Honor and Glory" (Rev)
M21, R81
"Most Holy Lord" (Rev)
M44
"All Heaven Declares" (Rev)
M58, R163
"Praise Adonai" (Rev)
M125
"Spirit Song" (John)
C352, R248, SP134, UM347
"Take Our Bread" (John, Communion)
C413, UM640
"Father, I Adore You" (John)
B256, F414, S2038, SF2038, SP194
"Cry of My Heart" (John)
S2165, SF2165, M39

Vocal Solos

"Look What You've Done" (Acts)
V-3 p. 122
"Worthy Is the Lamb" (Rev)
V-8 p. 228

Anthems

"Loving Shepherd of Thy Sheep" (John)
John Rutter; Hinshaw HMC 1192
SATB a cappella

"Feed My Lambs" (John)
Natalie Sleeth; Carl Fischer CM7777
Unison with keyboard and 2 flutes

Other Suggestions

Visuals:
Acts Light, blindfold, healing hand, Acts 9:4c or 10c
P Joy, singing, dancing, sackcloth, Ps 30:5c or 11a
E Lamb, praise, angel choir, four creatures
G Fish, bread, lamb, sheep, fire, boat, net, fish, ICTHUS
Introit: L214, R197, UM625. "Come, Let Us Eat" (John)
Greeting: N819 (Pss) or N821 (Rev) or N825 (Rev)
Canticle: N735. "Canticle to the Lamb" (Rev)
Readings: C89, F506, or F508 (John)
Prayer: C89. Christ Comes as One Unknown (John)
Blessing: N872 (John, Easter) or N874 (John)

Acts 9:36-43

[36]Now in Joppa there was a disciple whose name was Tabitha, which in Greek is Dorcas. She was devoted to good works and acts of charity. [37]At that time she became ill and died. When they had washed her, they laid her in a room upstairs. [38]Since Lydda was near Joppa, the disciples, who heard that Peter was there, sent two men to him with the request, "Please come to us without delay." [39]So Peter got up and went with them; and when he arrived, they took him to the room upstairs. All the widows stood beside him, weeping and showing tunics and other clothing that Dorcas had made while she was with them. [40]Peter put all of them outside, and then he knelt down and prayed. He turned to the body and said, "Tabitha, get up." Then she opened her eyes, and seeing Peter, she sat up. [41]He gave her his hand and helped her up. Then calling the saints and widows, he showed her to be alive. [42]This became known throughout Joppa, and many believed in the Lord. [43]Meanwhile he stayed in Joppa for some time with a certain Simon, a tanner.

Psalm 23

[1]The LORD is my shepherd, I shall not want. [2]He makes me lie down in green pastures; he leads me beside still waters; [3]he restores my soul. He leads me in right paths for his name's sake. [4]Even though I walk through the darkest valley, I fear no evil; for you are with me; your rod and your staff—they comfort me. [5]You prepare a table before me in the presence of my enemies; you anoint my head with oil; my cup overflows. [6]Surely goodness and mercy shall follow me all the days of my life, and I shall dwell in the house of the LORD my whole life long.

Revelation 7:9-17

[9]After this I looked, and there was a great multitude that no one could count, from every nation, from all tribes and peoples and languages, standing before the throne and before the Lamb, robed in white, with palm branches in their hands. [10]They cried out in a loud voice, saying, "Salvation belongs to our God who is seated on the throne, and to the Lamb!" [11]And all the angels stood around the throne and around the elders and the four living creatures, and they fell on their faces before the throne and worshiped God, [12]singing, "Amen! Blessing and glory and wisdom and thanksgiving and honor and power and might be to our God forever and ever! Amen."

[13]Then one of the elders addressed me, saying, "Who are these, robed in white, and where have they come from?" [14]I said to him, "Sir, you are the one that knows." Then he said to me, "These are they who have come out of the great ordeal; they have washed their robes and made them white in the blood of the Lamb. [15]For this reason they are before the throne of God, and worship him day and night within his temple, and the one who is seated on the throne will shelter them. [16]They will hunger no more, and thirst no more; the sun will not strike them, nor any scorching heat; [17]for the Lamb at the center of the throne will be their shepherd, and he will guide them to springs of the water of life, and God will wipe away every tear from their eyes."

John 10:22-30

[22]At that time the festival of the Dedication took place in Jerusalem. It was winter, [23]and Jesus was walking in the temple, in the portico of Solomon. [24]So the Jews gathered around him and said to him, "How long will you keep us in suspense? If you are the Messiah, tell us plainly." [25]Jesus answered, "I have told you, and you do not believe. The works that I do in my Father's name testify to me; [26]but you do not believe, because you do not belong to my sheep. [27]My sheep hear my voice. I know them, and they follow me. [28]I give them eternal life, and they will never perish. No one will snatch them out of my hand. [29]What my Father has given me is greater than all else, and no one can snatch it out of the Father's hand. [30]The Father and I are one."

Notes

Primary Hymns and Songs for the Day

"Come We That Love the Lord" (Rev) (O)
B525
H-3 Chr-71; Desc-39; Org-39
S-1 #129. Descant
E392, W552
H-3 Chr-166; Desc-102
N379, UM732, VU715
H-3 Chr-106, 167; Desc-97; Org-147
S-1 #311. Descant and harmonization
"Precious Lord, Take My Hand" (Acts, Pss)
B456, C628, F611, N472, P404, UM474, VU670
H-3 Chr-164; Org-116
"The Lord's My Shepherd, I'll Not Want" (Pss, John)
C79, F42, L451, N479, VU748
H-3 Chr-75, 188
F40, C78, P170, UM136, VU747
H-3 Hbl-96; Chr-188, 189; Desc-24; Org-21
"Lamb of God" (Pss, Rev, John)
S2113, SF2113
"Awesome God" (Rev)
R245, S2040, SF2040, SP11
"Savior, Like a Shepherd Lead Us" (Pss, John) (C)
B61, C558, F601, N252, P387, UM381 (PD)
H-3 Chr-167; Org-15
S-2 #29. Harmonization
E708
H-3 Chr-75, 116, 130; Desc-98; Org-151
L481
"Marching to Zion" (Rev) (C)
B524, C707, F550, N382, UM733 (PD), VU714
H-3 Chr-298

Additional Hymn Suggestions

"Send Me, Lord" (Acts., Pss)
C447, N360, R308, UM497, VU572
"He Leadeth Me: O Blessed Thought" (Pss)
B52, C545, F606, L501, UM128 (PD), VU657
"The King of Love My Shepherd Is" (Pss)
E645 and E646, L456, P171, R106, N248, UM138 (PD), VU273, W609
"Close to Thee" (Pss, John)
B464, F405, UM407 (PD)
"Jesus Walked This Lonesome Valley" (Pss)
C211, F217, P80, S2112, W427
"Without Seeing You" (Pss)
S2206, SF2206
"Lead Me, Guide Me" (Pss)
C583, R176, S2214, SF2214
"Maker, in Whom We Live" (Rev) (O)
UM88 (PD), VU321
"Ye Watchers and Ye Holy Ones" (Rev)
E618, L175, P451, UM90, W707
"Majesty, Worship His Majesty" (Rev)
B215, R63, SP73, UM176
"This Is the Feast of Victory" (Rev, Communion)
E417, P594, R199, UM638, VU904, W458
"Jesus, the Very Thought of Thee" (John)
B225, C102, F465, L316, N507, P310, UM175 (PD)

Additional Contemporary Suggestions

"You Are Good" (Pss)
M124
"Enough" (Pss, Rev)
M160
"Holy Ground" (Rev)
B224, C112, S2272, SF2272, SP86
"Blessing, Honor and Glory" (Rev, Easter)
M21, R81
"Hallelujah to the Lamb" (Rev, Easter)
M23
"White as Snow" (Rev)
M35
"All Who Are Thirsty" (Rev)
M159
"Healing Rain" (Rev)
M161
"He Reigns" (Rev)
M168
"My Tribute" ("To God Be the Glory") (Rev, John)
B153, C39, F365, N14, R68, UM99; V-8 p. 5 Vocal Solo
"Fill My Cup, Lord" (Rev, Communion)
C351, F481, UM641; S-2 stanzas for soloist

Vocal Solos

"God, Our Ever Faithful Shepherd" (Pss)
V-4 p. 15
"My Shepherd Will Supply My Need" (Pss)
V-10 p. 4

Anthems

"The King of Love My Shepherd Is" (Ps)
Laura and Russell Farnell; Kjos 9059
SATB with piano, opt. cello

"When I Can Read My Title Clear" (Rev)
Arr. Gregory M Pysh; Kjos 9058
SATB, instrument, and keyboard

Other Suggestions

Visuals:
Acts Shroud, basin/water, sewing, praying hands, touching
P Shepherd crook, pasture, water, path, shadow, table/oil
E White robe/palms, angels, Lamb, water, wiped tears
G Winter, Jesus, sheep, John 10:27
Greeting: N821 (Rev) or F350 (Pss)
Readings: B1, F25, or UM137 (Pss) and F666 (Rev)
Prayers: UM321 (Easter) and N852 or UM460 (Pss)
Responsive Prayer: C81. Knee-bowed and Body-bent (Pss)
Words of Assurance: N840 (Pss)

PLANNING NOTES

DO YOU HAVE THE BOOK YOU NEED?

We want you to have the best planner, designed to meet your specific needs. How do you know if you have the right resource? Simply complete this one-question quiz:

Do you lead worship in a United Methodist congregation?

☐ YES. Use *The United Methodist Music and Worship Planner, 2009–2010* (ISBN: 9780687649464) ➡

☐ NO. Use *Prepare! A Weekly Worship Planbook for Pastors and Musicians, 2009–2010* (ISBN: 9780687649365) ⬇

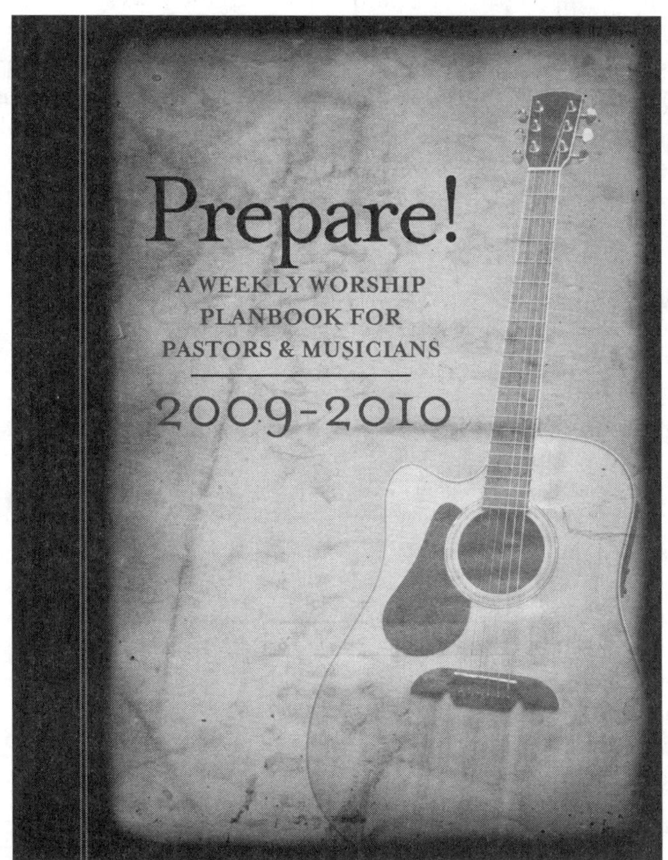

To order these resources, call Cokesbury Music Service toll-free at 1-877-877-8674, visit your local Cokesbury store, or shop online at www.cokesbury.com.

Do you find yourself rushing at the last minute to order your new planner? Subscribe today and receive your new *The United Methodist Music and Worship Planner* or *Prepare!* automatically next year and every year.

Call toll-free 1-800-672-1789 to request subscription.

Acts 11:1-18

[1]Now the apostles and the believers who were in Judea heard that the Gentiles had also accepted the word of God. [2] So when Peter went up to Jerusalem, the circumcised believers criticized him, [3]saying, "Why did you go to uncircumcised men and eat with them?" [4]Then Peter began to explain it to them, step by step, saying, [5]"I was in the city of Joppa praying, and in a trance I saw a vision. There was something like a large sheet coming down from heaven, being lowered by its four corners; and it came close to me. [6]As I looked at it closely I saw four-footed animals, beasts of prey, reptiles, and birds of the air. [7]I also heard a voice saying to me, 'Get up, Peter; kill and eat.' [8]But I replied, 'By no means, Lord; for nothing profane or unclean has ever entered my mouth.' [9]But a second time the voice answered from heaven, 'What God has made clean, you must not call profane.' [10]This happened three times; then everything was pulled up again to heaven. [11]At that very moment three men, sent to me from Caesarea, arrived at the house where we were. [12]The Spirit told me to go with them and not to make a distinction between them and us. These six brothers also accompanied me, and we entered the man's house. [13]He told us how he had seen the angel standing in his house and saying, 'Send to Joppa and bring Simon, who is called Peter; [14]he will give you a message by which you and your entire household will be saved.' [15]And as I began to speak, the Holy Spirit fell upon them just as it had upon us at the beginning. [16]And I remembered the word of the Lord, how he had said, 'John baptized with water, but you will be baptized with the Holy Spirit.' [17]If then God gave them the same gift that he gave us when we believed in the Lord Jesus Christ, who was I that I could hinder God?" [18]When they heard this, they were silenced. And they praised God, saying, "Then God has given even to the Gentiles the repentance that leads to life."

Psalm 148

[1]Praise the LORD! Praise the LORD from the heavens; praise him in the heights [2]Praise him, all his angels; praise him, all his host! [3]Praise him, sun and moon; praise him, all you shining stars! [4]Praise him, you highest heavens, and you waters above the heavens! [5]Let them praise the name of the LORD, for he commanded and they were created. [6]He established them forever and ever; he fixed their bounds, which cannot be passed. [7]Praise the LORD from the earth, you sea monsters and all deeps, [8]fire and hail, snow and frost, stormy wind fulfilling his command! [9] Mountains and all hills, fruit trees and all cedars! [10]Wild animals and all cattle, creeping things and flying birds! [11]Kings of the earth and all peoples, princes and all rulers of the earth! [12]Young men and women alike, old and young together! [13]Let them praise the name of the LORD, for his name alone is exalted; his glory is above earth and heaven. [14]He has raised up a horn for his people, praise for all his faithful, for the people of Israel who are close to him. Praise the LORD!

Revelation 21:1-6

[1]Then I saw a new heaven and a new earth; for the first heaven and the first earth had passed away, and the sea was no more. [2]And I saw the holy city, the new Jerusalem, coming down out of heaven from God, prepared as a bride adorned for her husband. [3]And I heard a loud voice from the throne saying, "See, the home of God is among mortals. He will dwell with them; they will be his peoples, and God himself will be with them; [4]he will wipe every tear from their eyes. Death will be no more; mourning and crying and pain will be no more, for the first things have passed away."

And the one who was seated on the throne said, "See, I am making all things new." Also he said, "Write this, for these words are trustworthy and true." [6]Then he said to me, "It is done! I am the Alpha and the Omega, the beginning and the end. To the thirsty I will give water as a gift from the spring of the water of life."

John 13:31-35

[31]When he had gone out, Jesus said, "Now the Son of Man has been glorified, and God has been glorified in him. [32]If God has been glorified in him, God will also glorify him in himself and will glorify him at once. [33]Little children, I am with you only a little longer. You will look for me; and as I said to the Jews so now I say to you, 'Where I am going, you cannot come.' [34]I give you a new commandment, that you love one another. Just as I have loved you, you also should love one another. [35]By this everyone will know that you are my disciples, if you have love for one another."

Notes

Primary Hymns and Songs for the Day

"All Creatures of Our God and King" (Pss, Communion) (O)
B27, C22, E400, F347, L527, N17, P455, R47, UM62, VU217 (Fr.), W520
H-3 Hbl-44; Chr-21; Desc-66; Org-73
S-1 #198-204. Various treatments

"Let All Things Now Living" (Pss) (O)
B640, C717, F389, L557, P554, R48, S2008, VU242, W559
C717 Descant
H-3 Chr-125; Org-9
S-1 #327. Descant

"O Holy City, Seen of John" (Rev)
E583, N613, P453, UM726, VU709
H-3 Chr-139, 145; Desc-77
S-1 #241-242. Orff arr. and descant

"O What Their Joy and Their Glory Must Be" (Rev)
E623, L337, N385, UM727 (PD)
H-3 Hbl-49; Chr-132; Desc-83; Org-103
S-1 #255. Harmonization and descant

"They'll Know We Are Christians" (John)
C494, S2223, SF2223

"In Christ There Is No East or West" (Acts) (C)
B385, C687, F685, N394, P439
H-3 Hbl-71; Chr-111-112; Desc-95; Org-143
S-2 #162. Harmonization
E529, L359, N394, P440, UM548, VU606, W659
H-3 Chr-111; Desc-74; Org-88
S-1 #231-233. Various treatments

"Love Divine, All Loves Excelling" (Acts, Rev, John) (C)
B208, C517, F21, N43, UM384 (PD)
H-3 Chr-134; Desc-18; Org-13
S-1 #41-42. Descant and harmonization
E657, L315, P376, R196, VU333, W588 (PD)
H-3 Hbl-46; Chr-26, 134; Desc-53; Org-56
S-1 #168-171. Various treatments

Additional Hymn Suggestions

"How Great Thou Art" (Pss)
B10, C33, F2, L532, N35, P467, R250, UM77, VU238 (Fr.)

"Spirit of the Living God" (Acts)
B244, C259, F155, N283, P322, R90, SP131, UM393, VU376

"Here, O Lord, Your Servants Gather" (Acts, Communion)
B179, C278, N72, P465, UM552, VU362 (Fr.)

"Help Us Accept Each Other" (Acts, John)
C487, UM560, P358, N388, W656 (different tunes)

"Sing a New Song to the Lord" (Pss)
S2045, SF2045, W550

"This Is a Day of New Beginnings" (Rev, Communion)
B370, C518, N417, UM383

"For the Healing of the Nations" (Rev)
C668, N576, UM428, VU678, W643

"O Love That Wilt Not Let Me Go" (Rev)
B292, C540, F404, L324, N485, P384, UM480 (PD), VU658

"Glorious Things of Thee Are Spoken" (Rev)
B398, C709, E522 (or 523), F376, L358, N307, P446, UM731 (PD)

"Blessed Quietness" (Rev)
F145, C267, N284, S2142, SF2142

"Jesus Loves Me" (John)
B344 (PD), C113, F226, N327, P304, UM191, VU365

"The Gift of Love" (John)
B423, C526, P335, R155, UM408, VU372

Additional Contemporary Suggestions

"Spirit Song" (Acts, Rev)
C352, R248, SP134, UM347

"Make Us One" (Acts, John)
S2224, SF2224, SP137

"God of Wonders" (Pss)
M80; V-3 p. 184 Vocal Solo

"Let Everything That Has Breath" (Pss)
M59

"Holy and Anointed One" (Rev, Easter, John)
M32

"All Who Are Thirsty" (Rev)
M159

"We Will Glorify" (Rev, John)
B213, S2087, SF2087, SP68

"Spirit Song" (Rev)
C352, R248, SP134, UM347

"Bind Us Together" (John)
R292, S2226, SF2226, SP140

"Live in Charity" ("Ubi Caritas") (John)
C523, R226, S2179, SF2179, W604

Vocal Solos

"All Creatures of Our God and King" (Pss)
V-6 p. 55

"This Is My Commandment" (John)
V-8 p. 284

Anthems

"Come and Sing!" (Pss)
Steve McManaman; Kjos 6341
SSA with opt. piano and percussion

"This Is My Commandment" (John)
Steve Sandberg; Kjos 9041
SATB a cappella

Other Suggestions

Visuals:
Acts Sheet, animals, baptism, Holy Spirit, rebirth
P Creation, sun/moon/stars, angels, nature, all ages, praise
E Newness, marriage, home, unity, water, A&O, baptism
G Newness, love, John 13:34a, b

Greeting: N824 (Pss)
Prayer: C682. God's Love for All People (Acts)

Acts 16:9-15

9During the night Paul had a vision: there stood a man
of Macedonia pleading with him and saying, "Come over
to Macedonia and help us." 10When he had seen the
vision, we immediately tried to cross over to Macedonia,
being convinced that God had called us to proclaim the
good news to them.

11We set sail from Troas and took a straight course to
Samothrace, the following day to Neapolis, 12and from
there to Philippi, which is a leading city of the district of
Macedonia and a Roman colony. We remained in this city
for some days. 13On the sabbath day we went outside the
gate by the river, where we supposed there was a place of
prayer; and we sat down and spoke to the women who
had gathered there. 14A certain woman named Lydia, a
worshiper of God, was listening to us; she was from the
city of Thyatira and a dealer in purple cloth. The Lord
opened her heart to listen eagerly to what was said by
Paul. 15When she and her household were baptized, she
urged us, saying, "If you have judged me to be faithful to
the Lord, come and stay at my home." And she prevailed
upon us.

Psalm 67

1May God be gracious to us and bless us and make his
face to shine upon us, 2that your way may be known upon
earth, your saving power among all nations. 3Let the peoples praise you, O God; let all the peoples praise you. 4Let
the nations be glad and sing for joy, for you judge the
peoples with equity and guide the nations upon earth.
5Let the peoples praise you, O God; let all the peoples
praise you. 6The earth has yielded its increase; God, our
God, has blessed us. 7May God continue to bless us; let all
the ends of the earth revere him.

Revelation 21:1-10, 22–22:5

1Then I saw a new heaven and a new earth; for the first
heaven and the first earth had passed away, and the sea
was no more. 2And I saw the holy city, the new Jerusalem,
coming down out of heaven from God, prepared as a
bride adorned for her husband. 3And I heard a loud voice
from the throne saying, "See, the home of God is among
mortals. He will dwell with them; they will be his peoples,
and God himself will be with them; 4he will wipe every
tear from their eyes. Death will be no more; mourning
and crying and pain will be no more, for the first things
have passed away."

5And the one who was seated on the throne said, "See, I
am making all things new." Also he said, "Write this, for
these words are trustworthy and true." 6Then he said to
me, "It is done! I am the Alpha and the Omega, the
beginning and the end. To the thirsty I will give water as a
gift from the spring of the water of life. 7Those who con-
quer will inherit these things, and I will be their God and
they will be my children. 8But as for the cowardly, the
faithless, the polluted, the murderers, the fornicators, the
sorcerers, the idolaters, and all liars, their place will be in
the lake that burns with fire and sulfur, which is the second death."

9Then one of the seven angels who had the seven bowls
full of the seven last plagues came and said to me, "Come,
I will show you the bride, the wife of the Lamb." 10And in
the spirit he carried me away to a great, high mountain
and showed me the holy city Jerusalem coming down out
of heaven from God.

22I saw no temple in the city, for its temple is the Lord
God the Almighty and the Lamb. 23And the city has no
need of sun or moon to shine on it, for the glory of God
is its light, and its lamp is the Lamb. 24The nations will
walk by its light, and the kings of the earth will bring their
glory into it. 25Its gates will never be shut by day—and
there will be no night there. 26People will bring into it the
glory and the honor of the nations. 27But nothing unclean
will enter it, nor anyone who practices abomination or
falsehood, but only those who are written in the Lamb's
book of life.

1Then the angel showed me the river of the water of
life, bright as crystal, flowing from the throne of God and
of the Lamb 2through the middle of the street of the city.
On either side of the river is the tree of life with its twelve
kinds of fruit, producing its fruit each month; and the
leaves of the tree are for the healing of the nations.
3Nothing accursed will be found there any more. But the
throne of God and of the Lamb will be in it, and his servants will worship him; 4they will see his face, and his
name will be on their foreheads. 5And there will be no
more night; they need no light of lamp or sun, for the
Lord God will be their light, and they will reign forever
and ever.

John 14:23-29

23 Jesus answered him, "Those who love me will keep my
word, and my Father will love them, and we will come to
them and make our home with them. 24 Whoever does
not love me does not keep my words; and the word that
you hear is not mine, but is from the Father who sent me.

25 "I have said these things to you while I am still with
you. 26 But the Advocate, the Holy Spirit, whom the
Father will send in my name, will teach you everything,
and remind you of all that I have said to you. 27 Peace I
leave with you; my peace I give to you. I do not give to you
as the world gives. Do not let your hearts be troubled, and
do not let them be afraid. 28 You heard me say to you, 'I
am going away, and I am coming to you.' If you loved me,
you would rejoice that I am going to the Father, because
the Father is greater than I. 29 And now I have told you
this before it occurs, so that when it does occur, you
may believe."

Primary Hymns and Songs for the Day

"Holy God, We Praise Thy Name" (Pss) (O)
E366 (PD), F385, L535, N276, P460, UM79, VU894 (Fr.), W524
H-3 Chr-78, 98; Desc-48; Org-48
S-1 #151-153. Harmonization and descants
"Immortal, Invisible, God Only Wise" (Rev) (O)
B6, C66, E423, F319, L526, N1, P263, R46, UM103 (PD), VU264, W512
H-3 Hbl-15, 71; Chr-65; Desc-93; Org-135
S-1 #300. Harmonization
"For the Healing of the Nations" (Rev)
C668, UM428
H-3 Hbl-25, 51, 58; Chr-89; Desc-26; Org-23
S-1 #76-77. Descant and harmonization
N576, VU678
H-3 Chr-49; Desc-103; Org-180
S-1 #346. Descant
"Now It Is Evening" (John, Evening)
C471, S2187, SF2187
"You Are Mine" (John)
S2218, SF2218
"Shall We Gather at the River" (Acts, Rev) (C)
B518, C701, N597, UM723 (PD), VU710
H-3 Chr-169

Additional Hymn Suggestions

"The Church of Christ, in Every Age" (Acts, John)
B402, C475, L433, N306, P421, UM589, VU601, W626
"Guide Me, O Thou Great Jehovah" (Rev) (O)
B56, C622, E690, F608, L343, N18 and N19, P281, UM127 (PD), VU651 (Fr.)
"I Love Thy Kingdom, Lord" (Rev)
B354, C274, E524, F545, L368, N312, P441, UM540
"Come, Thou Fount of Every Blessing" (Rev)
B15, C16, E686, F318, L499, N459, P356, UM400 (PD), VU559
"Blessed Quietness" (Rev)
F145, C267, N284, S2142, SF2142
"Just a Closer Walk with Thee" (Rev)
B448, C557, F591, S2158, SF2158
"We've a Story to Tell to the Nations" (Rev) (C)
B586, C484, F659, UM569 (PD)
"There's Within My Heart a Melody" (John)
B425, C550, UM380 (PD)
"The Gift of Love" (John)
B423, C526, P335, R155, UM408, VU372
"Happy the Home When God Is There" (John, Christian Home)
B505, F540, UM445
"Our Parent, by Whose Name" (John, Christian Home)
E587, L357, UM447, VU555, W570
"Come Down, O Love Divine" (John)
C582, E516, L508, N289, P313, UM475 (PD), VU367, W472
"Where Charity and Love Prevail" (John)
E581, L126, N396, UM549
"Your Love, O God, Has Called Us Here" (John)
B509, E353, N361, UM647
"Healer of Our Every Ill" (John)
C506, S2213, SF2213, VU619

Additional Contemporary Suggestions

"Shine, Jesus, Shine" (Rev)
B579, R247, S2173, SF2173, SP142
"Turn Your Eyes upon Jesus" (Rev)
B320, F621, SP218, UM349
"There's Something about That Name" (Rev)
B177, C115, F227, R26, SP89, UM171
"Soon and Very Soon" (Rev)
B192, R276, UM706; S-2 #187
"Spirit Song" (Rev, John)
C352, R248, SP134, UM347
"Blessing, Honor and Glory" (Rev, Easter)
M21, R81
"Who Can Satisfy My Soul Like You?" (Rev)
M28
"I Could Sing of Your Love Forever" (Rev)
M63; V-3 p. 22 Vocal Solo
"Did You Feel the Mountains Tremble?" (Rev)
M69; V-3 p. 140 Vocal Solo
"Offering" (Rev)
M130
"Holy Spirit, Rain Down" (John)
M88
"Dwell" (John)
M154

Vocal Solo

"Praise to the Lord, the Almighty" (Pss)
V-6 p. 18

Anthems

"You Are the Hands" (Christian Home)
Bailey and Mayo; Choristers Guild CGA1121
Unison/Two-part with piano

"No Greater Love" John
Michael Joncas; GIA G-3141
SATB with organ

Other Suggestions

Visuals:
Acts Purple cloth, women witnessing, ship/sails, open/closed door
P Thanksgiving, first garden fruit, rogation
E Light/lamp, nations, open gates, sing, Lamb, book, water
G Love, Word, Trinity, Spirit, John 14:27, briefcase, lamp, heart
Prayer: N818 (Rev) or N853 (John)
Canticle: C702. "All Things New" (Rev)
Blessing: F593. Take His Peace (John)

Acts 1:1-11

[1]In the first book, Theophilus, I wrote about all that Jesus did and taught from the beginning [2]until the day when he was taken up to heaven, after giving instructions through the Holy Spirit to the apostles whom he had chosen. [3]After his suffering he presented himself alive to them by many convincing proofs, appearing to them during forty days and speaking about the kingdom of God. [4]While staying with them, he ordered them not to leave Jerusalem, but to wait there for the promise of the Father. "This," he said, "is what you have heard from me; [5]for John baptized with water, but you will be baptized with the Holy Spirit not many days from now."

[6]So when they had come together, they asked him, "Lord, is this the time when you will restore the kingdom to Israel?" [7]He replied, "It is not for you to know the times or periods that the Father has set by his own authority. [8]But you will receive power when the Holy Spirit has come upon you; and you will be my witnesses in Jerusalem, in all Judea and Samaria, and to the ends of the earth." [9]When he had said this, as they were watching, he was lifted up, and a cloud took him out of their sight. [10]While he was going and they were gazing up toward heaven, suddenly two men in white robes stood by them. [11]They said, "Men of Galilee, why do you stand looking up toward heaven? This Jesus, who has been taken up from you into heaven, will come in the same way as you saw him go into heaven."

Psalm 47

[1]Clap your hands, all you peoples; shout to God with loud songs of joy. [2]For the LORD, the Most High, is awesome, a great king over all the earth. [3]He subdued peoples under us, and nations under our feet. [4]He chose our heritage for us, the pride of Jacob whom he loves. [5]God has gone up with a shout, the LORD with the sound of a trumpet. [6]Sing praises to God, sing praises; sing praises to our King, sing praises. [7]For God is the king of all the earth; sing praises with a psalm. [8]God is king over the nations; God sits on his holy throne. [9]The princes of the peoples gather as the people of the God of Abraham. For the shields of the earth belong to God; he is highly exalted.

Ephesians 1:15-23

[15]I have heard of your faith in the Lord Jesus and your love toward all the saints, and for this reason [16]I do not cease to give thanks for you as I remember you in my prayers. [17]I pray that the God of our Lord Jesus Christ, the Father of glory, may give you a spirit of wisdom and revelation as you come to know him, [18]so that, with the eyes of your heart enlightened, you may know what is the hope to which he has called you, what are the riches of his glorious inheritance among the saints, [19]and what is the immeasurable greatness of his power for us who believe, according to the working of his great power. [20]God put this power to work in Christ when he raised him from the dead and seated him at his right hand in the heavenly places, [21]far above all rule and authority and power and dominion, and above every name that is named, not only in this age but also in the age to come. [22]And he has put all things under his feet and has made him the head over all things for the church, [23]which is his body, the fullness of him who fills all in all.

Luke 24:44-53

[44]Then he said to them, "These are my words that I spoke to you while I was still with you—that everything written about me in the law of Moses, the prophets, and the psalms must be fulfilled." [45]Then he opened their minds to understand the scriptures, [46]and he said to them, "Thus it is written, that the Messiah is to suffer and to rise from the dead on the third day, [47]and that repentance and forgiveness of sins is to be proclaimed in his name to all nations, beginning from Jerusalem. [48]You are witnesses of these things. [49]And see, I am sending upon you what my Father promised; so stay here in the city until you have been clothed with power from on high."

[50]Then he led them out as far as Bethany, and, lifting up his hands, he blessed them. [51]While he was blessing them, he withdrew from them and was carried up into heaven. [52]And they worshiped him, and returned to Jerusalem with great joy; [53]and they were continually in the temple blessing God.

Notes

Primary Hymns and Songs for the Day
"Hail the Day That Sees Him Rise" (Acts) (O)
E214, UM312, W471 (PD)
H-3 Hbl-72; Chr-50; Desc-69; Org-78
S-1 #213-214. Transposition with descant
B165, N260, VU189
"Shout to the Lord" (Pss)
S2074, SF2074, M16; V-3 p. 56 Vocal Solo
"Christ Is Made the Sure Foundation" (Eph)
C275, E518, P416, UM559 (PD), VU325, W617
H-3 Chr-49; Desc-103; Org-180
S-1 #346. Descant
F557, N400, P417
H-3 Chr-30, 48, 62; Desc-89; Org-121
S-1 #280. Descant and harmonization
L367, B356 (PD)
"Open Our Eyes, Lord" (Eph)
B499, R91, S2086, SF2086, SP199
"Love Divine, All Loves Excelling" (Luke) (C)
B208, C517, F21, N43, UM384 (PD)
H-3 Chr-134; Desc-18; Org-13
S-1 #41-42. Descant and harmonization
E657, L315, P376, R196, VU333, W588 (PD)
H-3 Hbl-46; Chr-26, 134; Desc-53; Org-56
S-1 #168-171. Various treatments

Additional Hymn Suggestions
"All Hail the Power of Jesus' Name" (Acts) (O)
B202, C91, E450, F325, L328, N304, P142, R45, UM154 (PD), W494
B200, C92, F326, P143, UM155 (PD) (alternate tune)
B201, E451, F327, L329 (PD), VU334 (alternate tune)
"Hail Thee, Festival Day" (Acts, Luke) (O)
E216, L142, N262, P120, UM324, VU163
"Cristo Vive" ("Christ is Risen") (Acts, Luke)
B167, N235, P109, UM313
"Christ Jesus Lay in Death's Strong Bands" (Acts)
E186, L134, P110, UM319 (PD)
"Jesus Shall Reign" (Pss, Eph)
B587, C95, E544, F238, L530, N157, P423, R296, UM157 (PD), VU330, W492
"The Head That Once Was Crowned" (Pss, Eph)
E483, L173, P149, UM326 (PD), VU190, W464
"Crown Him with Many Crowns" (Pss, Eph, Luke)
B161, C234, E494, F345, L170, N301, P151, R56, UM327 (PD), VU211
"Hope of the World" (Eph)
E472, C538, L493, N46, P360, UM178, VU215, W565
"My Hope Is Built" (Eph)
B406, C537, F92, L293 and L294 (PD), N368, P379, UM368 (PD)
"For All the Saints" (Eph)
B355, C637, E287, F614, L174, N299, P526, UM711 (PD), VU705, W705
"Come, Let Us with Our Lord Arise" (Luke)
E49, R18, S2084, SF2084
"I'll Fly Away" (Luke, Ascension)
N595, S2282, SF2282
"Christ the Lord Is Risen Today" (Luke)
B159, C216, F289, N233, UM302 (PD), VU155 and VU157
"Christ Is Risen" (Luke, Communion) (C)
C222, P104, UM307

Additional Contemporary Suggestions
"Holy Spirit, Rain Down" (Acts, Luke)
M88
"Come, Holy Spirit" (Acts)
S2125, SF2125
"He Is Exalted" (Pss)
R238, S2070, SF2070, SP66
"Lord Most High" (Pss)
M120
"Forever" (Eph)
M68
"Above All" (Eph, Ascension)
M77; V-3 p. 17 Vocal Solo
"Lord God Almighty" (Luke)
R40, S2006, SF2006
"Lord, I Lift Your Name on High" (Luke, Ascension)
M2, R4, S2088, SF2088
"In Christ Alone" ("My Hope Is Found") (Ascension)
M138

Vocal Solos
"Jesus Christ is Risen Today" (Acts, Luke)
V-1 p. 50
"Ride On, Jesus" (Ascension)
V-7 p. 8

Anthems
"Psalm 47" (Pss)
Bradley Ellingboe; Kjos 8890
SATB a cappella with percussion

"Love Divine, All Loves Excelling" (Luke)
Mack Wilberg; Oxford 0-19-386490-8
SATB with organ

Other Suggestions
The Feast of the Ascension is celebrated on the fortieth day after Easter (the sixth Thursday of Easter) and may be celebrated on the Sunday that follows. These ideas may be used on Thursday, May 13, or on May 16, Ascension Sunday
Visuals:
Acts Baptism, Holy Spirit, Ascension, mantel
P Clasped hands, Ascension, trumpet, singing, feet
E Praying, heart, Bible, Christ/throne, names, church
G Mantel, Bible, witness, Ascension, worship, joy
Prayer: F300, F302, N856, UM323 (Luke, Ascension)
Reading: C271. The Church (Eph)
Call to Communion: C408, S2269, SF2269, VU469. "Come, Share the Lord" (Eph)
Blessing: N872 (Luke, Easter)

Acts 16:16-34

16 One day, as we were going to the place of prayer, we met a slave-girl who had a spirit of divination and brought her owners a great deal of money by fortune-telling. 17 While she followed Paul and us, she would cry out, 'These men are slaves of the Most High God, who proclaim to you a way of salvation.' 18 She kept doing this for many days. But Paul, very much annoyed, turned and said to the spirit, 'I order you in the name of Jesus Christ to come out of her.' And it came out that very hour.

19 But when her owners saw that their hope of making money was gone, they seized Paul and Silas and dragged them into the market-place before the authorities. 20 When they had brought them before the magistrates, they said, 'These men are disturbing our city; they are Jews 21 and are advocating customs that are not lawful for us as Romans to adopt or observe.' 22 The crowd joined in attacking them, and the magistrates had them stripped of their clothing and ordered them to be beaten with rods. 23 After they had given them a severe flogging, they threw them into prison and ordered the jailer to keep them securely. 24 Following these instructions, he put them in the innermost cell and fastened their feet in the stocks.

25 About midnight Paul and Silas were praying and singing hymns to God, and the prisoners were listening to them. 26 Suddenly there was an earthquake, so violent that the foundations of the prison were shaken; and immediately all the doors were opened and everyone's chains were unfastened. 27 When the jailer woke up and saw the prison doors wide open, he drew his sword and was about to kill himself, since he supposed that the prisoners had escaped. 28 But Paul shouted in a loud voice, 'Do not harm yourself, for we are all here.' 29 The jailer called for lights, and rushing in, he fell down trembling before Paul and Silas. 30 Then he brought them outside and said, 'Sirs, what must I do to be saved?' 31 They answered, 'Believe on the Lord Jesus, and you will be saved, you and your household.' 32 They spoke the word of the Lord to him and to all who were in his house. 33 At the same hour of the night he took them and washed their wounds; then he and his entire family were baptized without delay. 34 He brought them up into the house and set food before them; and he and his entire household rejoiced that he had become a believer in God.

Psalm 97

1 The LORD is king! Let the earth rejoice; let the many coastlands be glad! 2 Clouds and thick darkness are all around him; righteousness and justice are the foundation of his throne. 3 Fire goes before him, and consumes his adversaries on every side. 4 His lightnings light up the world; the earth sees and trembles. 5 The mountains melt like wax before the LORD, before the Lord of all the earth.

6 The heavens proclaim his righteousness; and all the peoples behold his glory. 7 All worshippers of images are put to shame, those who make their boast in worthless idols; all gods bow down before him. 8 Zion hears and is glad, and the towns of Judah rejoice, because of your judgments, O God.

9 For you, O LORD, are most high over all the earth; you are exalted far above all gods.

10 The LORD loves those who hate evil; he guards the lives of his faithful; he rescues them from the hand of the wicked.

11 Light dawns for the righteous, and joy for the upright in heart. 12 Rejoice in the LORD, O you righteous, and give thanks to his holy name!

Revelation 22:12-14, 16-17, 20-21

12 'See, I am coming soon; my reward is with me, to repay according to everyone's work. 13 I am the Alpha and the Omega, the first and the last, the beginning and the end.' 14 Blessed are those who wash their robes, so that they will have the right to the tree of life and may enter the city by the gates.

16 'It is I, Jesus, who sent my angel to you with this testimony for the churches. I am the root and the descendant of David, the bright morning star.' 17 The Spirit and the bride say, 'Come.' And let everyone who hears say, 'Come.' And let everyone who is thirsty come. Let anyone who wishes take the water of life as a gift.

20 The one who testifies to these things says, 'Surely I am coming soon.' Amen. Come, Lord Jesus! 21 The grace of the Lord Jesus be with all the saints. Amen.

John 17:20-26

20 'I ask not only on behalf of these, but also on behalf of those who will believe in me through their word, 21 that they may all be one. As you, Father, are in me and I am in you, may they also be in us, so that the world may believe that you have sent me. 22 The glory that you have given me I have given them, so that they may be one, as we are one, 23 I in them and you in me, that they may become completely one, so that the world may know that you have sent me and have loved them even as you have loved me. 24 Father, I desire that those also, whom you have given me, may be with me where I am, to see my glory, which you have given me because you loved me before the foundation of the world.

25 'Righteous Father, the world does not know you, but I know you; and these know that you have sent me. 26 I made your name known to them, and I will make it known, so that the love with which you have loved me may be in them, and I in them.'

Notes

Primary Hymns and Songs for the Day
"We Know That Christ Is Raised (Acts, Easter, Baptism) (O)
E296, L189, P495, UM610, VU448, W721
H-3 Hbl-100; Chr-214; Desc-; Org-37
S-1 #118-127. Various treatments
"And Can It Be that I Should Gain" (Acts)
B147, F260, R193, UM363 (PD)
"Stand By Me" (Acts)
C629, UM512
H-3 Chr-177
"O Morning Star, How Fair and Bright" (Rev)
C105, E497, L76, N158, P69, UM247, VU98, W390
H-3 Chr-147; Desc-104; Org-183
"O Blessed Spring" (Rev)
S2076, SF2076, VU632
H-3 Chr-200; Org-45
"All Hail King Jesus" (Rev)
S2069, SF2069, SP63
"Make Us One" (John)
S2224, SF2224, SP137
"Softly and Tenderly Jesus Is Calling" (Rev) (C)
B312, C340, F432, N449, R147, UM348
H-3 Chr-174

Additional Hymn Suggestions
"God Will Take Care of You" (Acts)
B64, F56, N460, UM130 (PD)
"Wash, O God, Our Sons and Daughters" (Acts, Baptism)
C365, UM605, VU442
"Wonder of Wonders" (Acts, Baptism)
C378, N328, P499, S2247
"I Love the Lord, Who Heard My Cry" (Acts)
P362, N511, VU617
"O Worship the King" (Pss)
B16, C17, E388, F336, L548 (PD), N26, P476, UM73, VU235
"How Great Thou Art" (Pss)
B10, C33, F2, L532, N35, P467, R250, UM77, VU238 (Fr.)
"Rejoice, Ye Pure in Heart" (Pss)
B39, C15, E556, F394, N55, P145, UM160 (PD)
E557, N71, P146, UM161
"Rejoice, the Lord Is King" (Pss)
B197, C699, F374, N303, P155, UM715 (PD), VU213, W493,
E481, L171 (PD), UM716
"We've a Story to Tell to the Nations" (Rev)
B586, C484, F659, UM569 (PD)
"Shall We Gather at the River" (Rev)
B518, C701, N597, UM723 (PD), VU710
"Blest Be the Tie That Binds" (John)
B387, C433, F560, L370, N393, P438, UM557 (PD), VU602
"Praise and Thanksgiving Be to God" (John, Baptism)
L191, UM604, VU441
"We Are God's People" (John)
B383, F546, S2220, SF2220
"In the Midst of New Dimensions" (John)
N391, S2238, SF2238

Additional Contemporary Suggestions
"Forever" (Pss)
M68
"Above All" (Pss)
M77; V-3 p. 17 Vocal Solo
"Lord Most High" (Pss)
M120
"Great Is the Lord" (Pss)
B12, R22, S2022, SF2022, SP30
"He Is Exalted" (Pss)
R238, S2070, SF2070, SP66
"We Will Glorify" (Rev)
B213, S2087, SF2087, SP68
"Jesus Is Alive" (Rev)
M20
"Come, Now Is the Time to Worship" (Rev)
M56; V-3 p. 114Vocal Solo
"I Could Sing of Your Love Forever"
M63; V-3 p. 22 Vocal Solo
"Do You Feel the Mountains Tremble?" (Rev)
M69; V-3 p. 140 Vocal Solo
"How Great Is Our God" (Rev)
M117
"They'll Know We Are Christians" (John)
C494, S2223, SF2223
"Bind Us Together" (John)
R292, S2226, SF2226, SP140

Vocal Solos
"O Glorious Love" (Acts)
V-8 p. 306
"These Thousand Hills" (Rev)
V-3 p. 30

Anthems
"E'en So, Lord Jesus Quickly Come" (Rev)
Paul Manz; Concordia 98-1054
SATB a cappella

"That We May Be One" (John)
James Moore; GIA G3311
SATB with keyboard

Other Suggestions
If celebration Ascension Sunday, see May 13 ideas.
Visuals:
Acts Fortune teller/money, rods/open shackles, chains, baptism
P Coast, clouds, lightning, shield/rescue
E Alpha/Omega, white robe, root, flame, bride, water, Rev 22:20b
G Jesus praying, hearts
Canticle: UM734. "Canticle of Hope" (Rev)

Acts 2:1-21

[1]When the day of Pentecost had come, they were all together in one place. [2]And suddenly from heaven there came a sound like the rush of a violent wind, and it filled the entire house where they were sitting. [3]Divided tongues, as of fire, appeared among them, and a tongue rested on each of them. [4]All of them were filled with the Holy Spirit and began to speak in other languages, as the Spirit gave them ability.

[5]Now there were devout Jews from every nation under heaven living in Jerusalem. [6]And at this sound the crowd gathered and was bewildered, because each one heard them speaking in the native language of each. [7]Amazed and astonished, they asked, "Are not all these who are speaking Galileans? [8]And how is it that we hear, each of us, in our own native language? [9]Parthians, Medes, Elamites, and residents of Mesopotamia, Judea and Cappadocia, Pontus and Asia, [10]Phrygia and Pamphylia, Egypt and the parts of Libya belonging to Cyrene, and visitors from Rome, both Jews and proselytes, [11]Cretans and Arabs—in our own languages we hear them speaking about God's deeds of power." [12]All were amazed and perplexed, saying to one another, "What does this mean?" [13]But others sneered and said, "They are filled with new wine."

[14]But Peter, standing with the eleven, raised his voice and addressed them, "Men of Judea and all who live in Jerusalem, let this be known to you, and listen to what I say. [15]Indeed, these are not drunk, as you suppose, for it is only nine o'clock in the morning. [16]No, this is what was spoken through the prophet Joel: [17]'In the last days it will be, God declares, that I will pour out my Spirit upon all flesh, and your sons and your daughters shall prophesy, and your young men shall see visions, and your old men shall dream dreams. [18]Even upon my slaves, both men and women, in those days I will pour out my Spirit; and they shall prophesy. [19]And I will show portents in the heaven above and signs on the earth below, blood, and fire, and smoky mist. [20]The sun shall be turned to darkness and the moon to blood, before the coming of the Lord's great and glorious day. [21]Then everyone who calls on the name of the Lord shall be saved.' "

Psalm 104:24-34, 35*b*

[24]O LORD, how manifold are your works! In wisdom you have made them all; the earth is full of your creatures. [25]Yonder is the sea, great and wide, creeping things innumerable are there, living things both small and great. [26]There go the ships, and Leviathan that you formed to sport in it. [27]These all look to you to give them their food in due season; [28]when you give to them, they gather it up; when you open your hand, they are filled with good things. [29]When you hide your face, they are dismayed; when you take away their breath, they die and return to their dust. [30]When you send forth your spirit, they are created; and you renew the face of the ground. [31]May the glory of the LORD endure forever; may the LORD rejoice in his works— [32]who looks on the earth and it trembles, who touches the mountains and they smoke. [33]I will sing to the LORD as long as I live; I will sing praise to my God while I have being. [34]May my meditation be pleasing to him, for I rejoice in the LORD.

[35b]Bless the LORD, O my soul. Praise the LORD!

Romans 8:14-17

[14]For all who are led by the Spirit of God are children of God. [15]For you did not receive a spirit of slavery to fall back into fear, but you have received a spirit of adoption. When we cry, "Abba! Father!" [16]it is that very Spirit bearing witness with our spirit that we are children of God, [17]and if children, then heirs, heirs of God and joint heirs with Christ—if, in fact, we suffer with him so that we may also be glorified with him.

John 14:8-17 (25-27)

[8]Philip said to him, "Lord, show us the Father, and we will be satisfied." [9]Jesus said to him, "Have I been with you all this time, Philip, and you still do not know me? Whoever has seen me has seen the Father. How can you say, 'Show us the Father'? [10]Do you not believe that I am in the Father and the Father is in me? The words that I say to you I do not speak on my own; but the Father who dwells in me does his works. [11]Believe me that I am in the Father and the Father is in me; but if you do not, then believe me because of the works themselves. [12]Very truly, I tell you, the one who believes in me will also do the works that I do and, in fact, will do greater works than these, because I am going to the Father. [13]I will do whatever you ask in my name, so that the Father may be glorified in the Son. [14]If in my name you ask me for anything, I will do it.

[15]"If you love me, you will keep my commandments. [16]And I will ask the Father, and he will give you another Advocate, to be with you forever. [17]This is the Spirit of truth, whom the world cannot receive, because it neither sees him nor knows him. You know him, because he abides with you, and he will be in you.

[25]"I have said these things to you while I am still with you. [26]But the Advocate, the Holy Spirit, whom the Father will send in my name, will teach you everything, and remind you of all that I have said to you. [27]Peace I leave with you; my peace I give to you. I do not give to you as the world gives. Do not let your hearts be troubled, and do not let them be afraid."

Primary Hymns and Songs for the Day
"O Worship the King" (Pss) (O)
B16, C17, E388, F336, L548 (PD), N26, P476, UM73, VU235
"Spirit Song" (Acts)
C352, R248, SP134, UM347
"Come Down, O Love Divine" (Acts)
C582, E516, L508, N289, P313, UM475 (PD), VU367, W472
Spirit of God" (Acts, John, Pentecost)
S2117, SF2117
"Blessed Quietness" (John)
F145, C267, N284, S2142, SF2142
"Love Divine, All Loves Excelling" (John) (C)
B208, C517, F21, N43, UM384 (PD)
H-3 Chr-134; Desc-18; Org-13
S-1 #41-42. Descant and harmonization
E657, L315, P376, R196, VU333, W588 (PD)
H-3 Hbl-46; Chr-26, 134; Desc-53; Org-56
S-1 #168-171. Various treatments

Additional Hymn Suggestions
"Like the Murmur of the Dove's Song" (Acts, John)
C245, E513, N270, P314, R280, UM544, VU205
"Spirit, Spirit of Gentleness" (Acts, Pentecost)
C249, N286, P319, S2120, VU375 (Fr.)
"Gather Us In" (Acts)
C284, S2236, SF2236, W665
"Deep in the Shadows of the Past" (Acts, Pentecost)
N320, P330, S2246
"Come, Share the Lord" (Acts, Communion)
C408, S2269, SF2269, VU469
"Every Time I Feel the Spirit" (Rom)
C592, N282, P315, UM404
"Source and Sovereign, Rock and Cloud" (John)
C12, UM113
"Because He Lives" (John)
B407, C562, F292, UM364
"There's Within My Heart a Melody" (John)
B425, C550, UM380 (PD)
"Loving Spirit" (Pentecost)
C244, P323, S2123, SF2123, VU387
"In the Midst of New Dimensions" (Pentecost) (C)
N391, S2238, SF2238
"The Spirit Sends Us Forth to Serve" (Pentecost) (C)
S2241, SF2241

Additional Contemporary Suggestions
"He Reigns" (Acts, Pentecost)
M168
"Holy Ground" (Acts)
B224, C112, S2272, SF2272, SP86
"Awesome In This Place" (Acts)
M36
"Holy Spirit, Rain Down" (Acts, John)
M88
"Spirit of the Living God" (Rom)
B244, C259, F155, N283, P322, R90, SP131, UM393, VU376
"Holy, Holy" (Rom, Pentecost)
B254, F149, P140, R206, S2039, SP141
"Surely the Presence of the Lord" (Acts, Pentecost)
C263, R167, SP243, UM328; S-2, #200 Stanzas for soloist
"Sweet, Sweet Spirit" (Acts)
B243, C261, F159, N293, P398, SP136, UM334
"Where the Spirit of the Lord Is" (Acts, Pentecost)
C264, S2119, SF2119
"Come, O Holy Spirit, Come" (Acts, Pentecost)
S2124, SF2124, VU383
"Let it Rise" (Pss, Pentecost)
M4
"Indescribable" (Pss)
M127
"Friend of God" (Rom)
M165
"Be Glorified" (John)
M13
"Dwell" (John, Pentecost)
M154

Vocal Solos
"Spirit of Faith Come Down" (Acts)
V-1 p. 43
"Light the Fire Again"
M144
"New Wind Blowin' " (Acts)
V-8 p. 192

Anthems
"Christ Calls Us Forth" (Acts)
K. Lee Scott; Hope C5003
SATB with organ and opt. brass

"There's Within My Heart a Melody" (John)
Luther B. Bridgers; Hope C5478
SATB with piano and opt. handbells

Other Suggestions
Visuals:
Acts Wind, flames, nature, wine, clock (9:00 a.m.), nations, blood
P Nature, ship/whale, open hand, volcano, joy
E Children, open shackles, adoption certificate, will
G Jesus, ministry, prayer, flames, Bible, John 14:27
Introit: N742. "Gathered Here" (Acts)
Greeting: N820 (John) or N824 (Pss)
Opening Prayer: N826 (Acts) or N827 (John)
Call to Prayer: C456. Prayer from the Heart (John)
Prayers: C52, C235, C238, C240, C243, N857 (Pentecost)
Blessing: N877 (Acts, Pentecost)

Proverbs 8:1-4, 22-31

[1]Does not wisdom call, and does not understanding raise her voice? [2]On the heights, beside the way, at the crossroads she takes her stand; [3]beside the gates in front of the town, at the entrance of the portals she cries out: [4]"To you, O people, I call, and my cry is to all that live.

[22]"The LORD created me at the beginning of his work, the first of his acts of long ago. [23]Ages ago I was set up, at the first, before the beginning of the earth. [24]When there were no depths I was brought forth, when there were no springs abounding with water. [25]Before the mountains had been shaped, before the hills, I was brought forth— [26]when he had not yet made earth and fields, or the world's first bits of soil. [27]When he established the heavens, I was there, when he drew a circle on the face of the deep, [28]when he made firm the skies above, when he established the fountains of the deep, [29]when he assigned to the sea its limit, so that the waters might not transgress his command, when he marked out the foundations of the earth, [30]then I was beside him, like a master worker; and I was daily his delight, rejoicing before him always, [31]rejoicing in his inhabited world and delighting in the human race."

Psalm 8

[1]O LORD, our Sovereign, how majestic is your name in all the earth! You have set your glory above the heavens. [2]Out of the mouths of babes and infants you have founded a bulwark because of your foes, to silence the enemy and the avenger. [3]When I look at your heavens, the work of your fingers, the moon and the stars that you have established; [4]what are human beings that you are mindful of them, mortals that you care for them? [5]Yet you have made them a little lower than God, and crowned them with glory and honor. [6]You have given them dominion over the works of your hands; you have put all things under their feet, [7]all sheep and oxen, and also the beasts of the field, [8]the birds of the air, and the fish of the sea, whatever passes along the paths of the seas. [9]O LORD, our Sovereign, how majestic is your name in all the earth!

Romans 5:1-5

[1]Therefore, since we are justified by faith, we have peace with God through our Lord Jesus Christ, [2]through whom we have obtained access to this grace in which we stand; and we boast in our hope of sharing the glory of God. [3]And not only that, but we also boast in our sufferings, knowing that suffering produces endurance, [4]and endurance produces character, and character produces hope, [5]and hope does not disappoint us, because God's love has been poured into our hearts through the Holy Spirit that has been given to us.

John 16:12-15

[12]"I still have many things to say to you, but you cannot bear them now. [13]When the Spirit of truth comes, he will guide you into all the truth; for he will not speak on his own, but will speak whatever he hears, and he will declare to you the things that are to come. [14]He will glorify me, because he will take what is mine and declare it to you. [15]All that the Father has is mine. For this reason I said that he will take what is mine and declare it to you."

Notes

Primary Hymns and Songs for the Day

"Holy, Holy, Holy" (Trinity)
B2, C4, E362, F323, L165, N277, P138, R204, UM64 and UM65, VU315, W485
N277 Descant
C4 Descant
H-3 Hbl-68; Chr-99; Desc-80; Org-97
S-1 #245-248. Various treatments.

"Immortal, Invisible, God Only Wise" (Prov) (O)
B6, C66, E423, F319, L526, N1, P263, R46, UM103 (PD), VU264, W512
H-3 Hbl-15, 71; Chr-65; Desc-93; Org-135
S-1 #300. Harmonization

"How Majestic Is Your Name" (Pss)
C63, R98, S2023, SF2023, SP14

"My Hope Is Built" (Rom)
B406, C537, F92, L293 and L294 (PD), N368, P379, UM368 (PD)
H-3 Chr-191
S-2 #171-172. Trumpet and vocal descants

"Come, Thou Almighty King" (John, Trinity)
B247, C27, E365, F341, L522, N275, P139, UM61 (PD), W487
H-3 Hbl-28, 49, 53; Chr-56; Desc-57; Org-63
S-1 #185-186. Descant and harmonization
VU314

Additional Hymn Suggestions

"All Creatures of Our God and King" (Prov, Pss, Trinity) (O)
B27, C22, E400, F347, L527, N17, P455, R47, UM62, VU217 (Fr.), W520

"For the Beauty of the Earth" (Prov, Pss)
B44, C56, E416, F1, L561, P473, N28, UM92 (PD), VU226, W557

"God Created Heaven and Earth" (Prov, Pss)
N33, P290, UM151, VU251

"I Sing the Almighty Power of God" (Prov, Pss)
B42, C64, E398, N12, P288 (PD), R54, UM152 (PD), VU231 (PD), W502 (PD)

"This Is My Father's World" (Prov, Pss)
B43, C59, E651, F6, L554, P293, UM144, VU296

"All Things Bright and Beautiful" (Prov,, Pss)
C61, E405, N31, P267, UM147 (PD), VU291, W505

"She Is the Spirit" (Prov)
C255

"Let Us with a Joyful Mind" (Prov, Pss)
E389, L521, N16, P244, S2012, SF2012VU234

"Bring Many Names" (Prov, Trinity)
C10, N11, S2047, SF2047, VU268

"Blessed Assurance" (Rom)
B334, C543, F67, N473, P341, UM369 (PD), VU337

"Standing on the Promises" (Rom, Trinity)
B335, C552, F69, UM374 (PD)

"O Love That Wilt Not Let Me Go" (Rom)
B292, C540, F404, L324, N485, P384, UM480 (PD), VU658

"We Walk by Faith" (Rom)
E209, N256, P399, S2196, SF2196, W572

"Come, Holy Ghost, Our Souls Inspire" (Rom, John)
E503 and E504, L472 and L473, N268 , P125, UM651 (PD), VU201

"Fairest Lord, Jesus" (John)
B176, C97, E383, F240, L518, N44, P306, R166, UM189 (PD), VU341

"Come Down, O Love Divine" (John) (C)
C582, E516, L508, N289, P313, UM475 (PD), VU367, W472

Additional Contemporary Suggestions

"God of Wonders" (Pss)
M80; V-3 p. 184 Vocal Solo

"Friend of God"
M165

"I Could Sing of Your Love Forever" (Rom)
M63; V-3 p. 22 Vocal Solo

"Spirit of the Living God" (John)
B244, C259, F155, N283, P322, R90, SP131, UM393, VU376

"Lord God Almighty" (Trinity)
R40, S2006, SF2006

"Holy, Holy" (Trinity)
B254, F149, P140, R206, S2039, SP141

Vocal Solos

"Be Thou My Vision" (Prov)
V-5 p. 3
V-6 p. 13

"Redeeming Grace" (Rom)
V-4 p. 47

Anthems

"Trinitarian Blessings" (Trinity)
Alice Parker: Hope AG7294
SATB a cappella

"Gloria Deo" (Trinity)
James E. Clemens; Kjos 9069
SATB divisi a cappella

Other Suggestions

Visuals:
O Crossroads, gate, nature, outer space, circle, joy
P Space, baby, moon/stars, Adam/Eve, animals, bird, fish
E Kairos/chronos, heart, pouring, flames
G Jesus, Spirit, Bible, kairos/chronos, preaching

Greeting: N824 (Pss)
Canticle: N740 or UM112. "Wisdom" (Prov)
Litany: C11. Names of God Litany (Trinity)

1 Kings 17:8-24

8Then the word of the LORD came to him, saying, 9"Go now to Zarephath, which belongs to Sidon, and live there; for I have commanded a widow there to feed you." 10so he set out and went to Zarephath. When he came to the gate of the town, a widow was there gathering sticks; he called to her and said, "Bring me a little water in a vessel, so that I may drink." 11As she was going to bring it, he called to her and said, "Bring me a morsel of bread in your hand." 12But she said, "As the LORD your God lives, I have nothing baked, only a handful of meal in a jar, and a little oil in a jug; I am now gathering a couple of sticks, so that I may go home and prepare it for myself and my son, that we may eat it, and die." 13Elijah said to her, "Do not be afraid; go and do as you have said; but first make me a little cake of it and bring it to me, and afterwards make something for yourself and your son. 14For thus says the LORD the God of Israel: The jar of meal will not be emptied and the jug of oil will not fail until the day that the LORD sends rain on the earth." 15She went and did as Elijah said, so that she as well as he and her household ate for many days. 16The jar of meal was not emptied, neither did the jug of oil fail, according to the word of the LORD that he spoke by Elijah.

17After this the son of the woman, the mistress of the house, became ill; his illness was so severe that there was no breath left in him. 18She then said to Elijah, "What have you against me, O man of God? You have come to me to bring my sin to remembrance, and to cause the death of my son!" 19But he said to her, "Give me your son." He took him from her bosom, carried him up into the upper chamber where he was lodging, and laid him on his own bed. 20He cried out to the Lord, "O LORD my God, have you brought calamity even upon the widow with whom I am staying, by killing her son?" 21Then he stretched himself upon the child three times, and cried out to the LORD, "O LORD my God, let this child's life come into him again." 22The LORD listened to the voice of Elijah; the life of the child came into him again, and he revived. 23Elijah took the child, brought him down from the upper chamber into the house, and gave him to his mother; then Elijah said, "See, your son is alive." 24So the woman said to Elijah, "Now I know that you are a man of God, and that the word of the LORD in your mouth is truth."

Psalm 146

1Praise the LORD! Praise the LORD, O my soul!

2I will praise the LORD as long as I live; I will sing praises to my God all my life long.

3Do not put your trust in princes, in mortals, in whom there is no help.

4When their breath departs, they return to the earth; on that very day their plans perish.

5Happy are those whose help is the God of Jacob, whose hope is in the LORD their God,

6who made heaven and earth, the sea, and all that is in them; who keeps faith forever;

7who executes justice for the oppressed; who gives food to the hungry. The LORD sets the prisoners free;

8the LORD opens the eyes of the blind. The LORD lifts up those who are bowed down; the LORD loves the righteous.

9The LORD watches over the strangers; he upholds the orphan and the widow, but the way of the wicked he brings to ruin.

10The LORD will reign forever, your God, O Zion, for all generations. Praise the LORD!

Galatians 1:11-24

11For I want you to know, brothers and sisters, that the gospel that was proclaimed by me is not of human origin; 12for I did not receive it from a human source, nor was I taught it, but I received it through a revelation of Jesus Christ.

13You have heard, no doubt, of my earlier life in Judaism. I was violently persecuting the church of God and was trying to destroy it. 14I advanced in Judaism beyond many among my people of the same age, for I was far more zealous for the traditions of my ancestors. 15But when God, who had set me apart before I was born and called me through his grace, was pleased 16to reveal his Son to me, so that I might proclaim him among the Gentiles, I did not confer with any human being, 17nor did I go up to Jerusalem to those who were already apostles before me, but I went away at once into Arabia, and afterwards I returned to Damascus.

18Then after three years I did go up to Jerusalem to visit Cephas and stayed with him fifteen days; 19but I did not see any other apostle except James the Lord's brother. 20In what I am writing to you, before God, I do not lie! 21Then I went into the regions of Syria and Cilicia, 22and I was still unknown by sight to the churches of Judea that are in Christ; 23they only heard it said, "The one who formerly was persecuting us is now proclaiming the faith he once tried to destroy." 24And they glorified God because of me.

Luke 7:11-17

11Soon afterwards he went to a town called Nain, and his disciples and a large crowd went with him. 12As he approached the gate of the town, a man who had died was being carried out. He was his mother's only son, and she was a widow; and with her was a large crowd from the town. 13When the Lord saw her, he had compassion for her and said to her, "Do not weep." 14Then he came forward and touched the bier, and the bearers stood still. And he said, "Young man, I say to you, rise!" 15The dead man sat up and began to speak, and Jesus gave him to his mother. 16Fear seized all of them; and they glorified God, saying, "A great prophet has risen among us!" and "God has looked favorably on his people!" 17This word about him spread throughout Judea and all the surrounding country.

Notes

Primary Hymns and Songs for the Day

"I'll Praise My Maker While I've Breath" (Pss) (O)
B35, C20, E429 (PD), P253, UM60, VU867
H-3 Chr-109; Org-105
S-2 #141. Harmonization

"Lord, When I Came Into This Life" (Gal)
N354, P522

"Children of the Heavenly Father" (1 Kgs, Luke)
B55, F89, L474, N487, UM141
H-3 Chr-46; Desc-102
S-2 #180-185. Various treatments.

"Healer of Our Every Ill" (1 Kgs, Luke)
C506, S2213, SF2213, VU619

"This Is a Day of New Beginnings" (1 Kgs, Gal, Luke, Communion)
B370, C518, N417, UM383
H-3 Chr-196

"Give to the Winds Thy Fears" (1 Kgs, Pss, Luke) (C)
P286 (PD)
H-3 Hbl-61; Chr-71; Desc-93; Org-133
UM129 (PD)
H-3 Chr-71; Desc-39; Org-39
S-1 #129. Descant
N404, VU636 (PD)

Additional Hymn Suggestions

"O For a Thousand Tongues to Sing" (Pss) (O)
B216, C5, E493, F349, L559, N42, P466, R32, UM57 (PD) and UM59, VU326

"O That I Had a Thousand Voices" (Luke)
L560, P475, W546

"It's Me, It's Me, O Lord" (1 Kgs)
C579, N519, UM352

"Cuando El Pobre" ("When the Poor Ones") (1 Kgs, Pss)
C662, P407, UM434, VU702

"Hope of the World" (1 Kgs, Pss)
C538, E472, L493, N46, P360, UM178, VU215, W565

"When God Restored our Common Life" (Pss)
S2182, SF2182

"Holy Spirit, Come, Confirm Us" (Gal, Luke)
N264, UM331

"Have Thine Own Way, Lord" (Gal)
B294, C588, F400, UM382 (PD)

"Lord, Speak to Me" (Gal)
B568, F625, L403, N531, P426, UM463 (PD), VU589

"Since Jesus Came into My Heart" (Gal)
B441, F639, S2140, SF2140

"Living for Jesus" (Gal)
B282, C610, F462, S2149, SF2149

"I'm Gonna Live So God Can Use Me" (Gal)
C614, P369, S2153, VU575

"Lord of the Dance" (Luke)
P302, UM261, VU352, W636

"Now the Green Blade Riseth" (Luke)
C230, E204, L148, N238, UM311, VU186, W453

"Love Divine, All Loves Excelling" (Luke)
B208, C517, F21, N43, UM384 (PD)
E657, L315, P376, R196, VU333, W588 (PD)

Additional Contemporary Suggestions

"Days of Elijah" (1 Kgs)
M139

"My Life Is in You, Lord" (Pss)
S2032, SF2032, SP204

"God of Wonders" (Pss)
M80; V-3 p. 184 Vocal Solo

"Give Thanks" (Pss)
C528, R266, S2036, SF2036, SP170

"Someone Asked the Question" (Pss)
N523, S2144, SF2144

"Song of Hope" (Pss)
P432, S2186, VU424

"I Know the Lord's Laid His Hands on Me" (Gal)
S2139, SF2139

"You Are My King" ("Amazing Love") (Gal)
M82

"Forever" (Gal)
M68

"Trading My Sorrows" (Gal, Luke)
M75

"Christ the Lord Is Risen" (Luke)
S2116, SF2116

Vocal Solos

"O for a Thousand Tongues to Sing" (Pss)
V-1 p. 32
V-6 p. 28

"Ocean" (Pss)
V-3 p. 78

Anthems

"How Blest Are They" (Pss)
Claude Bass; MorningStar 50-5201
SATB with Piano

"Praise the Goodness of God" (Pss)
Allen Pote; Choristers Guild CGA733
SATB with keyboard

Other Suggestions

Visuals:
O Water vessel, sticks, meal/oil, child (sick/healed)
P praise/singing, creation, justice (scales), food, open Shackles, woman/child
E Paul, shackles, Christ, Peter
G Jesus, woman, bier/bearers, man sitting up, hug

Opening Prayer: C771 (1 Kgs, Gal)
Opening Prayer: N831 (1 Kgs, Luke)
Prayer of Confession: N835 (Gal)
Prayer: N863. Justice (1 Kgs, Pss, Gal, Luke)
Blessing: N872 (Luke)
Alternate Lessons: 1 Kgs 17:17-24; Ps 30 (see Scripture Index in this, or previous, editions of *Prepare!*).

1 Kings 21:1-21*a*

1 Later the following events took place: Naboth the Jezreelite had a vineyard in Jezreel, beside the palace of King Ahab of Samaria. 2 And Ahab said to Naboth, "Give me your vineyard, so that I may have it for a vegetable garden, because it is near my house; I will give you a better vineyard for it; or, if it seems good to you, I will give you its value in money." 3But Naboth said to Ahab, "The LORD forbid that I should give you my ancestral inheritance." 4Ahab went home resentful and sullen because of what Naboth the Jezreelite had said to him; for he had said, "I will not give you my ancestral inheritance." He lay down on his bed, turned away his face, and would not eat.

5His wife Jezebel came to him and said, "Why are you so depressed that you will not eat?" 6He said to her, "Because I spoke to Naboth the Jezreelite and said to him, 'Give me your vineyard for money; or else, if you prefer, I will give you another vineyard for it'; but he answered, 'I will not give you my vineyard.' " 7His wife Jezebel said to him, "Do you now govern Israel? Get up, eat some food, and be cheerful; I will give you the vineyard of Naboth the Jezreelite."

8So she wrote letters in Ahab's name and sealed them with his seal; she sent the letters to the elders and the nobles who lived with Naboth in his city. 9She wrote in the letters, "Proclaim a fast, and seat Naboth at the head of the assembly; 10seat two scoundrels opposite him, and have them bring a charge against him, saying, 'You have cursed God and the king.' Then take him out, and stone him to death." 11The men of his city, the elders and the nobles who lived in his city, did as Jezebel had sent word to them. Just as it was written in the letters that she had sent to them, 12they proclaimed a fast and seated Naboth at the head of the assembly. 13The two scoundrels came in and sat opposite him; and the scoundrels brought a charge against Naboth, in the presence of the people, saying, "Naboth cursed God and the king." So they took him outside the city, and stoned him to death. 14Then they sent to Jezebel, saying, "Naboth has been stoned; he is dead."

15As soon as Jezebel heard that Naboth had been stoned and was dead, Jezebel said to Ahab, "Go, take possession of the vineyard of Naboth the Jezreelite, which he refused to give you for money; for Naboth is not alive, but dead." 16As soon as Ahab heard that Naboth was dead, Ahab set out to go down to the vineyard of Naboth the Jezreelite, to take possession of it.

17Then the word of the LORD came to Elijah the Tishbite, saying: 18Go down to meet King Ahab of Israel, who rules in Samaria; he is now in the vineyard of Naboth, where he has gone to take possession. 19You shall say to him, "Thus says the LORD: Have you killed, and also taken possession?" You shall say to him, "Thus says the LORD: In the place where dogs licked up the blood of Naboth, dogs will also lick up your blood."

20Ahab said to Elijah, "Have you found me, O my enemy?" He answered, "I have found you. Because you have sold yourself to do what is evil in the sight of the LORD, 21a I will bring disaster on you."

Psalm 5:1-8

1Give ear to my words, O LORD; give heed to my sighing. 2Listen to the sound of my cry, my King and my God, for to you I pray. 3O LORD, in the morning you hear my voice; in the morning I plead my case to you, and watch. 4For you are not a God who delights in wickedness; evil will not sojourn with you. 5The boastful will not stand before your eyes; you hate all evildoers. 6You destroy those who speak lies; the LORD abhors the bloodthirsty and deceitful. 7But I, through the abundance of your steadfast love, will enter your house, I will bow down toward your holy temple in awe of you. 8Lead me, O LORD, in your righteousness because of my enemies; make your way straight before me.

Galatians 2:15-21

15We ourselves are Jews by birth and not Gentile sinners; 16yet we know that a person is justified not by the works of the law but through faith in Jesus Christ. And we have come to believe in Christ Jesus, so that we might be justified by faith in Christ, and not by doing the works of the law, because no one will be justified by the works of the law. 17But if, in our effort to be justified in Christ, we ourselves have been found to be sinners, is Christ then a servant of sin? Certainly not! 18But if I build up again the very things that I once tore down, then I demonstrate that I am a transgressor. 19For through the law I died to the law, so that I might live to God. I have been crucified with Christ; 20and it is no longer I who live, but it is Christ who lives in me. And the life I now live in the flesh I live by faith in the Son of God, who loved me and gave himself for me. 21I do not nullify the grace of God; for if justification comes through the law, then Christ died for nothing.

Luke 7:36–8:3

36One of the Pharisees asked Jesus to eat with him, and he went into the Pharisee's house and took his place at the table. 37And a woman in the city, who was a sinner, having learned that he was eating in the Pharisee's house, brought an alabaster jar of ointment. 38 She stood behind him at his feet, weeping, and began to bathe his feet with her tears and to dry them with her hair. Then she continued kissing his feet and anointing them with the ointment. 39Now when the Pharisee who had invited him saw it, he said to himself, "If this man were a prophet, he would have known who and what kind of woman this is who is touching him—that she is a sinner." 40Jesus spoke up and said to him, "Simon, I have something to say to you." "Teacher," he replied, "speak." 41"A certain creditor had two debtors; one owed five hundred denarii, and the other fifty. 42When they could not pay, he canceled the debts for both of them. Now which of them will love him more?" 43Simon answered, "I suppose the one for whom he canceled the greater debt." And Jesus said to him, "You have judged rightly." 44Then turning toward the woman, he said to Simon, "Do you see this woman? I entered your house; you gave me no water for my feet, but she has bathed my feet with her tears and dried them with her hair. 45You gave me no kiss, but from the time I came in she has not stopped kissing my feet. 46You did not anoint my head with oil, but she has anointed my feet with ointment. 47Therefore, I tell you, her sins, which were many, have been forgiven; hence she has shown great love. But the one to whom little is forgiven, loves little." 48Then he said to her, "Your sins are forgiven." 49But those who were at the table with him began to say among themselves, "Who is this who even forgives sins?" 50And he said to the woman, "Your faith has saved you; go in peace."

1Soon afterwards he went on through cities and villages, proclaiming and bringing the good news of the kingdom of God. The twelve were with him, 2as well as some women who had been cured of evil spirits and infirmities: Mary, called Magdalene, from whom seven demons had gone out, 3and Joanna, the wife of Herod's steward Chuza, and Susanna, and many others, who provided for them out of their resources.

Primary Hymns and Songs for the Day

"Alleluia, Alleluia" (Gal) (O)
B170, E178, P106, R271, UM162, VU179, W441
"What Does the Lord Require" (1 Kgs, Gal, Luke)
E605, P405, UM441, W624
H-3 Chr-211
C659
"Lead Me, Lord" (Pss)
C593, N774, R175, UM473 (PD), VU662
"Pues Si Vivimos" ("When We Are Living") (Gal)
C536, N499, P400, UM356, VU581
S-1 #320. Orff instrument arrangement
H-3 Chr-218; Org-155
"Come, Ye Sinners, Poor and Needy" (Luke)
B323 (PD), R141, UM340, W756
S-1 #283. Choral harmonization
"We Walk by Faith" (Gal) (C)
N256, P399, W572
H-3 Chr-67
S2196, SF2196
H-3 Chr-21
E209

Additional Hymn Suggestions

"Dear Lord, Lead Me Day by Day" (Pss) (O)
B459, UM411, VU568
"God Hath Spoken by the Prophets" (1 Kgs, Luke)
L238, UM108 (PD), W516
"O God of Every Nation" (1 Kgs, Pss)
C680, E607, L416, P289, UM435, VU677, W650
"Lead Me, Guide Me" (Pss)
C583, R176, S2214, SF2214
"Walk with Me" (Pss, Luke)
S2242, SF2242, VU649
"Alas! And Did My Savior Bleed" (Gal)
B145, F274, L98, N200, P78, UM294 (PD)
"I Sought the Lord" (Gal)
E689, UM341 (PD), W593
"Pass Me Not, O Gentle Savior" (Gal)
B308, F416, N551, UM351 (PD), VU665
"Faith Is Patience in the Night" (Gal)
S2211, SF2211
"Woman in the Night" (Luke)
C188, UM274
"Forgive Our Sins As We Forgive" (Luke)
E674, L307, P347, R184, UM390, VU364, W754
"My Faith Looks Up to Thee" (Luke)
B416, C576, E691, F84, L479, P383, UM452 (PD), VU663
"Two Fishermen" (Luke)
S2101, SF2101, W633
"The Summons" (Luke)
S2130, SF2130, VU567
"God, How Can We Forgive" (Luke)
S2169, SF2169
"He Touched Me" (Luke) (C)
C564, F628, UM367

Additional Contemporary Suggestions

"Days of Elijah" (1 Kings)
M139
"Grace Alone" (Gal)
M100, S2162, SF2162
"O How He Loves You and Me!" (Gal)
B146, F622, R27, S2108, SF2108, SP113
"We Fall Down" (Gal)
M66
"Grace Flows Down" (Gal)
M162
"Jesus, Your Name" (Luke)
M3
"I Believe in Jesus" (Luke)
M7
"Everyday" (Luke)
M150
"Something Beautiful" (Luke)
F656, UM394
"I Have Decided to Follow Jesus" (Luke)
B305, C344, S2129, SF2129
"I'm So Glad Jesus Lifted Me" (Luke)
C529, N474, S2151, SF2151
"Go Now in Peace" (Luke)
B660, C437, R293, UM665, VU964

Vocal Solos

"And Can It Be That I Should Gain" (Gal)
V-1 p. 29
"Grace Greater Than Our Sin" (Gal)
V-8 p. 180
"Redeeming Grace" (Gal, Luke)
V-4 p. 47

Anthems

"We Wait for Thy Loving Kindness, O God" (Pss)
William McKie; Oxford A 124
SATB with tenor solo and organ

"None Other Lamb" (Gal, Luke)
Larry B. Peterson; Curtis Music Press C9307
SATB divisi with organ

Other Suggestions

Visuals:
O Vineyard, garden, bed, sad, seal, stones, money
P Weeping, prayer, bowing, straight path, ruler
E Christ, build/destroy, cross, justify (margin)
G Table, broken jar, woman/hair/feet, Jesus
Opening Prayer: N818 (Pss)
Prayers: C508, F88, N863, and UM403 (Pss, Luke)
Reading: F280. Justified by Faith (Gal)
Blessing: C449 or N874 (Luke)
Alternate Lessons: 2 Sam 11:26-12:10, 13-15; Ps 32 (see Scripture Index in this, or previous, editions of *Prepare!*).

1 Kings 19:1-15*a*

1Ahab told Jezebel all that Elijah had done, and how he had killed all the prophets with the sword. 2Then Jezebel sent a messenger to Elijah, saying, "So may the gods do to me, and more also, if I do not make your life like the life of one of them by this time tomorrow." 3Then he was afraid; he got up and fled for his life, and came to Beer-sheba, which belongs to Judah; he left his servant there.

4But he himself went a day's journey into the wilderness, and came and sat down under a solitary broom tree. He asked that he might die: "It is enough; now, O LORD, take away my life, for I am no better than my ancestors." 5Then he lay down under the broom tree and fell asleep. Suddenly an angel touched him and said to him, "Get up and eat." 6He looked, and there at his head was a cake baked on hot stones, and a jar of water. He ate and drank, and lay down again. 7The angel of the LORD came a second time, touched him, and said, "Get up and eat, otherwise the journey will be too much for you." 8He got up, and ate and drank; then he went in the strength of that food forty days and forty nights to Horeb the mount of God. 9At that place he came to a cave, and spent the night there.

Then the word of the LORD came to him, saying, "What are you doing here, Elijah?" 10He answered, "I have been very zealous for the LORD, the God of hosts; for the Israelites have forsaken your covenant, thrown down your altars, and killed your prophets with the sword. I alone am left, and they are seeking my life, to take it away."

11He said, "Go out and stand on the mountain before the LORD, for the LORD is about to pass by." Now there was a great wind, so strong that it was splitting mountains and breaking rocks in pieces before the LORD, but the LORD was not in the wind; and after the wind an earthquake, but the LORD was not in the earthquake; 12and after the earthquake a fire, but the LORD was not in the fire; and after the fire a sound of sheer silence. 13When Elijah heard it, he wrapped his face in his mantle and went out and stood at the entrance of the cave. Then there came a voice to him that said, "What are you doing here, Elijah?" 14He answered, "I have been very zealous for the LORD, the God of hosts; for the Israelites have forsaken your covenant, thrown down your altars, and killed your prophets with the sword. I alone am left, and they are seeking my life, to take it away." 15aThen the LORD said to him, "Go, return on your way to the wilderness of Damascus."

Psalm 42

1As a deer longs for flowing streams, so my soul longs for you, O God. 2My soul thirsts for God, for the living God. When shall I come and behold the face of God? 3My tears have been my food day and night, while people say to me continually, "Where is your God?" 4These things I remember, as I pour out my soul: how I went with the throng, and led them in procession to the house of God, with glad shouts and songs of thanksgiving, a multitude keeping festival. 5Why are you cast down, O my soul, and why are you disquieted within me? Hope in God; for I shall again praise him, my help 6and my God. My soul is cast down within me; therefore I remember you from the land of Jordan and of Hermon, from Mount Mizar. 7Deep calls to deep at the thunder of your cataracts; all your waves and your billows have gone over me. 8By day the LORD commands his steadfast love, and at night his song is with me, a prayer to the God of my life. 9I say to God, my rock, "Why have you forgotten me? Why must I walk about mournfully because the enemy oppresses me?" 10As with a deadly wound in my body, my adversaries taunt me, while they say to me continually, "Where is your God?" 11Why are you cast down, O my soul, and why are you disquieted within me? Hope in God; for I shall again praise him, my help and my God.

Galatians 3:23-29

23Now before faith came, we were imprisoned and guarded under the law until faith would be revealed. 24Therefore the law was our disciplinarian until Christ came, so that we might be justified by faith. 25But now that faith has come, we are no longer subject to a disciplinarian, 26for in Christ Jesus you are all children of God through faith. 27As many of you as were baptized into Christ have clothed yourselves with Christ. 28There is no longer Jew or Greek, there is no longer slave or free, there is no longer male and female; for all of you are one in Christ Jesus. 29And if you belong to Christ, then you are Abraham's offspring, heirs according to the promise.

Luke 8:26-39

26Then they arrived at the country of the Gerasenes, which is opposite Galilee. 27As he stepped out on land, a man of the city who had demons met him. For a long time he had worn no clothes, and he did not live in a house but in the tombs. 28When he saw Jesus, he fell down before him and shouted at the top of his voice, "What have you to do with me, Jesus, Son of the Most High God? I beg you, do not torment me"— 29for Jesus had commanded the unclean spirit to come out of the man. (For many times it had seized him; he was kept under guard and bound with chains and shackles, but he would break the bonds and be driven by the demon into the wilds.) 30Jesus then asked him, "What is your name?" He said, "Legion"; for many demons had entered him. 31They begged him not to order them to go back into the abyss.

32Now there on the hillside a large herd of swine was feeding; and the demons begged Jesus to let them enter these. So he gave them permission. 33Then the demons came out of the man and entered the swine, and the herd rushed down the steep bank into the lake and was drowned.

34When the swineherds saw what had happened, they ran off and told it in the city and in the country. 35Then people came out to see what had happened, and when they came to Jesus, they found the man from whom the demons had gone sitting at the feet of Jesus, clothed and in his right mind. And they were afraid. 36Those who had seen it told them how the one who had been possessed by demons had been healed. 37Then all the people of the surrounding country of the Gerasenes asked Jesus to leave them; for they were seized with great fear. So he got into the boat and returned. 38The man from whom the demons had gone begged that he might be with him; but Jesus sent him away, saying, 39"Return to your home, and declare how much God has done for you." So he went away, proclaiming throughout the city how much Jesus had done for him.

Primary Hymns and Songs for the Day

"In Christ There Is No East or West" (Gal) (O)
B385, C687, F685, N394, P439
H-3 Hbl-71; Chr-111-112; Desc-95; Org-143
S-2 #162. Harmonization
E529, L359, N394, P440, UM548, VU606, W659
H-3 Chr-111; Desc-74; Org-88
S-1 #231-233. Various treatments
"As the Deer" (Pss)
R9, S2025, SF2025, SP200, VU766
"Baptized in Water" (Gal)
B362, E294, P492, S2248, W720
H-3 Hbl-77; Chr-136; Desc-21; Org-16
S-1 #50-51. Flute and vocal descants
"One Bread, One Body" (Gal, Communion) (C)
C393, UM620, VU467
H-3 Chr-156

Additional Hymn Suggestions

"Guide Me, O Thou Great Jehovah" (1 Kgs) (O)
B56, C622, E690, F608, L343, N18 and N19, P281, UM127 (PD), VU651 (Fr.)
"Give to the Winds Thy Fears" (1 Kgs, Pss)
N404, P286 (PD), UM129 (PD), VU636 (PD)
"If Thou but Suffer God to Guide Thee" (1 Kgs, Pss)
B57, C565, E635, L453, N410, P282, UM142 (PD), VU285 (Fr.) and VU286
"Dear Lord and Father of Mankind" (1 Kings)
B267, C594, E652 and E653, F422, L506, N502, P345, UM358 (PD), VU608
"Rock of Ages" (1 Kgs, Pss)
B342, C214, E685, F108, L327, N596, UM361 (PD)
"Spirit, Spirit of Gentleness" (1 Kgs)
C249, N286, P319, S2120, VU375 (Fr.)
"Loving Spirit" (1 Kgs, Pss)
C244, P323, S2123, SF2123, VU387
"There Is a Balm in Gilead" (1 Kgs, Pss, Luke)
B269 (PD), C501, E676, F48, N553, P394, UM375, VU612, W608
"Healer of Our Every Ill" (1 Kgs, Luke)
C506, S2213, SF2213, VU619
"The Church of Christ, in Every Age" (Gal)
B402, C475, L433, N306, P421, UM589, VU601, W626
"We Walk by Faith" (Gal)
E209, N256, P399, S2196, SF2196, W572
"Who Is My Mother, Who Is My Brother" (Gal)
C486, S2225, SF2225
"Come, Share the Lord" (Gal, Communion)
C408, S2269, SF2269, VU469
"Heal Me, Hands of Jesus" (Luke)
C504, UM262, VU621
"Silence, Frenzied, Unclean Spirit" (Luke)
C186, N176, UM264, VU620, W751
"Christ Is Risen" (Luke)
C222, P104, UM307
"O Young and Fearless Prophet" (Luke)
C669, UM444 (PD)
"This Little Light of Mine" (Luke)
N525, UM585
"Blessed Quietness" (Luke)
F145, C267, N284, S2142, SF2142

Additional Contemporary Suggestions

"Days of Elijah" (1 Kings)
M139
"Praise the Name of Jesus" (Pss)
R7, S2066, SF2066, SP87
"Cry of My Heart" (Pss)
S2165, SF2165, M39
"Who Can Satisfy My Soul Like You?" (Pss)
M28
"Draw Me Close" (Pss)
M29
"Knowing You" ("All I Once Held Dear") (Pss)
M30
"Jesus, You Are My Life" (Pss)
M33
"Breathe" (Pss)
M61; V-3 p. 42 Vocal Solo
"Show Me Your Ways" (Pss)
M107
"Enough" (Pss)
M160
"I'm So Glad Jesus Lifted Me" (Luke)
C529, N474, S2151, SF2151

Vocal Solos

"Joy" (Pss)
V-3 p. 94
"So Art Thou with Me" (Pss)
V-9 p. 34

Anthems

"Balm in Gilead" (1 Kgs, Pss, Luke)
arr. Mark Shepperd; Augsburg 11-10923
SATB with keyboard

"As The Deer" (Pss)
Michael Joncas; GIA G-4883
SATB with keyboard

Other Suggestions

Visuals:
O Run, tree, cake/stone/jar, overturned altar
P Deer, stream, tears, procession, waterfall, waves
E Shackles, ruler, switch, child, baptism, unity
G Tombstone, man(naked/clothed), chains, pigs
Greeting: N819 (Pss)
Opening Prayer: N831 (Luke)
Prayer: C524, UM423. Prayer of the Restless (1 Kgs, Pss)
Blessing: N873 (Gal)
Alternate Lessons: Isa 62:1-9; Ps 16 (see Scripture Index in this, or previous, editions of *Prepare!*).

2 Kings 2:1-2, 6-14

[1]Now when the LORD was about to take Elijah up to heaven by a whirlwind, Elijah and Elisha were on their way from Gilgal. [2]Elijah said to Elisha, "Stay here; for the LORD has sent me as far as Bethel." But Elisha said, "As the LORD lives, and as you yourself live, I will not leave you." So they went down to Bethel.

[6]Then Elijah said to him, "Stay here; for the LORD has sent me to the Jordan." But he said, "As the LORD lives, and as you yourself live, I will not leave you." So the two of them went on. [7]Fifty men of the company of prophets also went, and stood at some distance from them, as they both were standing by the Jordan. [8]Then Elijah took his mantle and rolled it up, and struck the water; the water was parted to the one side and to the other, until the two of them crossed on dry ground.

[9]When they had crossed, Elijah said to Elisha, "Tell me what I may do for you, before I am taken from you." Elisha said, "Please let me inherit a double share of your spirit." [10]He responded, "You have asked a hard thing; yet, if you see me as I am being taken from you, it will be granted you; if not, it will not." [11]As they continued walking and talking, a chariot of fire and horses of fire separated the two of them, and Elijah ascended in a whirlwind into heaven. [12]Elisha kept watching and crying out, "Father, father! The chariots of Israel and its horsemen!" But when he could no longer see him, he grasped his own clothes and tore them in two pieces.

[13]He picked up the mantle of Elijah that had fallen from him, and went back and stood on the bank of the Jordan. [14]He took the mantle of Elijah that had fallen from him, and struck the water, saying, "Where is the LORD, the God of Elijah?" When he had struck the water, the water was parted to the one side and to the other, and Elisha went over.

Psalm 77:1-2, 11-20

[1]I cry aloud to God, aloud to God, that he may hear me. [2]In the day of my trouble I seek the Lord; in the night my hand is stretched out without wearying; my soul refuses to be comforted.

[11]I will call to mind the deeds of the LORD; I will remember your wonders of old. [12]I will meditate on all your work, and muse on your mighty deeds. [13]Your way, O God, is holy. What god is so great as our God? [14]You are the God who works wonders; you have displayed your might among the peoples. [15]With your strong arm you redeemed your people, the descendants of Jacob and Joseph. [16]When the waters saw you, O God, when the waters saw you, they were afraid; the very deep trembled. [17]The clouds poured out water; the skies thundered; your arrows flashed on every side. [18]The crash of your thunder was in the whirlwind; your lightnings lit up the world; the earth trembled and shook. [19]Your way was through the sea, your path, through the mighty waters; yet your footprints were unseen. [20]You led your people like a flock by the hand of Moses and Aaron.

Galatians 5:1, 13-25

[1]For freedom Christ has set us free. Stand firm, therefore, and do not submit again to a yoke of slavery.

[13]For you were called to freedom, brothers and sisters; only do not use your freedom as an opportunity for self-indulgence, but through love become slaves to one another. [14]For the whole law is summed up in a single commandment, "You shall love your neighbor as yourself." [15]If, however, you bite and devour one another, take care that you are not consumed by one another.

[16]Live by the Spirit, I say, and do not gratify the desires of the flesh. [17]For what the flesh desires is opposed to the Spirit, and what the Spirit desires is opposed to the flesh; for these are opposed to each other, to prevent you from doing what you want. [18]But if you are led by the Spirit, you are not subject to the law. [19]Now the works of the flesh are obvious: fornication, impurity, licentiousness, [20]idolatry, sorcery, enmities, strife, jealousy, anger, quarrels, dissensions, factions, [21]envy, drunkenness, carousing, and things like these. I am warning you, as I warned you before: those who do such things will not inherit the kingdom of God.

[22]By contrast, the fruit of the Spirit is love, joy, peace, patience, kindness, generosity, faithfulness, [23]gentleness, and self-control. There is no law against such things. [24]And those who belong to Christ Jesus have crucified the flesh with its passions and desires. [25]If we live by the Spirit, let us also be guided by the Spirit.

Luke 9:51-62

[51]When the days drew near for him to be taken up, he set his face to go to Jerusalem. [52]And he sent messengers ahead of him. On their way they entered a village of the Samaritans to make ready for him; [53]but they did not receive him, because his face was set toward Jerusalem. [54]When his disciples James and John saw it, they said, "Lord, do you want us to command fire to come down from heaven and consume them?" [55]But he turned and rebuked them. [56]Then they went on to another village.

[57]As they were going along the road, someone said to him, "I will follow you wherever you go." [58]And Jesus said to him, "Foxes have holes, and birds of the air have nests; but the Son of Man has nowhere to lay his head." [59]To another he said, "Follow me." But he said, "Lord, first let me go and bury my father." [60]But Jesus said to him, "Let the dead bury their own dead; but as for you, go and proclaim the kingdom of God." [61]Another said, "I will follow you, Lord; but let me first say farewell to those at my home." [62]Jesus said to him, "No one who puts a hand to the plow and looks back is fit for the kingdom of God."

Primary Hymns and Songs for the Day

"O God, Our Help in Ages Past" (Pss) (O)
B74, C67, E680, F370, L320, N25, P210, UM117 (PD), VU806, W579
H-3 Hbl-33, 80; Chr-143; Desc-93; Org-132
S-1 #293-296. Various treatments

"Spirit of God, Descend upon My Heart" (2 Kgs, Gal)
B245, C265, F147, L486, N290, P326, UM500 (PD), VU378
H-3 Chr-175; Desc-77; Org-94
S-2 #125-128. Various treatments

"Swing Low, Sweet Chariot" (2 Kgs)
C643, UM703
H-3 Chr-177

"Wade in the Water" (2 Kgs, Gal)
C371, S2107, SF2107

"Of All the Spirit's Gifts to Me" (Gal)
UM336
S-2 #121. Descant
B442, C270

"Holy Spirit, Truth Divine" (Gal)
L257, P321, UM465 (PD)
H-3 Chr-63, 100
S-1 #53. Descant
C241, N63, VU368

"O Jesus, I Have Promised" (Luke) (C)
B276, C612, F402, N493, P388, UM396 (PD)
S-2 #9. Descant
E655, L503 (PD), P389, VU120

Additional Hymn Suggestions

"Children of the Heavenly Father" (2 Kgs, Pss)
B55, F89, L474, N487, UM141

"Spirit of the Living God" (2 Kgs, Gal)
B244, C259, F155, N283, P322, R90, SP131, UM393, VU376

"Come, Holy Ghost, Our Souls Inspire" (2 Kgs, Gal)
E503 and E504, L472 and L473, N268, P125, UM651 (PD), VU201

"I Sing the Almighty Power of God" (Pss)
B42, C64, E398, N12, P288 (PD), R54, UM152 (PD), VU231 (PD), W502 (PD)

"By the Babylonian Rivers" (Pss)
P246, S2217, VU859, W426

"Where Charity and Love Prevail" (Gal)
E581, L126, N396, UM549

"Healer of Our Every Ill" (Gal)
C506, S2213, SF2213, VU619

"In Remembrance of Me" (Gal, Communion)
B365, C403, S2254

"O for a Closer Walk with God" (Gal)
E684, P396, N450

"I Want to Walk as a Child of the Light" (Luke)
E490, R152, UM206, W510

"Where He Leads Me" (Luke)
B288, C346, F607, UM338 (PD)

"Jesus Calls Us" (Luke)
B293, C337, F399, L494, N171 and N172, UM398 (PD), VU562

"Lord, I Want to Be a Christian" (Luke)
B489, C589, F421, N454, P372 (PD), R145, UM402

"Take Up Thy Cross" (Luke) (C)
B494, E675, L398, N204, P393, UM415 (PD), VU561, W634

Additional Contemporary Suggestions

"Days of Elijah" (1 Kgs)
M139

"How Great Is Our God" (Pss)
M117

"Step By Step" (Pss, Luke)
M51

"Holy Spirit, Come to Us" (Gal)
S2118, SF2118, W473

"Live in Charity" ("Ubi Caritas") (Gal)
C523, R226, S2179, SF2179, W604

"I've Got Peace Like a River" (Gal)
B418, C530, N478, P368, S2145, VU577

"Jesu, Jesu" (Gal)
B501, C600, E602, N498, P367, R289, UM432, VU593, W431

"Cry of My Heart" (Luke)
S2165, SF2165, M39

"Lead Me, Lord" (Luke)
M108

Vocal Solos

"Swing Low, Sweet Chariot!" (2 Kgs)
V-7 p. 36

"Because You Are God's Chosen Ones" (Gal)
V-8 p. 286

Anthems

"Will You Come and Follow Me" (Luke)
John Bell; GIA G4384
SATB with keyboar

"A Vineyard Grows" (Gal)
K. Lee Scott; MorningStar 509010
SATB with organ

Other Suggestions

Visuals:
O Tornado, mantel, parted water, torn clothes
P Prayer, arm, rain, clouds, storm, sea, Exodus
E Open shackles, love, brokenness, warning
G Jesus, fire, fox, nest, pillow, coffin, plow

Prayer: C89. Christ Comes as One Unknown (Luke)
Prayers: F371 (Gal) and F511 (Gal, Luke)
Blessing: N875 (Gal)
Alternate Lessons: 1 Kgs 19:15-16, 19-21; Ps 16 (see Scripture Index in this, or previous, editions of *Prepare!*).

2 Kings 5:1-14

1Naaman, commander of the army of the king of Aram, was a great man and in high favor with his master, because by him the LORD had given victory to Aram. The man, though a mighty warrior, suffered from leprosy. 2Now the Arameans on one of their raids had taken a young girl captive from the land of Israel, and she served Naaman's wife. 3She said to her mistress, "If only my lord were with the prophet who is in Samaria! He would cure him of his leprosy." 4So Naaman went in and told his lord just what the girl from the land of Israel had said. 5And the king of Aram said, "Go then, and I will send along a letter to the king of Israel."

He went, taking with him ten talents of silver, six thousand shekels of gold, and ten sets of garments. 6He brought the letter to the king of Israel, which read, "When this letter reaches you, know that I have sent to you my servant Naaman, that you may cure him of his leprosy." 7When the king of Israel read the letter, he tore his clothes and said, "Am I God, to give death or life, that this man sends word to me to cure a man of his leprosy? Just look and see how he is trying to pick a quarrel with me."

8But when Elisha the man of God heard that the king of Israel had torn his clothes, he sent a message to the king, "Why have you torn your clothes? Let him come to me, that he may learn that there is a prophet in Israel." 9So Naaman came with his horses and chariots, and halted at the entrance of Elisha's house. 10Elisha sent a messenger to him, saying, "Go, wash in the Jordan seven times, and your flesh shall be restored and you shall be clean." 11But Naaman became angry and went away, saying, "I thought that for me he would surely come out, and stand and call on the name of the LORD his God, and would wave his hand over the spot, and cure the leprosy! 12Are not Abana and Pharpar, the rivers of Damascus, better than all the waters of Israel? Could I not wash in them, and be clean?" He turned and went away in a rage. 13But his servants approached and said to him, "Father, if the prophet had commanded you to do something difficult, would you not have done it? How much more, when all he said to you was, 'Wash, and be clean'?" 14So he went down and immersed himself seven times in the Jordan, according to the word of the man of God; his flesh was restored like the flesh of a young boy, and he was clean.

Psalm 30

1I will extol you, O LORD, for you have drawn me up, and did not let my foes rejoice over me. 2O LORD my God, I cried to you for help, and you have healed me. 3O LORD, you brought up my soul from Sheol, restored me to life from among those gone down to the Pit. 4Sing praises to the LORD, O you his faithful ones, and give thanks to his holy name. 5For his anger is but for a moment; his favor is for a lifetime. Weeping may linger for the night, but joy comes with the morning. 6As for me, I said in my prosperity, "I shall never be moved." 7By your favor, O LORD, you had established me as a strong mountain; you hid your face; I was dismayed. 8To you, O LORD, I cried, and to the LORD I made supplication: 9"What profit is there in my death, if I go down to the Pit? Will the dust praise you? Will it tell of your faithfulness? 10Hear, O LORD, and be gracious to me! O LORD, be my helper!" 11You have turned my mourning into dancing; you have taken off my sackcloth and clothed me with joy, 12so that my soul may praise you and not be silent. O LORD my God, I will give thanks to you forever.

Galatians 6:(1-6) 7-16

1My friends, if anyone is detected in a transgression, you who have received the Spirit should restore such a one in a spirit of gentleness. Take care that you yourselves are not tempted. 2Bear one another's burdens, and in this way you will fulfill the law of Christ. 3For if those who are nothing think they are something, they deceive themselves. 4All must test their own work; then that work, rather than their neighbor's work, will become a cause for pride. 5For all must carry their own loads.

6Those who are taught the word must share in all good things with their teacher.

7Do not be deceived; God is not mocked, for you reap whatever you sow. 8If you sow to your own flesh, you will reap corruption from the flesh; but if you sow to the Spirit, you will reap eternal life from the Spirit. 9So let us not grow weary in doing what is right, for we will reap at harvest time, if we do not give up. 10So then, whenever we have an opportunity, let us work for the good of all, and especially for those of the family of faith.

11See what large letters I make when I am writing in my own hand! 12It is those who want to make a good showing in the flesh that try to compel you to be circumcised—only that they may not be persecuted for the cross of Christ. 13Even the circumcised do not themselves obey the law, but they want you to be circumcised so that they may boast about your flesh. 14May I never boast of anything except the cross of our Lord Jesus Christ, by which the world has been crucified to me, and I to the world. 15For neither circumcision nor uncircumcision is anything; but a new creation is everything! 16As for those who will follow this rule—peace be upon them, and mercy, and upon the Israel of God.

Luke 10:1-11, 16-20

1After this the Lord appointed seventy others and sent them on ahead of him in pairs to every town and place where he himself intended to go. 2He said to them, "The harvest is plentiful, but the laborers are few; therefore ask the Lord of the harvest to send out laborers into his harvest. 3Go on your way. See, I am sending you out like lambs into the midst of wolves. 4Carry no purse, no bag, no sandals; and greet no one on the road. 5Whatever house you enter, first say, 'Peace to this house!' 6And if anyone is there who shares in peace, your peace will rest on that person; but if not, it will return to you. 7Remain in the same house, eating and drinking whatever they provide, for the laborer deserves to be paid. Do not move about from house to house. 8Whenever you enter a town and its people welcome you, eat what is set before you; 9cure the sick who are there, and say to them, 'The kingdom of God has come near to you.' 10 But whenever you enter a town and they do not welcome you, go out into its streets and say, 11'Even the dust of your town that clings to our feet, we wipe off in protest against you. Yet know this: the kingdom of God has come near.'

16"Whoever listens to you listens to me, and whoever rejects you rejects me, and whoever rejects me rejects the one who sent me."

17The seventy returned with joy, saying, "Lord, in your name even the demons submit to us!" 18He said to them, "I watched Satan fall from heaven like a flash of lightning. 19See, I have given you authority to tread on snakes and scorpions, and over all the power of the enemy; and nothing will hurt you. 20Nevertheless, do not rejoice at this, that the spirits submit to you, but rejoice that your names are written in heaven."

Primary Hymns and Songs for the Day

"Praise, My Soul, the King of Heaven" (2 Kgs, Pss) (O)
B32, C23, E410, F339, L549, P478 or 479, R53, UM66 (PD), VU240, W530
H-3 Hbl-88; Chr-162; Desc-67; Org-75
S-1 #205. Harmonization
#206. Descant

"Joy Comes with the Dawn" (Pss)
S2210, SF2210, VU166

"In the Cross of Christ I Glory" (Pss, Gal)
B554, C207, E441, F251, L104, N193, P84, UM295 (PD)
H-3 Hbl-72; Chr-113; Desc-89; Org-119
S-1 #276-277. Harmonization with descant

"When I Survey the Wondrous Cross" (Gal)
B144, C195, F258, N224, P101, R236, UM298 (PD)
H-3 Hbl-6, 102; Chr-213; Desc-49; Org-49
S-1 #155. Descant
E474, L482, P100, UM299 (PD), VU149 (Fr.), W433
H-3 Hbl-47; Chr-214; Desc-90; Org-127
S-1 #288. Transposition to E-flat major

"Lord, You Give the Great Commission" (Luke) (C)
C459, P429, R305, UM584, VU512, W470
H-3 Hbl-61; Chr-132; Org-2
S-1 #4-5. Instrumental and vocal descants

"Sent Out in Jesus' Name" ("Enviado Soy de Dios") (C)
S2184, SF2184

Additional Hymn Suggestions

"Wash, O God, Our Sons and Daughters" (2 Kgs, Baptism)
C365, UM605, VU442

"Come, We That Love the Lord" (Pss)
B525, E392, N379, UM732, VU715, W552

"Marching to Zion" (Pss)
B524, C707, F550, N382, UM733 (PD), VU714

"Ask Ye What Great Think I Know" (Gal)
B538, N49, UM163 (PD), VU338

"Beneath the Cross of Jesus" (Gal)
B291, C197, E498, F253, L107, N190, P92, UM297 (PD), VU135

"Jesus, Keep Me Near the Cross" (Gal)
B280, C587, N197, UM301 (PD), VU142

"Thine Be the Glory" (Gal)
B163, C218, F291, L145, N253, P122, UM308, VU173

"Blest Be the Tie That Binds" (Gal)
B387, C433, F560, L370, N393, P438, UM557 (PD), VU602

"Healer of Our Every Ill" (Gal, Luke)
C506, S2213, SF2213, VU619

"Who Is My Mother, Who Is My Brother" (Gal)
C486, S2225, SF2225

"We've a Story to Tell to the Nations" (Luke)
B586, C484, F659, UM569 (PD)

"O Zion, Haste" (Luke)
B583, C482, E539, F658, L397, UM573 (PD)

"Here I Am, Lord" (Luke)
C452, P525, R149, UM593, VU509

"In Remembrance of Me" (Luke, Communion)
B365, C403, S2254

Additional Contemporary Suggestions

"Spirit of the Living God" (2 Kgs)
B244, C259, F155, N283, P322, R90, SP131, UM393, VU376

"Water, River, Spirit, Grace" (2 Kgs, Baptism)
C66, S2253, SF2253

"Someone Asked the Question" (Pss)
N523, S2144, SF2144

"Trading My Sorrows" (Pss)
M75

"Let It Be Said of Us" (Gal)
M53

"The Wonderful Cross" (Gal)
M76

"Make Us One" (Gal, Communion)
S2224, SF2224, SP137

"The Servant Song" (Gal)
C490, N539, R148, S2222, SF2222, SP193, VU595

"Make Me a Channel of Your Peace" (Luke)
S2171, SF2171, VU684

"Song of Hope" (Luke)
P432, S2186, VU424

"Days of Elijah" (Luke)
M139

Vocal Solos

"Standin' In De Need of Prayer" (2 Kgs, Pss)
V-7 p. 40

"Reach Out to Your Neighbor" (Gal, Luke)
V-8 p. 372

Anthems

"Sing Praises to the Lord" (Pss)
Timothy Shaw; Kjox 6330
Unison/Two-part with keyboard and C Instrument

"Beneath the Cross of Jesus" (Gal)
arr. Benjamin Harlan; Augsburg 0-8006-7800-1
SATB with organ and violin

Other Suggestions

Visuals:
O Letter, torn clothes, healing, water/river
P Oil/cruet, joy/dance, mourn/sackcloth
E Pairs, harvest/workers, cross, butterfly/chrysalis
G Oil, no. 70/pairs, harvest, lamb/wolf, ministry, reject, joy

Greeting: F340 or N819 (Pss)
Call to Confession: N833 (Gal)
Prayer of Confession: N836 (Gal)
Prayer: C723. A Prayer for the Nation (Independence Day)
Litany: C209. The Wondrous Cross (Gal)
Prayer: F410 or N844 (Gal, Luke)
Alternate Lessons: Isa 66:10-14; Ps 66:1-9 (see Scripture Index in this, or previous, editions of *Prepare!*).

Amos 7:7-17

[7]This is what he showed me: the Lord was standing beside a wall built with a plumb line, with a plumb line in his hand. [8]And the LORD said to me, "Amos, what do you see?" And I said, "A plumb line." Then the Lord said, "See, I am setting a plumb line in the midst of my people Israel; I will never again pass them by; [9]the high places of Isaac shall be made desolate, and the sanctuaries of Israel shall be laid waste, and I will rise against the house of Jeroboam with the sword."

[10]Then Amaziah, the priest of Bethel, sent to King Jeroboam of Israel, saying, "Amos has conspired against you in the very center of the house of Israel; the land is not able to bear all his words. [11]For thus Amos has said, 'Jeroboam shall die by the sword, and Israel must go into exile away from his land.' " [12]And Amaziah said to Amos, "O seer, go, flee away to the land of Judah, earn your bread there, and prophesy there; [13]but never again prophesy at Bethel, for it is the king's sanctuary, and it is a temple of the kingdom."

[14]Then Amos answered Amaziah, "I am no prophet, nor a prophet's son; but I am a herdsman, and a dresser of sycamore trees, [15]and the LORD took me from following the flock, and the LORD said to me, 'Go, prophesy to my people Israel.' [16]"Now therefore hear the word of the LORD. You say, 'Do not prophesy against Israel, and do not preach against the house of Isaac.' [17]Therefore thus says the LORD: 'Your wife shall become a prostitute in the city, and your sons and your daughters shall fall by the sword, and your land shall be parceled out by line; you yourself shall die in an unclean land, and Israel shall surely go into exile away from its land.' "

Psalm 82

[1]God has taken his place in the divine council; in the midst of the gods he holds judgment: [2]"How long will you judge unjustly and show partiality to the wicked? [3]Give justice to the weak and the orphan; maintain the right of the lowly and the destitute. [4]Rescue the weak and the needy; deliver them from the hand of the wicked." [5]They have neither knowledge nor understanding, they walk around in darkness; all the foundations of the earth are shaken. [6]I say, "You are gods, children of the Most High, all of you; [7]nevertheless, you shall die like mortals, and fall like any prince." [8]Rise up, O God, judge the earth; for all the nations belong to you!

Colossians 1:1-14

[1]Paul, an apostle of Christ Jesus by the will of God, and Timothy our brother,

[2]To the saints and faithful brothers and sisters in Christ in Colossae:

Grace to you and peace from God our Father.

[3]In our prayers for you we always thank God, the Father of our Lord Jesus Christ, [4]for we have heard of your faith in Christ Jesus and of the love that you have for all the saints, [5]because of the hope laid up for you in heaven. You have heard of this hope before in the word of the truth, the gospel [6]that has come to you. Just as it is bearing fruit and growing in the whole world, so it has been bearing fruit among yourselves from the day you heard it and truly comprehended the grace of God. [7]This you learned from Epaphras, our beloved fellow servant. He is a faithful minister of Christ on your behalf, [8]and he has made known to us your love in the Spirit.

[9]For this reason, since the day we heard it, we have not ceased praying for you and asking that you may be filled with the knowledge of God's will in all spiritual wisdom and understanding, [10]so that you may lead lives worthy of the Lord, fully pleasing to him, as you bear fruit in every good work and as you grow in the knowledge of God. [11]May you be made strong with all the strength that comes from his glorious power, and may you be prepared to endure everything with patience, while joyfully [12]giving thanks to the Father, who has enabled you to share in the inheritance of the saints in the light. [13]He has rescued us from the power of darkness and transferred us into the kingdom of his beloved Son, [14]in whom we have redemption, the forgiveness of sins.

Luke 10:25-37

[25]Just then a lawyer stood up to test Jesus. "Teacher," he said, "what must I do to inherit eternal life?" [26]He said to him, "What is written in the law? What do you read there?" [27]He answered, "You shall love the Lord your God with all your heart, and with all your soul, and with all your strength, and with all your mind; and your neighbor as yourself." [28]And he said to him, "You have given the right answer; do this, and you will live."

[29]But wanting to justify himself, he asked Jesus, "And who is my neighbor?" [30]Jesus replied, "A man was going down from Jerusalem to Jericho, and fell into the hands of robbers, who stripped him, beat him, and went away, leaving him half dead. [31]Now by chance a priest was going down that road; and when he saw him, he passed by on the other side. [32]So likewise a Levite, when he came to the place and saw him, passed by on the other side. [33]But a Samaritan while traveling came near him; and when he saw him, he was moved with pity. [34]He went to him and bandaged his wounds, having poured oil and wine on them. Then he put him on his own animal, brought him to an inn, and took care of him. [35]The next day he took out two denarii, gave them to the innkeeper, and said, 'Take care of him; and when I come back, I will repay you whatever more you spend.' [36]Which of these three, do you think, was a neighbor to the man who fell into the hands of the robbers?" [37]He said, "The one who showed him mercy." Jesus said to him, "Go and do likewise."

Good Samaritan

Primary Hymns and Songs for the Day

"God of Grace and God of Glory" (Pss) (O)
B395, C464, E594, F528, L415, N436, P420, R301, UM577
H-3 Hbl-25, 51, 58; Chr-89; Desc-26; Org-23
S-1 #76-77. Descant and harmonization
VU686

"What Does the Lord Require" (Amos)
E605, P405, UM441, W624
H-3 Chr-211
C659

"We Meet You, O Christ" (Luke)
C183, UM257
S-2 #166. Descant
P311
H-3 Chr-76
VU183

"Love the Lord Your God" (Luke)
S2168, SF2168

"The Summons" (Luke)
S2130, SF2130, VU567
H-3 Chr-220

"Pues Si Vivimos" ("When We Are Living") (Col, Luke) (C)
C536, N499, P400, UM356, VU581
S-1 #320. Orff instrument arrangement
H-3 Chr-218; Org-155

Additional Hymn Suggestions

"God Hath Spoken By the Prophets" (Amos)
L238, UM108 (PD), W516

"The Battle Hymn of the Republic" (Amos, Pss)
B633, C705, F692, L332, N610, UM717 (PD), W686

"Rejoice in God's Saints" (Amos, Col)
C476, UM708

"For the Healing of the Nations" (Pss)
C668, N576, UM428, VU678

"This Is My Song" (Pss)
C722, N591, UM437

"Bring Many Names" (Pss)
C10, N11, S2047, SF2047, VU268

"Mothering God, You Gave Me Birth" (Col)
C83, N467, S2050, SF2050, VU320

"There's a Spirit in the Air" (Col, Luke)
B393, C257, N292, P433, R282, UM192, VU582, W531

"Lord, I Want to Be a Christian" (Luke)
B489, C589, F421, N454, P372 (PD), R145, UM402

"Where Cross the Crowded Ways of Life" (Luke)
C665, E609, F665, L429, N543, P408, UM427 (PD), VU681

"Spirit of God, Descend upon My Heart" (Luke)
B245, C265, F147, L486, N290, P326, UM500 (PD), VU378

"Sunday's Palms Are Wednesday's Ashes" (Luke)
S2138, SF2138, VU107

"Healer of Our Every Ill" (Luke)
C506, S2213, SF2213, VU619

"In Remembrance of Me" (Luke, Communion)
B365, C403, S2254

Additional Contemporary Suggestions

"Give Thanks" (Pss, Col)
C528, R266, S2036, SF2036, SP170

"In the Lord I'll Be Ever Thankful" (Col)
S2195, SF2195

"Make Me a Channel of Your Peace" (Luke)
S2171, SF2171, VU684

"Live in Charity" ("Ubi Caritas") (Luke)
C523, R226, S2179, SF2179, W604

"Jesu, Jesu" (Luke)
B501, C600, E602, N498, P367, R289, UM432, VU593, W431

"More Love, More Power" (Luke)
M40

"You're Worthy of My Praise" (Luke)
M41

"Refresh My Heart" (Luke)
M49

"Let It Be Said of Us" (Luke)
M53

"Rise Up and Praise Him" (Luke)
M62

"Just Let Me Say" (Luke)
M83

"With All of My Heart" (Luke)
M86, SP187

"Take This Life"
M98

Vocal Solo

"A Song About Me" (Luke)
V-8 p. 364

Anthems

"Celtic Benediction" (Col)
Sue Orrell; Kjos 6337
Two-part with piano

"Children of the Heavenly Father" (Col, Luke)
arr. Bradley Ellingboe; Kjos 8787
SATB a cappella

Other Suggestions

Visuals:
O Wall, plumb line, sword, scales of justice
P Scales, ministry with poor, children, earthquake
E Pray, Bible, fruit/globe, joy, light, rescue
G Briefcase, bloody clothes, bandages, oil, wine, coins

Opening Prayer: N817 (Col)
Prayer of Confession: N835 (Amos, Pss)
Prayer: F624 or N861 (Amos, Pss Luke)
Prayer: C31. Prayer of St. Augustine (Col)
Readings: F678 or UM449 (Amos, Pss)
Alternate Lessons: Deut 30:9-14; Ps 25:1-10 (see Scripture Index in this, or previous, editions of *Prepare!*).

Amos 8:1-12

[1]This is what the Lord GOD showed me—a basket of summer fruit. [2]He said, "Amos, what do you see?" And I said, "A basket of summer fruit." Then the LORD said to me, "The end has come upon my people Israel; I will never again pass them by. [3]The songs of the temple shall become wailings in that day," says the Lord GOD; "the dead bodies shall be many, cast out in every place. Be silent!"
[4]Hear this, you that trample on the needy, and bring to ruin the poor of the land, [5]saying, "When will the new moon be over so that we may sell grain; and the sabbath, so that we may offer wheat for sale? We will make the ephah small and the shekel great, and practice deceit with false balances, [6]buying the poor for silver and the needy for a pair of sandals, and selling the sweepings of the wheat." [7]The LORD has sworn by the pride of Jacob: Surely I will never forget any of their deeds. [8]Shall not the land tremble on this account, and everyone mourn who lives in it, and all of it rise like the Nile, and be tossed about and sink again, like the Nile of Egypt? [9]On that day, says the Lord GOD, I will make the sun go down at noon, and darken the earth in broad daylight. [10]I will turn your feasts into mourning, and all your songs into lamentation; I will bring sackcloth on all loins, and baldness on every head; I will make it like the mourning for an only son, and the end of it like a bitter day. [11]The time is surely coming, says the Lord GOD, when I will send a famine on the land; not a famine of bread, or a thirst for water, but of hearing the words of the LORD. [12]They shall wander from sea to sea, and from north to east; they shall run to and fro, seeking the word of the LORD, but they shall not find it.

Psalm 52

[1]Why do you boast, O mighty one, of mischief done against the godly? All day long [2]you are plotting destruction. Your tongue is like a sharp razor, you worker of treachery. [3]You love evil more than good, and lying more than speaking the truth. [4]You love all words that devour, O deceitful tongue. [5]But God will break you down forever; he will snatch and tear you from your tent; he will uproot you from the land of the living. [6]The righteous will see, and fear, and will laugh at the evildoer, saying, [7]"See the one who would not take refuge in God, but trusted in abundant riches, and sought refuge in wealth!" [8]But I am like a green olive tree in the house of God. I trust in the steadfast love of God forever and ever. [9]I will thank you forever, because of what you have done. In the presence of the faithful I will proclaim your name, for it is good.

Colossians 1:15-28

[15]He is the image of the invisible God, the firstborn of all creation; [16]for in him all things in heaven and on earth were created, things visible and invisible, whether thrones or dominions or rulers or powers—all things have been created through him and for him. [17]He himself is before all things, and in him all things hold together. [18]He is the head of the body, the church; he is the beginning, the firstborn from the dead, so that he might come to have first place in everything. [19]For in him all the fullness of God was pleased to dwell, [20]and through him God was pleased to reconcile to himself all things, whether on earth or in heaven, by making peace through the blood of his cross.

[21]And you who were once estranged and hostile in mind, doing evil deeds, [22]he has now reconciled in his fleshly body through death, so as to present you holy and blameless and irreproachable before him— [23]provided that you continue securely established and steadfast in the faith, without shifting from the hope promised by the gospel that you heard, which has been proclaimed to every creature under heaven. I, Paul, became a servant of this gospel.

[24]I am now rejoicing in my sufferings for your sake, and in my flesh I am completing what is lacking in Christ's afflictions for the sake of his body, that is, the church. [25]I became its servant according to God's commission that was given to me for you, to make the word of God fully known, [26]the mystery that has been hidden throughout the ages and generations but has now been revealed to his saints. [27]To them God chose to make known how great among the Gentiles are the riches of the glory of this mystery, which is Christ in you, the hope of glory. [28]It is he whom we proclaim, warning everyone and teaching everyone in all wisdom, so that we may present everyone mature in Christ.

Luke 10:38-42

[38]Now as they went on their way, he entered a certain village, where a woman named Martha welcomed him into her home. [39]She had a sister named Mary, who sat at the Lord's feet and listened to what he was saying. [40]But Martha was distracted by her many tasks; so she came to him and asked, "Lord, do you not care that my sister has left me to do all the work by myself? Tell her then to help me." [41]But the Lord answered her, "Martha, Martha, you are worried and distracted by many things; [42]there is need of only one thing. Mary has chosen the better part, which will not be taken away from her."

Notes

Primary Hymns and Songs for the Day

"Immortal, Invisible, God Only Wise" (Col) (O)
B6, C66, E423, F319, L526, N1, P263, R46, UM103 (PD), VU264, W512
H-3 Hbl-15, 71; Chr-65; Desc-93; Org-135
S-1 #300. Harmonization
"All Who Love and Serve Your City" (Amos, Luke)
C670, E571, P413, UM433
H-3 Chr-26, 65; Org-19
S-1 #62. Descant
E570, L436, W621
"What Does the Lord Require" (Amos)
E605, P405, UM441, W624
H-3 Chr-211
C659
"It Is Well With My Soul" (Col) (C)
B410, C561, F495, L346, N438, UM377 (PD)
H-3 Chr-113

Additional Hymn Suggestions

"When the Church of Jesus" (Amos)
B396, C470, UM592
"My Lord, What a Morning" (Amos)
C708, P449, UM719, VU708
"Why Stand So Far Away, My God?" (Amos, Pss)
C671, S2180, SF2180
"O God of Earth and Altar (Amos)
C724, E591, L428, N582, P291
"Beneath the Cross of Jesus" (Col)
B291, C197, E498, F253, L107, N190, P92, UM297 (PD), VU135
"Jesus, Keep Me Near the Cross" (Col)
B280, C587, N197, UM301 (PD), VU142
"Praise the Source of Faith and Learning" (Col)
N411, S2004, SF2004
"O Holy Spirit, Root of Life" (Col)
C251, N57, S2121, SF2121, VU379
"Christ Beside Me" (Col)
R164, S2166, SF2166
"We Are God's People" (Col)
B383, F546, S2220, SF2220
"Dear Lord and Father of Mankind" (Luke)
(alternate text, "Parent of Us All")
B267, C594, E652 and E653, F422, L506, N502, P345, UM358 (PD), VU608
O Jesus, I Have Promised (Luke)
B276, C612, F402, N493, P388, UM396 (PD)
E655, L503 (PD), P389, VU120
"Take My Life, and Let It Be" (Luke)
B277, C609, P391
B283, E707, L406, N448, R133, UM399 (PD), VU506
"Be Thou My Vision" (Luke)
B60, C595, E488, F468, N451, P339, R151, UM451, VU642
"Jesus, Priceless Treasure" (Luke)
F277, L457 and L458 (PD), N480 P365, UM532 (PD), VU667 and VU668 (Fr.)
"Come and Find the Quiet Center" (Luke)
C575, S2128, SF2128, VU374
"I'm Gonna Live So God Can Use Me" (Luke)
C614, P369, S2153, VU575

Additional Contemporary Suggestions

"Forever" (Pss)
M68
"Hallelujah" ("Your Love Is Amazing") (Pss)
M118
"Your Love, Oh Lord" (Pss)
M189
"Sanctuary" (Col)
M52, R185, S2164, SF2164
"Shine, Jesus, Shine" (Col)
B579, R247, S2173, SF2173, SP142
"Holy Ground" (Col)
B224, C112, S2272, SF2272, SP86
"That's Why We Praise Him" (Col)
M94
"Every Move I Make" (Luke)
M122
"Turn Your Eyes upon Jesus" (Luke)
B320, F621, SP218, UM349

Vocal Solos

"Jesus Revealed in Me" (Col)
V-8 p. 347
"Be Thou My Vision" (Col, Luke)
V-6 p. 13

Anthems

"Rise, Shine!" (Col, Luke)
Dale Wood; Augsburg 11-10737
SATB with organ

"Thee We Adore" (Col, Luke)
arr. Ralph M. Johnson; Kjos 6261
Two-part mixed with piano

Other Suggestions

Visuals:
O Basket/fruit, new moon, silver, sandals, sackcloth
P Uprooted tree, wealth, olive tree, joy, laugh
E Risen Christ, glue, blood/cross, service
G Pots/pans, dust cloth, mop, dishes, Jesus/two women
Greeting: N822 (Pss) or N824 (Col)
Opening Prayer: N830 (Col)
Words of Assurance: N839 (Pss)
Prayer: C660, UM446. Serving the Poor (Amos)
Prayer: N858. Providence of God (Eph)
Reading: C271, F233, or F445 (Col)
Reading: F680. Can This World Be Fed? (Amos)
Alternate Lessons: Gen 18:1-10a; Ps 15 (see Scripture Index in this, or previous, editions of *Prepare!*).

Hosea 1:2-10

[2]When the LORD first spoke through Hosea, the LORD said to Hosea, "Go, take for yourself a wife of whoredom and have children of whoredom, for the land commits great whoredom by forsaking the LORD." [3]So he went and took Gomer daughter of Diblaim, and she conceived and bore him a son.

[4]And the LORD said to him, "Name him Jezreel; for in a little while I will punish the house of Jehu for the blood of Jezreel, and I will put an end to the kingdom of the house of Israel. [5]On that day I will break the bow of Israel in the valley of Jezreel."

[6]She conceived again and bore a daughter. Then the LORD said to him, "Name her Lo-ruhamah, for I will no longer have pity on the house of Israel or forgive them. [7]But I will have pity on the house of Judah, and I will save them by the LORD their God; I will not save them by bow, or by sword, or by war, or by horses, or by horsemen."

[8]When she had weaned Lo-ruhamah, she conceived and bore a son. [9]Then the LORD said, "Name him Lo-ammi, for you are not my people and I am not your God."

[10]Yet the number of the people of Israel shall be like the sand of the sea, which can be neither measured nor numbered; and in the place where it was said to them, "You are not my people," it shall be said to them, "Children of the living God."

Psalm 85

[1]LORD, you were favorable to your land; you restored the fortunes of Jacob. [2]You forgave the iniquity of your people; you pardoned all their sin. [3]You withdrew all your wrath; you turned from your hot anger. [4]Restore us again, O God of our salvation, and put away your indignation toward us. [5]Will you be angry with us forever? Will you prolong your anger to all generations? [6]Will you not revive us again, so that your people may rejoice in you? [7]Show us your steadfast love, O LORD, and grant us your salvation. [8]Let me hear what God the LORD will speak, for he will speak peace to his people, to his faithful, to those who turn to him in their hearts. [9]Surely his salvation is at hand for those who fear him, that his glory may dwell in our land. [10]Steadfast love and faithfulness will meet; righteousness and peace will kiss each other. [11]Faithfulness will spring up from the ground, and righteousness will look down from the sky. [12]The LORD will give what is good, and our land will yield its increase. [13]Righteousness will go before him, and will make a path for his steps.

Colossians 2:6-15 (16-19)

[6]As you therefore have received Christ Jesus the Lord, continue to live your lives in him, [7]rooted and built up in him and established in the faith, just as you were taught, abounding in thanksgiving.

[8]See to it that no one takes you captive through philosophy and empty deceit, according to human tradition, according to the elemental spirits of the universe, and not according to Christ. [9]For in him the whole fullness of deity dwells bodily, [10]and you have come to fullness in him, who is the head of every ruler and authority. [11]In him also you were circumcised with a spiritual circumcision, by putting off the body of the flesh in the circumcision of Christ; [12]when you were buried with him in baptism, you were also raised with him through faith in the power of God, who raised him from the dead. [13]And when you were dead in trespasses and the uncircumcision of your flesh, God made you alive together with him, when he forgave us all our trespasses, [14]erasing the record that stood against us with its legal demands. He set this aside, nailing it to the cross. [15]He disarmed the rulers and authorities and made a public example of them, triumphing over them in it.

[16]Therefore do not let anyone condemn you in matters of food and drink or of observing festivals, new moons, or sabbaths. [17]These are only a shadow of what is to come, but the substance belongs to Christ. [18]Do not let anyone disqualify you, insisting on self-abasement and worship of angels, dwelling on visions, puffed up without cause by a human way of thinking, [19]and not holding fast to the head, from whom the whole body, nourished and held together by its ligaments and sinews, grows with a growth that is from God.

Luke 11:1-13

[1]He was praying in a certain place, and after he had finished, one of his disciples said to him, "Lord, teach us to pray, as John taught his disciples." [2]He said to them, "When you pray, say: Father, hallowed be your name. Your kingdom come. [3]Give us each day our daily bread. [4]And forgive us our sins, for we ourselves forgive everyone indebted to us. And do not bring us to the time of trial."

[5]And he said to them, "Suppose one of you has a friend, and you go to him at midnight and say to him, 'Friend, lend me three loaves of bread; [6]for a friend of mine has arrived, and I have nothing to set before him.' [7]And he answers from within, 'Do not bother me; the door has already been locked, and my children are with me in bed; I cannot get up and give you anything.' [8]I tell you, even though he will not get up and give him anything because he is his friend, at least because of his persistence he will get up and give him whatever he needs.

[9]"So I say to you, Ask, and it will be given you; search, and you will find; knock, and the door will be opened for you. [10]For everyone who asks receives, and everyone who searches finds, and for everyone who knocks, the door will be opened. [11]Is there anyone among you who, if your child asks for a fish, will give a snake instead of a fish? [12]Or if the child asks for an egg, will give a scorpion? [13]If you then, who are evil, know how to give good gifts to your children, how much more will the heavenly Father give the Holy Spirit to those who ask him!"

Primary Hymns and Songs for the Day

"The Church's One Foundation" (Col) (O)
UM546, VU331
H-3 Hbl-94; Chr-180; Desc-16; Org-9
S-1 #25-26. Descant and harmonization
B350, C272, E525, F547, L369, N386, P442, UM545 (PD), VU332 (Fr.)
C272 Descant
H-3 Hbl-94; Chr-180; Desc-16; Org-9
S-1 #25-26. Descant and harmonization

"God, How Can We Forgive" (Hos, Pss, Luke)
S2169, SF2169
H-3 Hbl-62, 95; Chr-59; Org-77
S-1 #211. Harmonization

"Seek Ye First" (Luke)
B478, C354, E711, P333, UM405, SP182, VU356, W580

"The Lord's Prayer" (Luke)
S2278, SF2278
C308, P589, R180, UM271

"O Master, Let Me Walk with Thee" (Col) (C)
B279, C602, E660, F442, L492, N503, P357, UM430 (PD), VU560
H-3 Hbl-81; Chr-147; Desc-74; Org-87
S-2 #118. Descant
E659

Additional Hymn Suggestions

"Come Away with Me" (Luke) (O)
S2202, SF2202

"Whom Shall I Send?" (Hos)
UM582

"O God, Our Help in Ages Past" (Pss)
B74, C67, E680, F370, L320, N25, P210, UM117 (PD), VU806, W579

"O God in Heaven" (Pss)
N279, UM119

"Forgive Our Sins as We Forgive" (Pss, Col, Luke)
E674, L307, P347, R184, UM390, VU364, W754

"Why Stand So Far Away, My God?" (Hos, Pss)
C671, S2180, SF2180

"How Long, O Lord" (Hos, Pss)
S2209, SF2209

"By the Babylonian Rivers" (Hos, Pss)
P246, S2217, VU859, W426

"Lead On, O Cloud of Presence" (Hos, Pss)
C633, S2234, SF2234, VU421

"It is Well with My Soul" (Col)
B410, C561, F495, L346, N438, UM377 (PD)

"I Want Jesus to Walk with Me" (Col)
B465, C627, N490, P363, UM521

"Christ Is Made the Sure Foundation" (Col)
B356 (PD), C275, E518, F557, L367, N400, P416 and P417, UM559 (PD), VU325, W617

"We Know That Christ Is Raised" (Col, Baptism)
E296, L189, P495, UM610, VU448, W721

"We Are God's People" (Col)
B383, F546, S2220, SF2220

"Come, Share the Lord" (Col, Luke, Communion)
C408, S2269, SF2269, VU469

"This Is My Song" (Luke)
C722, N591, UM437

"Let There Be Light" (Luke)
UM440, VU679, W653

"Prayer is the Soul's Sincere Desire" (Luke)
F446 (PD), N508 (PD), UM492 (PD)

"We Walk by Faith" (Luke)
E209, N256, P399, S2196, SF2196, W572

Additional Contemporary Suggestions

"You Are My All in All" (Col, Luke)
SP220

"Make Me a Channel of Your Peace" (Luke)
S2171, SF2171, VU684

"Lord, Listen to Your Children" (Luke)
S2207, SF2207

"This Kingdom" (Luke)
M17

"Step By Step" (Luke)
M51

"Breathe" (Luke)
M61; V-3 p. 42 Vocal Solo

Vocal Solos

"Patiently Have I Waited for the Lord" (Pss)
V-4 p. 24

"It is Well with My Soul" (Col)
V-5 p. 3

"The Lord's Prayer" (Luke)
V-8 p. 39

"O Father in Heaven" (Luke)
V-8 p. 122

Anthems

"I Want Jesus to Walk With Me" (Col)
arr. Joe Cox; Abingdon Press 9780687 651450
SATB a cappella

"Seek Ye First" (Luke)
arr. Douglas Wagner; Hope C5196
SATB with keyboard and opt. handbells

Other Suggestions

Visuals:
O Broken bow, newborn, sand
P Revival, kiss, growing plants, sky, harvest, path
E Roots, building, Christ, cross/crown, eraser
G Jesus, pray, three loaves, lock, open door, gifts, Trinity

Prayer: S2201, SF2201. "Prayers of the People" (Luke)
Prayer: N862. Those in Need (Luke)
Reading: C271. The Church (Col)
Alternate Lessons: Gen 18:20-32; Ps 138 (see Scripture Index in this, or previous, editions of *Prepare!*).

Hosea 11:1-11

1When Israel was a child, I loved him, and out of Egypt I called my son. 2The more I called them, the more they went from me; they kept sacrificing to the Baals, and offering incense to idols. 3Yet it was I who taught Ephraim to walk, I took them up in my arms; but they did not know that I healed them. 4I led them with cords of human kindness, with bands of love. I was to them like those who lift infants to their cheeks. I bent down to them and fed them. 5They shall return to the land of Egypt, and Assyria shall be their king, because they have refused to return to me. 6The sword rages in their cities, it consumes their oracle-priests, and devours because of their schemes. 7My people are bent on turning away from me. To the Most High they call, but he does not raise them up at all. 8How can I give you up, Ephraim? How can I hand you over, O Israel? How can I make you like Admah? How can I treat you like Zeboiim? My heart recoils within me; my compassion grows warm and tender. 9I will not execute my fierce anger; I will not again destroy Ephraim; for I am God and no mortal, the Holy One in your midst, and I will not come in wrath. 10They shall go after the LORD, who roars like a lion; when he roars, his children shall come trembling from the west. 11They shall come trembling like birds from Egypt, and like doves from the land of Assyria; and I will return them to their homes, says the LORD.

Psalm 107:1-9, 43

1O give thanks to the LORD, for he is good; for his steadfast love endures forever. 2Let the redeemed of the LORD say so, those he redeemed from trouble 3and gathered in from the lands, from the east and from the west, from the north and from the south. 4Some wandered in desert wastes, finding no way to an inhabited town; 5hungry and thirsty, their soul fainted within them. 6Then they cried to the LORD in their trouble, and he delivered them from their distress; 7he led them by a straight way, until they reached an inhabited town. 8Let them thank the LORD for his steadfast love, for his wonderful works to humankind. 9For he satisfies the thirsty, and the hungry he fills with good things.

43Let those who are wise give heed to these things, and consider the steadfast love of the LORD.

Colossians 3:1-11

1So if you have been raised with Christ, seek the things that are above, where Christ is, seated at the right hand of God. 2Set your minds on things that are above, not on things that are on earth, 3for you have died, and your life is hidden with Christ in God. 4When Christ who is your life is revealed, then you also will be revealed with him in glory.

5Put to death, therefore, whatever in you is earthly: fornication, impurity, passion, evil desire, and greed (which is idolatry). 6On account of these the wrath of God is coming on those who are disobedient. 7These are the ways you also once followed, when you were living that life. 8But now you must get rid of all such things—anger, wrath, malice, slander, and abusive language from your mouth. 9Do not lie to one another, seeing that you have stripped off the old self with its practices 10and have clothed yourselves with the new self, which is being renewed in knowledge according to the image of its creator. 11In that renewal there is no longer Greek and Jew, circumcised and uncircumcised, barbarian, Scythian, slave and free; but Christ is all and in all!

Luke 12:13-21

13Someone in the crowd said to him, "Teacher, tell my brother to divide the family inheritance with me." 14But he said to him, "Friend, who set me to be a judge or arbitrator over you?" 15And he said to them, "Take care! Be on your guard against all kinds of greed; for one's life does not consist in the abundance of possessions." 16Then he told them a parable: "The land of a rich man produced abundantly. 17And he thought to himself, 'What should I do, for I have no place to store my crops?' 18Then he said, 'I will do this: I will pull down my barns and build larger ones, and there I will store all my grain and my goods. 19And I will say to my soul, Soul, you have ample goods laid up for many years; relax, eat, drink, be merry.' 20But God said to him, 'You fool! This very night your life is being demanded of you. And the things you have prepared, whose will they be?' 21So it is with those who store up treasures for themselves but are not rich toward God."

Notes

Primary Hymns and Songs for the Day

"Sing Praise to God Who Reigns Above" (Hos) (O)
B20, C6, E408, F343, N6, P483, R52, UM126 (PD), VU216, W528
H-3 Hbl-92; Chr-173; Desc-76; Org-91
S-1 #237. Descant
"Loving Spirit" (Hos, Pss)
C244, P323, VU387
H-3 Chr-67, 134; Org-108
S2123, SF2123
H-3 Chr-67
S-2 #63-64. Descant and harmonization
"All Who Love and Serve Your City" (Luke)
C670, E571, P413, UM433
H-3 Chr-26, 65; Org-19
S-1 #62. Descant
E570, L436, W621
"Now Thank We All Our God" (Hos, Pss, Col) (C)
B638, C715, E396 or E397, F525, L533 or L534, N419, P555, UM102 (PD), VU236 (Fr.), W560
H-3 Hbl-78; Chr-140; Desc-81; Org-98
S-1 #252-254. Various treatments

Additional Hymn Suggestions

"Lead On, O Cloud of Presence" (Hos, Pss) (O)
C633, S2234, SF2234, VU421
"Praise, My Soul, the King of Heaven" (Hos, Pss)
B32, C23, E410, F339, L549, P478 or 479, R53, UM66 (PD), VU240, W530
"There's a Wideness in God's Mercy" (Hos)
B25, C73, E469 and E470, F115, L290, N23, P298, UM121, VU271, W595 and W596
"Guide Me, O Thou Great Jehovah" (Hos, Pss)
B56, C622, E690, F608, L343, N18 and N19, P281, UM127 (PD), VU651 (Fr.)
"Great is Thy Faithfulness" (Hos, Pss)
B54, C86, F98, N423, P276, R249, UM140, VU288
"If Thou but Suffer God to Guide Thee (Hos, Pss)
B57, C565, E635, L453, N410, P282, UM142 (PD), VU285 (Fr.) and VU286
"Let Us with a Joyful Mind" (Pss, Col)
E389, N16, P244, S2012, SF2012, VU234
All Who Hunger" (Pss)
C419, S2126, SF2126, VU460
"In Christ There Is No East or West" (Col)
B385, C687, F685, N394, P439
E529, L359, N394, P440, UM548, VU606, W659
"Blest Be the Tie That Binds" (Col)
B387, C433, F560, L370, N393, P438, UM557 (PD), VU602
"Help Us Accept Each Other" (Col)
C487, N388, P358, UM560, W656
"I Come with Joy" (Col, Communion)
B371, C420, E304, N349, P607, R195, UM617, VU477 W726
"Woke Up This Morning" (Col)
C623, N85, S2082, SF2082
"Come, Share the Lord" (Col, Communion)
C408, S2269, SF2269, VU469
"Take My Life, and Let It Be" (Luke)
B277, C609, E707, L406, N448, P391, R133, UM399 (PD), VU506

Additional Contemporary Suggestions

"We Bring the Sacrifice of Praise" (Pss)
R3, S2031, SF2031, SP1
"Give Thanks" (Pss)
C528, R266, S2036, SF2036, SP170
"Hungry" ("Falling On My Knees") (Pss)
M155
"All Who Are Thirsty" (Pss)
M159
"Enough"
M160
"In the Secret" ("I Want to Know You") (Col)
M38,; V-3 p. 36 Vocal Solo
"Let It Be Said of Us" (Col)
M53
"Jesus, Draw Me Close" (Col, Luke)
S2159, SF2159, M48
"Seek Ye First" (Luke)
B478, C354, E711, P333, UM405, SP182, VU356, W580

Vocal Solos

"My Father's Heart" (Col)
V-3 p. 134
"Take My Life" (Luke)
V-5 p. 28
V-8 p. 262

Anthems

"Psalm 107" (Pss)
Robert C. Clatterbuck; Hope Publishing A-510
SATB with keyboard

"Treasures in Heaven" (Luke)
Allen Pote; Hinshaw HMC1059
SATB with keyboard

Other Suggestions

Visuals:
O Child, incense, cords/bands, heart, lion, birds/dove
P N/S/E/W, desert, food/drink, straight path, Ps 107:2a
E Christ, crown, Bible, baptism, white robe, open shackles
G Will, possessions, barns, grain, party, death
Greeting: N822 (Pss) or N825 (Hos)
Opening Prayer: N826 (Col)
Call to Confession: N833 (Luke)
Prayer of Confession: N835 or N836 (Luke)
Blessing: C268 or F643 (Col)
Alternate Lessons: Eccl 1:2, 12-14; 2:18-23; Ps 49:1-12 (see Scripture Index in this, or previous, editions of *Prepare!*).

Isaiah 1:1, 10-20

[1]The vision of Isaiah son of Amoz, which he saw concerning Judah and Jerusalem in the days of Uzziah, Jotham, Ahaz, and Hezekiah, kings of Judah.

[10]Hear the word of the LORD, you rulers of Sodom! Listen to the teaching of our God, you people of Gomorrah! [11]What to me is the multitude of your sacrifices? says the LORD; I have had enough of burnt offerings of rams and the fat of fed beasts; I do not delight in the blood of bulls, or of lambs, or of goats. [12]When you come to appear before me, who asked this from your hand? Trample my courts no more; [13]bringing offerings is futile; incense is an abomination to me. New moon and sabbath and calling of convocation—I cannot endure solemn assemblies with iniquity. [14]Your new moons and your appointed festivals my soul hates; they have become a burden to me, I am weary of bearing them. [15]When you stretch out your hands, I will hide my eyes from you; even though you make many prayers, I will not listen; your hands are full of blood. [16]Wash yourselves; make yourselves clean; remove the evil of your doings from before my eyes; cease to do evil, [17]learn to do good; seek justice, rescue the oppressed, defend the orphan, plead for the widow. [18]Come now, let us argue it out, says the LORD: though your sins are like scarlet, they shall be like snow; though they are red like crimson, they shall become like wool. [19]If you are willing and obedient, you shall eat the good of the land; [20]but if you refuse and rebel, you shall be devoured by the sword; for the mouth of the LORD has spoken.

Psalm 50:1-8, 22-23

[1]The mighty one, God the LORD, speaks and summons the earth from the rising of the sun to its setting. [2]Out of Zion, the perfection of beauty, God shines forth. [3]Our God comes and does not keep silence, before him is a devouring fire, and a mighty tempest all around him. [4]He calls to the heavens above and to the earth, that he may judge his people: [5] "Gather to me my faithful ones, who made a covenant with me by sacrifice!" [6]The heavens declare his righteousness, for God himself is judge. [7]"Hear, O my people, and I will speak, O Israel, I will testify against you. I am God, your God. [8]Not for your sacrifices do I rebuke you; your burnt offerings are continually before me.

[22]"Mark this, then, you who forget God, or I will tear you apart, and there will be no one to deliver. [23]Those who bring thanksgiving as their sacrifice honor me; to those who go the right way I will show the salvation of God."

Hebrews 11:1-3, 8-16

[1]Now faith is the assurance of things hoped for, the conviction of things not seen. [2]Indeed, by faith our ancestors received approval. [3]By faith we understand that the worlds were prepared by the word of God, so that what is seen was made from things that are not visible.

[8]By faith Abraham obeyed when he was called to set out for a place that he was to receive as an inheritance; and he set out, not knowing where he was going. [9]By faith he stayed for a time in the land he had been promised, as in a foreign land, living in tents, as did Isaac and Jacob, who were heirs with him of the same promise. [10]For he looked forward to the city that has foundations, whose architect and builder is God. [11]By faith he received power of procreation, even though he was too old—and Sarah herself was barren—because he considered him faithful who had promised. [12]Therefore from one person, and this one as good as dead, descendants were born, "as many as the stars of heaven and as the innumerable grains of sand by the seashore."

[13]All of these died in faith without having received the promises, but from a distance they saw and greeted them. They confessed that they were strangers and foreigners on the earth, [14]for people who speak in this way make it clear that they are seeking a homeland. [15]If they had been thinking of the land that they had left behind, they would have had opportunity to return. [16]But as it is, they desire a better country, that is, a heavenly one. Therefore God is not ashamed to be called their God; indeed, he has prepared a city for them.

Luke 12:32-40

[32]"Do not be afraid, little flock, for it is your Father's good pleasure to give you the kingdom. [33]Sell your possessions, and give alms. Make purses for yourselves that do not wear out, an unfailing treasure in heaven, where no thief comes near and no moth destroys. [34]For where your treasure is, there your heart will be also.

[35]"Be dressed for action and have your lamps lit; [36]be like those who are waiting for their master to return from the wedding banquet, so that they may open the door for him as soon as he comes and knocks. [37]Blessed are those slaves whom the master finds alert when he comes; truly I tell you, he will fasten his belt and have them sit down to eat, and he will come and serve them. [38]If he comes during the middle of the night, or near dawn, and finds them so, blessed are those slaves.

[39]"But know this: if the owner of the house had known at what hour the thief was coming, he would not have let his house be broken into. [40]You also must be ready, for the Son of Man is coming at an unexpected hour."

Primary Hymns and Songs for the Day

"How Firm a Foundation" (Heb, Luke) (O)
B338, C618, E636, F32, L507, N407, P361, UM529 (PD), VU660, W585
H-3 Hbl-27, 69; Chr-102; Desc-41; Org-41
S-1 #133. Harmonization
#134. Performance note

"Faith, While Trees Are Still in Blossom" (Heb)
C535, UM508, VU643
H-3 Chr-67
S-2 #63-64. Descant and harmonization

"Faith of Our Fathers" (Heb)
B352, C635, F526, L500, N381, UM710 (PD), VU580, W571
H-3 Hbl-57; Chr-63; Desc-93; Org-133

"O Day of God, Draw Nigh" (Luke) (C)
B623, C700, E601, N611, P452, UM730 (PD), VU688 and VU689 (Fr.)
H-3 Hbl-79; Chr-141; Desc-95; Org-143

Additional Hymn Suggestions

"Lift Every Voice and Sing" (Heb, Luke) (O)
B627, C631, E599, L562, N593, P563, UM519, W641

"The Voice of God Is Calling" (Isa)
C666, UM436 (PD)

"What Does the Lord Require" (Isa, Pss)
C659, E605, P405, UM441, W624
C661, S2174, SF2174, VU701

"Here Am I" (Isa)
C654, S2178, SF2178

"All My Hope Is Firmly Grounded" (Heb)
E665, N408, UM132, VU654 and VU655

"For All the Saints" (Heb)
B355, C637, E287, F614, L174, N299, P526, UM711 (PD), VU705, W705

"We Walk by Faith" (Heb)
E209, N256, P399, S2196, SF2196, W572

"Deep in the Shadows of the Past" (Heb)
N320, P330, S2246

"I Sing a Song of the Saints of God" (Heb, Luke)
E293, N712, P364, UM712 (PD)

"I Know Whom I Have Believed" (Heb, Luke)
B337, F631, UM714 (PD)

"Give to the Winds Thy Fears" (Luke)
N404, P286 (PD), UM129 (PD), VU636 (PD)

"Take Time to Be Holy" (Luke)
B446, C572, F457, UM395 (PD), VU672

"My Lord, What a Morning" (Luke)
C708, P449, UM719, VU708

"Wake, Awake, for Night Is Flying" (Luke)
E61, L31, P17, UM720 (PD), VU711, W371

"I Want to Be Ready" (Luke)
N616, UM722

"Since Jesus Came into My Heart" (Luke)
B441, F639, S2140, SF2140

Additional Contemporary Suggestions

"White as Snow" (Isa)
M35

"From the Rising of the Sun" (Pss)
S2024, SF2024

"We Bring the Sacrifice of Praise" (Pss)
R3, S2031, SF2031, SP1

"Praise to the Lord" (Pss)
S2029, SF2029, VU835

"God Is Here Today" ("Dios Esta' Aqui') (Pss)
S2049, SF2049

"I Stand Amazed" (Pss)
M79

"It Is You" (Pss)
M134

"I Will Not Forget You" (Pss)
M211

"All I Need Is You" (Luke)
S2080, SF2080

"You Are My All in All" (Luke)
SP220

"When It's All Been Said and Done" (Luke)
M115

"In Christ Alone" (Luke)
M138

"Sing to the King" (Luke)
M141

"Be the Centre" (Luke)
M156

Vocal Solos

"Spirit of Faith Come Down" (Heb)
V-1 p. 43

"Lord Over All" (Luke)
V-3 p. 84

Anthems

"Treasures in Heaven" (Luke)
Joseph W. Clokey; Summy-Birchard Company B-2010
SATB with organ

Keep Your Lamps" (Luke)
Andre Thomas; Hinshaw HMC577
SATB with piano

Other Suggestions

Visuals:
O Bloody hands, wash hands, scarlet / snow / wool
P Sunrise/set, fire, storm, heaven/earth, praise
E Creation, crowd, tents, T-square, baby, star/sand
G Flock, purse, wedding banquet, lit lamp, clock

Greeting: N822 (Pss), N823 (Luke), or F329 (Luke)
Opening Prayer: N816 or N818 (Luke)
Prayer: C567 or UM676 or N865 or F113 (Isa, Pss, Luke)
Blessing: N875 (Heb)
Alternate Lessons: Gen 15:1-6; Ps 33:12-22 (see Scripture Index in this, or previous, editions of *Prepare!*).

Isaiah 5:1-7

[1]Let me sing for my beloved my love-song concerning
his vineyard: My beloved had a vineyard on a very fertile
hill. [2]He dug it and cleared it of stones, and planted it
with choice vines; he built a watchtower in the midst of it,
and hewed out a wine vat in it; he expected it to yield
grapes, but it yielded wild grapes. [3]And now, inhabitants
of Jerusalem and people of Judah, judge between me and
my vineyard. [4]What more was there to do for my vineyard
that I have not done in it? When I expected it to yield
grapes, why did it yield wild grapes? [5]And now I will tell
you what I will do to my vineyard. I will remove its hedge,
and it shall be devoured; I will break down its wall, and it
shall be trampled down. [6] I will make it a waste; it shall not
be pruned or hoed, and it shall be overgrown with briers
and thorns; I will also command the clouds that they rain
no rain upon it. [7]For the vineyard of the LORD of hosts is
the house of Israel, and the people of Judah are his pleas-
ant planting; he expected justice, but saw bloodshed; righteousness, but heard a cry!

Psalm 80:1-2, 8-19

[1]Give ear, O Shepherd of Israel, you who lead Joseph
like a flock! You who are enthroned upon the cherubim,
shine forth [2]before Ephraim and Benjamin and
Manasseh. Stir up your might, and come to save us!

[8]You brought a vine out of Egypt; you drove out the
nations and planted it. [9]You cleared the ground for it; it
took deep root and filled the land. [10]The mountains were
covered with its shade, the mighty cedars with its branches;
[11]it sent out its branches to the sea, and its shoots to the
River. [12]Why then have you broken down its walls, so that
all who pass along the way pluck its fruit? [13] The boar from
the forest ravages it, and all that move in the field feed on
it. [14]Turn again, O God of hosts; look down from heaven,
and see; have regard for this vine, [15]the stock that your
right hand planted. [16]They have burned it with fire, they
have cut it down; may they perish at the rebuke of your
countenance. [17]But let your hand be upon the one at your
right hand, the one whom you made strong for yourself.
[18]Then we will never turn back from you; give us life, and
we will call on your name. [19]Restore us, O LORD God of
hosts; let your face shine, that we may be saved.

Hebrews 11:29–12:2

[29]By faith the people passed through the Red Sea as if it
were dry land, but when the Egyptians attempted to do so
they were drowned. [30]By faith the walls of Jericho fell after
they had been encircled for seven days. [31]By faith Rahab
the prostitute did not perish with those who were disobedient, because she had received the spies in peace.

[32]And what more should I say? For time would fail me to
tell of Gideon, Barak, Samson, Jephthah, of David and
Samuel and the prophets— [33]who through faith con-
quered kingdoms, administered justice, obtained promises, shut the mouths of lions, [34]quenched raging fire,
escaped the edge of the sword, won strength out of weakness, became mighty in war, put foreign armies to flight.
[35]Women received their dead by resurrection. Others were
tortured, refusing to accept release, in order to obtain a
better resurrection. [36]Others suffered mocking and flogging, and even chains and imprisonment. [37]They were
stoned to death, they were sawn in two, they were killed by
the sword; they went about in skins of sheep and goats,
destitute, persecuted, tormented— [38]of whom the world
was not worthy. They wandered in deserts and mountains,
and in caves and holes in the ground.

[39]Yet all these, though they were commended for their
faith, did not receive what was promised, [40]since God had
provided something better so that they would not, apart
from us, be made perfect.

[1]Therefore, since we are surrounded by so great a cloud
of witnesses, let us also lay aside every weight and the sin
that clings so closely, and let us run with perseverance the
race that is set before us, [2]looking to Jesus the pioneer
and perfecter of our faith, who for the sake of the joy that
was set before him endured the cross, disregarding its
shame, and has taken his seat at the right hand of the
throne of God.

Luke 12:49-56

[49]"I came to bring fire to the earth, and how I wish it
were already kindled! [50]I have a baptism with which to be
baptized, and what stress I am under until it is completed!
[51]Do you think that I have come to bring peace to the
earth? No, I tell you, but rather division! [52]From now on
five in one household will be divided, three against two
and two against three; [53]they will be divided: father against
son and son against father, mother against daughter and
daughter against mother, mother-in-law against her daughter-in-law and daughter-in-law against mother-in-law."

[54]He also said to the crowds, "When you see a cloud rising in the west, you immediately say, 'It is going to rain';
and so it happens. [55]And when you see the south wind
blowing, you say, 'There will be scorching heat'; and it
happens. [56]You hypocrites! You know how to interpret the
appearance of earth and sky, but why do you not know
how to interpret the present time?"

Notes

Primary Hymns and Songs for the Day
"How Firm a Foundation" (Heb, Luke) (O)
B338, C618, E636, F32, L507, N407, P361, UM529 (PD), VU660, W585
H-3 Hbl-27, 69; Chr-102; Desc-41; Org-41
S-1 #133. Harmonization
#134. Performance note
"Am I a Soldier of the Cross" (Heb, Luke)
B481, F411, UM511 (PD)
H-3 Chr-27
S-1 #22-23. Descant and harmonization
"Guide My Feet" (Heb)
N497, P354, S2208
"O Day of God, Draw Nigh" (Isa, Pss, Luke) (C)
B623, C700, E601, N611, P452, UM730 (PD), VU688 and VU689 (Fr.)
H-3 Hbl-79; Chr-141; Desc-95; Org-143
S-1 #306-308. Various treatments

Additional Hymn Suggestions
"O God of Every Nation" (Isa, Pss)
C680, E607, L416, P289, UM435, VU677, W650
"Out of the Depths" (Isa., Pss)
C510, N554, S2136, SF2136, VU611
"Holy God, We Praise Thy Name" (Heb)
E366 (PD), F385, L535, N276, P460, UM79, VU894 (Fr.), W524
"O God in Heaven" (Pss, Heb)
N279, UM119
"I Want to Walk as a Child of the Light" (Heb)
E490, R152, UM206, W510
"Rejoice in God's Saints" (Heb)
C476, UM708
"Faith of Our Fathers" (Heb)
B352, C635, F526, L500, N381, UM710 (PD), VU580, W571
"For All the Saints" (Heb)
B355, C637, E287, F614, L174, N299, P526, UM711 (PD), VU705, W705
"O What Their Joy and Glory Must Be" (Heb)
E623, L337, N385, UM727 (PD)
"Faith Is Patience in the Night" (Heb)
S2211, SF2211
"Deep in the Shadows of the Past" (Heb)
N320, P330, S2246
"For All the Saints" (Heb)
S2283, SF2283
"By Gracious Powers" (Heb, Luke)
E695 and E696, N413, P342, UM517, W577
"All Who Love and Serve Your City" (Luke)
C670, E570 and E571, L436, P413, UM433, W621
"My Lord, What a Morning" (Luke)
C708, P449, UM719, VU708
"God of Grace and God of Glory" (Heb) (C)
B395, C464, E594, F528, L415, N436, P420, R301, UM577, VU686

Additional Contemporary Suggestions
"Refiner's Fire" (Isa)
M50
"Light the Fire Again" (Pss)
M144
"Soon and Very Soon" (Heb)
B192, R276, UM706; S-2 #187
"I Will Never Be" (the Same Again) (Heb)
M34
"In the Secret" ("I Want to Know You") (Heb)
M38; V-3 p. 36 Vocal Solo
"Let It Be Said of Us" (Heb)
M53
"Once Again" (Heb)
M78
"He Who Began a Good Work in You" (Heb)
S2163, SF2163, SP180, R134
"May You Run and Not Be Weary" (Heb)
S2281, SF2281
"The Battle Belongs to the Lord" (Luke)
SP158, R244
"Days of Elijah" (Luke)
M139

Vocal Solos
"Joy" (Heb)
V-3 p. 94
"Come, O Thou Traveler Unknown" (Heb, Luke)
V-1 p. 21
"Guide My Feet, Lord" (Heb, Luke)
V-7 p. 15

Anthems
"We've Come This Far by Faith" (Heb)
Gary Alan Smith; Abingdon Press 9780687 651160
SATB with piano

"Ain'-a That Good News" (Luke)
arr. Mark Patterson; Choristers Guild CGA1029
Unison/Two-part with piano

Other Suggestions
Visuals:
O Vine/grapes, stones, tower, hedge, vat, wall
P Shepherd, vine/grapes, wall fire, shears
E Walls, lions, fire, rising, weights, race, cross
G Fire, baptism, cross, wall, division, clock
Greeting: N819 (Pss)
Opening Prayer: N831 (Heb)
Prayer of Confession: N837 (Isa, Heb)
Assurance: N840 (Pss)
Prayer: UM677 (Pss) or UM574 (Heb)
Readings: F503 (Isa, Luke), F463 or F615 (Heb)
Alternate Lessons: Jer 23:23-29; Ps 82 (see Scripture Index in this, or previous, editions of *Prepare!*).

Jeremiah 1:4-10

4 Now the word of the LORD came to me saying, 5 "Before I formed you in the womb I knew you, and before you were born I consecrated you; I appointed you a prophet to the nations." 6 Then I said, "Ah, Lord GOD! Truly I do not know how to speak, for I am only a boy." 7 But the LORD said to me, "Do not say, 'I am only a boy'; for you shall go to all to whom I send you, and you shall speak whatever I command you. 8 Do not be afraid of them, for I am with you to deliver you, says the LORD." 9 Then the LORD put out his hand and touched my mouth; and the LORD said to me, "Now I have put my words in your mouth. 10 See, today I appoint you over nations and over kingdoms, to pluck up and to pull down, to destroy and to overthrow, to build and to plant."

Psalm 71:1-6

1 In you, O LORD, I take refuge; let me never be put to shame. 2 In your righteousness deliver me and rescue me; incline your ear to me and save me. 3 Be to me a rock of refuge, a strong fortress, to save me, for you are my rock and my fortress. 4 Rescue me, O my God, from the hand of the wicked, from the grasp of the unjust and cruel. 5 For you, O Lord, are my hope, my trust, O LORD, from my youth. 6 Upon you I have leaned from my birth; it was you who took me from my mother's womb. My praise is continually of you.

Hebrews 12:18-29

18 You have not come to something that can be touched, a blazing fire, and darkness, and gloom, and a tempest, 19 and the sound of a trumpet, and a voice whose words made the hearers beg that not another word be spoken to them. 20 (For they could not endure the order that was given, "If even an animal touches the mountain, it shall be stoned to death." 21 Indeed, so terrifying was the sight that Moses said, "I tremble with fear.") 22 But you have come to Mount Zion and to the city of the living God, the heavenly Jerusalem, and to innumerable angels in festal gathering, 23 and to the assembly of the firstborn who are enrolled in heaven, and to God the judge of all, and to the spirits of the righteous made perfect, 24 and to Jesus, the mediator of a new covenant, and to the sprinkled blood that speaks a better word than the blood of Abel.

25 See that you do not refuse the one who is speaking; for if they did not escape when they refused the one who warned them on earth, how much less will we escape if we reject the one who warns from heaven! 26 At that time his voice shook the earth; but now he has promised, "Yet once more I will shake not only the earth but also the heaven." 27 This phrase, "Yet once more," indicates the removal of what is shaken—that is, created things—so that what cannot be shaken may remain. 28 Therefore, since we are receiving a kingdom that cannot be shaken, let us give thanks, by which we offer to God an acceptable worship with reverence and awe; 29 for indeed our God is a consuming fire.

Luke 13:10-17

10 Now he was teaching in one of the synagogues on the sabbath. 11 And just then there appeared a woman with a spirit that had crippled her for eighteen years. She was bent over and was quite unable to stand up straight. 12 When Jesus saw her, he called her over and said, "Woman, you are set free from your ailment." 13 When he laid his hands on her, immediately she stood up straight and began praising God. 14 But the leader of the synagogue, indignant because Jesus had cured on the sabbath, kept saying to the crowd, "There are six days on which work ought to be done; come on those days and be cured, and not on the sabbath day." 15 But the Lord answered him and said, "You hypocrites! Does not each of you on the sabbath untie his ox or his donkey from the manger, and lead it away to give it water? 16 And ought not this woman, a daughter of Abraham whom Satan bound for eighteen long years, be set free from this bondage on the sabbath day?" 17 When he said this, all his opponents were put to shame; and the entire crowd was rejoicing at all the wonderful things that he was doing.

Notes

Primary Hymns and Songs for the Day

"Glorious Things of Thee Are Spoken" (Heb) (O)
B398, C709, E522 (or 523), F376, L358, N307, P446, UM731 (PD)
H-3 Hbl-61; Chr-72; Desc-17; Org-11
S-1 #27. Descant
#28. Harmonization in F major

"Stand Up and Bless the Lord" (Heb)
B30, UM662 (PD)
H-3 Hbl-79; Chr-141; Desc-95; Org-143
S-1 #306-308. Various treatments
P491

"Lord of the Dance" (Luke)
P302, UM261, VU352, W636
H-3 Chr-106; Org-81

"Jesus' Hands Were Kind Hands" (Luke)
B477, UM273, VU570
S-2 #17-19. Various treatments

"Here I Am, Lord" (Jer) (C)
C452, P525, R149, UM593, VU509
H-3 Chr-97; Org-54

"Healer of Our Every Ill" (Luke)
C506, S2213, SF2213, VU619

Additional Hymn Suggestions

"Praise to the Lord, the Almighty" (Pss) (O)
B14 (PD), C25, E390, F337, L543, N22, P482, R57, UM139, VU220 (Fr.) and VU221, W547
H-3 Hbl-89; Chr-163; Desc-69; Org-79
S-1 #218-222. Various treatments

"O Master, Let Me Walk with Thee" (Jer, Luke)
B279, C602, E659 and E660, F442, L492, N503, P357, UM430 (PD), VU560

"Lord, Speak to Me" (Jer)
B568, F625, L403, N531, P426, UM463 (PD), VU589

"Womb of Life" (Jer)
C14, N274, S2046, SF2046

"I Was There to Hear Your Borning Cry" (Jer, Pss)
C75, N351, S2051, SF2051, VU644

"Loving Spirit" (Jer)
C244, P323, S2123, SF2123, VU387

Here Am I" (Jer, Luke)
C654, S2178, SF2178

"O God, Our Help in Ages Past" (Pss)
B74, C67, E680, F370, L320, N25, P210, UM117 (PD), VU806, W579

"Rock of Ages, Cleft for Me" (Pss)
B342, C214, E685, F108, L327, N596, UM361 (PD)

"Immortal, Invisible, God Only Wise" (Heb)
B6, C66, E423, F319, L526, N1, P263, R46, UM103 (PD), VU264, W512

"O Holy City, Seen of John" (Heb)
E583, N613, P453, UM726, VU709

"O God Beyond All Praising" (Heb)
S2009, SF2009, VU256, W541

"Wonder of Wonders" (Heb, Baptism)
C378, N328, P499, S2247

"Heal Me, Hands of Jesus" (Luke)
C504, UM262, VU621

"O Young and Fearless Prophet" (Luke)
C669, UM444 (PD)

Additional Contemporary Suggestions

"I Know the Lord's Laid His Hands on Me" (Jer, Luke)
S2139, SF2139

"My Life Is in You, Lord" (Pss)
S2032, SF2032, SP204

"Praise the Name of Jesus" (Pss)
R7, S2066, SF2066, SP87

"Rock of Ages" (Pss)
M93

"Let My Words Be Few" (Heb)
M105

"Awesome God" (Heb)
R245, S2040, SF2040, SP11

"Holy, Holy" (Heb)
B254, F149, P140, R206, S2039, SP141

"I'm So Glad Jesus Lifted Me" (Luke)
C529, N474, S2151, SF2151

"People Need the Lord" (Luke)
B557, S2244, SF2244

Vocal Solos

"Be Thou My Vision" (Jer)
V-6 p. 13
V-5 p. 13

"Jesus, Thou Art Watching Ever" (Pss)
V-4 p. 6

"Prayer" (Pss)
V-9 p. 32

Anthem

"I Was There to Hear Your Borning Cry" (Jer, Pss)
Arr. John Helgen; Kjos 8826
SAATB with keyboard and C instrument

"With Awe and Confidence" (Heb)
George Brandon; GIA 1883
SATB with keyboard

Other Suggestions

Visuals:
O Pregnant, young boy, hand to mouth, fear
P Rescue, rock, fortress, Ps 71:5, newborn
E Fire, darkness, storm, trumpet, stones, angels, throne, Christ, New Testament, praise
G Jesus, woman/cane/praise, donkey/water, open shackles

Introit: C654, S2178, SF2178. "Here Am I" (Jer, Luke)
Opening Prayer: N831 (Jer)
Prayer: N860 or UM460 or F649 (Luke)
Alternate Lessons: Isa 58:9b-14; Ps 103:1-8 (see Scripture Index in this, or previous, editions of *Prepare!*).

Jeremiah 2:4-13

[4]Hear the word of the LORD, O house of Jacob, and all the families of the house of Israel. [5]Thus says the LORD: What wrong did your ancestors find in me that they went far from me, and went after worthless things, and became worthless themselves? [6]They did not say, "Where is the LORD who brought us up from the land of Egypt, who led us in the wilderness, in a land of deserts and pits, in a land of drought and deep darkness, in a land that no one passes through, where no one lives?" [7]I brought you into a plentiful land to eat its fruits and its good things. But when you entered you defiled my land, and made my heritage an abomination. [8]The priests did not say, "Where is the LORD?" Those who handle the law did not know me; the rulers transgressed against me; the prophets prophesied by Baal, and went after things that do not profit. [9]Therefore once more I accuse you, says the LORD, and I accuse your children's children. [10]Cross to the coasts of Cyprus and look, send to Kedar and examine with care; see if there has ever been such a thing. [11]Has a nation changed its gods, even though they are no gods? But my people have changed their glory for something that does not profit. [12]Be appalled, O heavens, at this, be shocked, be utterly desolate, says the LORD, [13]for my people have committed two evils: they have forsaken me, the fountain of living water, and dug out cisterns for themselves, cracked cisterns that can hold no water.

Psalm 81:1, 10-16

[1]Sing aloud to God our strength; shout for joy to the God of Jacob.

[10]"I am the LORD your God, who brought you up out of the land of Egypt. Open your mouth wide and I will fill it. [11]But my people did not listen to my voice; Israel would not submit to me. [12]So I gave them over to their stubborn hearts, to follow their own counsels. [13]O that my people would listen to me, that Israel would walk in my ways! [14]Then I would quickly subdue their enemies, and turn my hand against their foes. [15]Those who hate the LORD would cringe before him, and their doom would last forever. [16]I would feed you with the finest of the wheat, and with honey from the rock I would satisfy you."

Hebrews 13:1-8, 15-16

[1]Let mutual love continue. [2]Do not neglect to show hospitality to strangers, for by doing that some have entertained angels without knowing it. [3]Remember those who are in prison, as though you were in prison with them; those who are being tortured, as though you yourselves were being tortured. [4]Let marriage be held in honor by all, and let the marriage bed be kept undefiled; for God will judge fornicators and adulterers. [5]Keep your lives free from the love of money, and be content with what you have; for he has said, "I will never leave you or forsake you." [6]So we can say with confidence, "The Lord is my helper; I will not be afraid. What can anyone do to me?"

[7]Remember your leaders, those who spoke the word of God to you; consider the outcome of their way of life, and imitate their faith. [8]Jesus Christ is the same yesterday and today and forever.

[15]Through him, then, let us continually offer a sacrifice of praise to God, that is, the fruit of lips that confess his name. [16]Do not neglect to do good and to share what you have, for such sacrifices are pleasing to God.

Luke 14:1, 7-14

[1]On one occasion when Jesus was going to the house of a leader of the Pharisees to eat a meal on the sabbath, they were watching him closely.

[7]When he noticed how the guests chose the places of honor, he told them a parable. [8]"When you are invited by someone to a wedding banquet, do not sit down at the place of honor, in case someone more distinguished than you has been invited by your host; [9]and the host who invited both of you may come and say to you, 'Give this person your place,' and then in disgrace you would start to take the lowest place. [10]But when you are invited, go and sit down at the lowest place, so that when your host comes, he may say to you, 'Friend, move up higher'; then you will be honored in the presence of all who sit at the table with you. [11]For all who exalt themselves will be humbled, and those who humble themselves will be exalted."

[12]He said also to the one who had invited him, "When you give a luncheon or a dinner, do not invite your friends or your brothers or your relatives or rich neighbors, in case they may invite you in return, and you would be repaid. [13]But when you give a banquet, invite the poor, the crippled, the lame, and the blind. [14]And you will be blessed, because they cannot repay you, for you will be repaid at the resurrection of the righteous."

Notes

Primary Hymns and Songs for the Day
"Gather Us In" (Luke, Communion) (O)
C284, S2236, SF2236, W665
"We Bring the Sacrifice of Praise" (Heb) (O)
S2031, SF2031, R3, SP1
"Jesu, Jesu" (Heb, Luke)
B501, C600, E602, N498, P367, R289, UM432, VU593, W431
H-3 Chr-114; Org-19
S-1 #63. Vocal part
"You Satisfy the Hungry Heart" (Pss, Communion)
C429, P521, UM629, R217, VU478, W736
S-1 #144. Four-part setting of refrain
"Blest Be the Tie That Binds" (Heb) (C)
B387, C433, F560, L370, N393, P438, UM557 (PD), VU602
H-3 Hbl-49; Chr-14; Desc-27; Org-25

Additional Hymn Suggestions
"O For a Thousand Tongues to Sing" (Pss, Luke) (O)
B216, C5, E493, F349, L559, N42, P466, R32, UM57 (PD) and UM59, VU326
"How Firm a Foundation" (Heb) (O)
B338, C618, E636, F32, L507, N407, P361, UM529 (PD), VU660, W585
"We Utter Our Cry" (Jer)
B631, UM439
"O God Who Shaped Creation" (Jer, Pss)
UM443, VU276
"Creator of the Earth and Skies" (Jer, Pss)
E148, UM450
"God Weeps" (Jer, Pss)
S2048, SF2048
"The Trees of the Field" (Pss)
R302, S2279, SF2279, SP128, VU884
"Lord God, Your Love Has Called Us Here" (Heb, Luke)
P353, UM579
"O God Beyond All Praising" (Heb)
S2009, SF2009, VU256, W541
"The Summons" (Heb)
S2130, SF2130, VU567
"Together We Serve" (Heb, Luke)
S2175, SF2175
"Here Am I" (Heb)
C654, S2178, SF2178
"As We Gather at Your Table" (Heb, Luke, Communion)
S2268, SF2268. N332, VU457
"Come, Ye Sinners, Poor and Needy" (Luke)
B323 (PD), R141, UM340, W756
"Christ for the World We Sing" (Luke)
E537, F686, R299, UM568 (PD)
"Lord of All Hopefulness" (Luke)
E482, L469, R174, S2197, SF2197, W568
"Lord, Whose Love through Humble Service" (Luke) (C)
C461, L423, UM581, R286

Contemporary Song Suggestions
"Lord God Almighty" (Pss)
R40, S2006, SF2006
"You Who Are Thirsty" (Jer, Pss)
S2132, SF2132
"Someone Asked the Question" (Pss)
N523, S2144, SF2144
"Trading My Sorrows" (Pss)
M75
"Made Me Glad" (Pss)
M123
"Make Me a Servant" (Heb, Luke)
S2176, SF2176, SP193
"Live in Charity" ("Ubi Caritas") (Heb)
C523, R226, S2179, SF2179, W604
"Jesus, We Crown You with Praise" (Heb)
M24
"I Stand Amazed" (Heb)
M79
"I Will Not Forget You" (Heb)
M211
"Humble Thyself in the Sight of the Lord" (Heb, Luke)
S2131, SF2131, R188, SP223

Vocal Solos
"Look What You've Done" (Heb)
V-3 p. 122
"Praise the Lord, He Never Changes" (Heb)
V-8 p. 62
"Author of Life Divine" (Luke, Communion)
V-1 p. 39

Anthems
"Song of Gentleness" (Heb, Luke)
Douglas Wagner; Beckenhorst Press BP1192
Unison with keyboard or handbells

"Welcome Table" (Luke)
Mark Hayes; Augsburg 0800676033
SATB with piano

Other Suggestions
Visuals:
O Exodus, abundance, fountain, broken cistern
P Singing, Exodus, hard hearts, wheat, honey/rock
E Welcome, prison ministry, marriage certificate, money, Heb 13:6 or 8, Jesus
G Meal, marriage feast, table, poor, maimed, lame, blind
Dance or Drama: Process or dance in a full feast, including Communion elements as "Gather Us In" is sung; mime or dance the Scripture as Luke 14:7-14 is read.
Prayer: C541. Draw Compassion from Us (Heb)
Prayer: F624 or N863 (Luke)
Reading: F620. I Stand by the Door (Heb, Luke)
Alternate Lessons: Sir 10:12-18; Ps 112 (see Scripture Index in this, or previous, editions of *Prepare!*).

SCRIPTURE INDEX

SCRIPTURE INDEX

SCRIPTURE INDEX

WORSHIP PLANNING SHEET 1

Date: ____________________ Color: ____________________

Preacher: ____

Liturgist: ____

Selected Scripture: ____

Selected Hymns	No.	Placement

Psalter #____________________

Keyboard Selections

Title	Composer	Placement

Anthems

Title	Choir	Composer	Placement

Vocal Solos

Title	Singer	Composer	Placement

Other Ideas:

Acolytes: ____

Head Usher: ____

Altar Guild Contact: ____

Other Participants:

____

WORSHIP PLANNING SHEET 2

Date: ______________________ Sunday: ________________________________ Color: ________________________

Preacher: ____

Liturgist: ____

Opening Voluntary Composer

____

Hymn Tune Name No.

____

Opening Prayer: ____

Prayer for Illumination: ____

First Lesson: ____

Psalter: ____

Second Lesson: ____

Gospel Lesson: ____

Hymn Tune Name No.

____

Response to the Word: ____

Prayers of the People: ____

Offertory Composer

____

Communion Setting: ____

Communion Hymns Tune Name No.

____

____

____

Closing Hymn Tune Name No.

____

Benediction: ____

Closing Voluntary Composer

____

CONTEMPORARY WORSHIP PLANNING SHEET

You will want to adjust this planning sheet to meet the needs of your worship planning team. A common order used would consist of three to four opening praise choruses and lively hymns, a time of informal prayers of the congregation along with songs of prayer, reading of the primary scripture for the day, a drama or video to illustrate the day's theme, a message from the preacher, a testimony on the theme for the day (if a drama or video was not presented earlier), followed by closing songs appropriate to the mood of the service and the message. Any offering would usually be taken early in the service, and Holy Communion would normally take place following the message. Special music (solos, duets, instrumental music) can be used wherever it best expresses the theme of the service.

Date: ______________________________ Sunday: ______________________________

Thematic Emphasis or Topic: ______________________________

Color: ______________________________ Visual Focus: ______________________________

Opening Songs:

____

____

Prayer Songs:

____

Scripture Selection(s):

____

Drama or Video: ______________________________

Message Title: ______________________________

Testimony: ______________________________

Special Music:

____

Closing Songs:

____

Preacher: ______________________________ Music Leader: ______________________________

Worship Facilitator: ______________________________ Prayer Leader: ______________________________

PLANNING NOTES

PLANNING NOTES

PLANNING NOTES

PLANNING NOTES